Revolutionizing Interfaces: Mastering User Experience in Operating Systems

Table of Content

Chapter 1: Unveiling the UI Landscape

- Define the concept of User Interface and its critical role in the digital world.
- Discuss the impact of UI on user experience and the overall interaction with operating systems.
- Explore various types of UIs, including graphical user interfaces (GUIs), command-line interfaces (CLIs), and touch-based interfaces.
- Discuss the strengths and weaknesses of each type, highlighting their applications and user demographics.
- Break down the essential elements that constitute a user interface.
- Explore common UI components such as buttons, menus, icons, and their significance in facilitating user interaction.
- Trace the historical evolution of user interface design.
- Highlight key milestones, paradigm shifts, and influential technologies that have shaped the UI landscape over time.
- Discuss challenges and solutions in designing UIs that work seamlessly across different platforms.
- Explore the importance of responsive design and cross-platform consistency for a unified user experience.

Chapter 2: The Evolution of Operating System Interfaces

- Establish the context for the evolution of operating system interfaces.
- Discuss the relationship between hardware advancements, user expectations, and the progression of interface design.
- Explore the early days of computing, focusing on command-line interfaces.
- Discuss the limitations and benefits of CLIs and their influence on subsequent interface developments.
- Examine the emergence of GUIs and their transformative impact on user interactions.
- Highlight iconic GUI-based operating systems and the shift towards more intuitive and visually oriented interfaces.
- Discuss the evolution of interfaces with the advent of touch-based interactions.
- Explore the impact of mobile devices on shaping user expectations and interface design trends.
- Provide insights into the contemporary landscape of OS interfaces.
- Discuss recent developments, such as minimalistic design, voice interfaces, and immersive experiences.

Chapter 3: Design Principles for Intuitive User Interaction

- Define the fundamental principles that guide intuitive user interaction.
- Emphasize the importance of a user-centric approach in UI design.
- Discuss the significance of maintaining consistency in UI elements and layout.
- Explore how consistent design fosters familiarity and ease of use.
- Explore the principles of organizing information hierarchically for optimal user comprehension.
- Discuss how a well-structured information hierarchy enhances the user's ability to navigate.
- Highlight the role of feedback mechanisms in user interfaces.
- Discuss how providing timely feedback enhances the user's understanding of their interactions.
- Emphasize the importance of simplicity and clarity in UI design.
- Discuss strategies for avoiding unnecessary complexity and promoting a straightforward user experience.

Chapter 4: Navigating the UI: A Deep Dive into User Experience

- Define User Experience and its connection to UI design.
- Discuss how positive UX is crucial for user satisfaction and overall system usability.
- Explore common navigation patterns in UI design.
- Discuss how understanding user flow contributes to creating intuitive and efficient interfaces.
- Highlight the significance of usability testing in refining UI designs.
- Discuss the iterative design process and how user feedback informs improvements.
- Explore the role of interactive elements in enhancing user engagement.
- Discuss the impact of animations, transitions, and interactive feedback on the overall user experience.
- Discuss the importance of designing interfaces that adapt to various screen sizes and devices.
- Explore responsive design principles for creating a seamless experience across platforms.

Chapter 5: Accessibility and Inclusivity in OS Interfaces

- Define accessibility and its significance in creating interfaces that cater to diverse user needs.
- Discuss the impact of inclusive design on user experience.
- Explore design considerations for making UI elements accessible to users with disabilities.
- Discuss features such as alternative text, keyboard navigation, and screen reader compatibility.
- Discuss strategies for creating visually inclusive interfaces.
- Explore color contrast, font choices, and other design elements that accommodate users with visual impairments.
- Highlight the importance of user testing specifically focused on accessibility.
- Discuss how involving users with diverse abilities contributes to a more inclusive interface.
- Discuss legal requirements and ethical considerations related to accessibility.
- Explore the impact of accessibility regulations on UI design practices.

Chapter 6: Innovations in UI Technology: Past, Present, and Future

- Establish the dynamic nature of UI technology and its continuous evolution.
- Discuss the symbiotic relationship between technological advancements and interface innovations.
- Explore historical milestones in UI technology.
- Discuss innovations such as the mouse, touchscreens, and gesture controls that shaped the UI landscape.
- Discuss the contemporary technological landscape in UI design.
- Explore current trends, such as augmented reality, voice interfaces, and AI-driven interactions.
- Explore emerging technologies expected to impact UI design in the future.
- Discuss the potential influence of technologies like virtual reality, brain-computer interfaces, and immersive experiences.
- Discuss ongoing research in the field of Human-Computer Interaction.
- Explore how HCI research contributes to shaping the future of UI technology.

Chapter 7: Security Measures in Operating System Interfaces

- Define the importance of security in operating system interfaces.
- Discuss the potential risks and consequences of insecure interfaces.
- Explore mechanisms for user authentication and authorization in UI design.
- Discuss the role of secure login procedures and permission management.
- Discuss strategies for securing data transmission within the UI.
- Explore the use of encryption and secure protocols to protect user data.
- Explore the integration of biometric authentication in operating system interfaces.
- Discuss the advantages and challenges of biometric security measures.
- Highlight the importance of user education in maintaining secure UI interactions.
- Discuss security best practices and how users can actively contribute to system security.

Chapter 8: UI Customization: Tailoring Your OS Experience

- Define UI customization and its role in personalizing the user experience.
- Discuss how customizable interfaces contribute to user satisfaction.
- Explore options for customizing the visual aspects of the interface.
- Discuss themes, color schemes, and icon customization.
- Discuss features that allow users to personalize their preferences.
- Explore options for customizing layouts, menus, and interactive elements.
- Discuss adaptive UI design principles for varying screen sizes and devices.
- Explore how interfaces can dynamically adjust to different platforms.
- Explore the integration of third-party extensions and plugins for UI customization.
- Discuss the benefits and considerations associated with external modifications.

Introduction

In the dynamic and ever-evolving landscape of technology, the user interface (UI) of operating systems stands as a linchpin, intricately weaving the fabric of our digital interactions. The essence of this pivotal role is encapsulated in the comprehensive exploration embarked upon in "Revolutionizing Interfaces: Mastering User Experience in Operating Systems." This literary voyage is more than a guide; it is an immersive journey that delves into the depths of UI design, unraveling its evolutionary trajectory, fundamental principles, and the profound impact it wields over our daily computing experiences.

The title itself, "Revolutionizing Interfaces," reflects the transformative nature of the subject matter. In the nascent stages of computing, interfaces were predominantly command-line driven, a far cry from the visually intuitive experiences we now take for granted. This exploration commences with an insightful retrospective in the early chapters, tracing the historical journey of interfaces through the eras of command-line interfaces (CLIs) and the revolutionary advent of Graphical User Interfaces (GUIs). These chapters not only chronicle the metamorphosis of UI design but also underscore the symbiotic relationship between hardware advancements, user expectations, and the perpetual evolution of interface aesthetics.

As the narrative unfolds, the guiding principles for crafting intuitive user interactions take center stage. "Design Principles for Intuitive User Interaction" becomes a compass, steering readers through the intricate labyrinth of creating interfaces that not only meet functional requirements but also resonate with users on a visceral level. Concepts such as consistency, hierarchy, and simplicity are dissected, revealing the alchemy behind designs that effortlessly guide users through the digital realm.

User Experience (UX), a concept synonymous with successful interface design, is given its due prominence in the chapters that follow. "Navigating the UI: A Deep Dive into User Experience" transcends the surface, exploring the psychological nuances of user interactions. It encapsulates the art of crafting seamless navigational patterns, usability testing methodologies, and the indispensable role of responsive design in an era where devices vary widely in form and function.

The narrative thread extends into the realm of inclusivity and accessibility with "Accessibility and Inclusivity in OS Interfaces." In this chapter, the importance of designing interfaces that cater to users with diverse abilities is underscored. Features ensuring accessibility, such as alternative text, keyboard navigation, and inclusivity in visual design, unfold as integral elements in the grand tapestry of interface design.

The exploration then delves into the technological metamorphosis that interfaces undergo in "Innovations in UI Technology: Past, Present, and Future." From the humble mouse to the realms of augmented reality and artificial intelligence, this chapter navigates the annals of technological advancements that have redefined the boundaries of UI design. It doesn't merely dwell in the past or present; it extends a visionary gaze into the future, contemplating the potential impact of emerging technologies on the UI landscape.

Security, an omnipresent concern in our interconnected world, takes center stage in "Security Measures in Operating System Interfaces." This chapter delves into the intricacies of securing UIs, encompassing aspects like authentication, data encryption, and user education. It unravels the layers of protection essential to ensure user data remains confidential and interactions secure.

The final chapter, "UI Customization: Tailoring Your OS Experience," transforms the narrative into a user-centric exploration. Here, the spotlight shifts to empowering users with the ability to personalize their operating system experiences. Customization, whether in visual elements, user preferences, or adaptive designs, emerges as the gateway to fostering a sense of ownership and comfort in the digital realm.

In conclusion, "Revolutionizing Interfaces" is not merely a compendium of design principles; it is an odyssey through the past, present, and future of user interfaces in operating systems. It illuminates the intricate dance between form and function, aesthetics and accessibility, technology and humanity. As the digital landscape continues to evolve, this exploration serves as a timeless guide, inviting readers to master the art of user experience in operating systems—a journey that is as profound as the digital interactions it seeks to enhance.

Chapter 1: Unveiling the UI Landscape

Define the concept of User Interface and its critical role in the digital world.

The User Interface (UI) serves as the pivotal link between humans and the digital realm, encapsulating the design elements and interactive components that facilitate user interactions with software, applications, and devices. Its critical role in the digital world lies in its ability to bridge the gap between the complexities of underlying technologies and the user's cognitive capacity, rendering the digital landscape accessible, intuitive, and efficient. UI encompasses a myriad of visual and interactive elements, ranging from graphical interfaces to touchscreens, voice commands, and gestures, each tailored to cater to diverse user preferences and requirements.

At its core, UI is not merely about aesthetics but is deeply intertwined with usability, aiming to enhance the overall user experience by minimizing friction and cognitive load. A well-designed user interface seamlessly guides users through functionalities, making navigation and interaction with digital systems an intuitive and enjoyable experience. Elements such as layout, color schemes, typography, and iconography are meticulously orchestrated to convey information, hierarchy, and functionality, contributing to the overall usability and aesthetics of the interface.

In the dynamic landscape of the digital world, the significance of UI extends beyond traditional computing devices to encompass a plethora of platforms, including smartphones, tablets, wearables, and emerging technologies like augmented reality (AR) and virtual reality (VR). The adaptability and responsiveness of UI become paramount as users engage with a diverse array of devices, each demanding a tailored interface that aligns with its unique form factor and input modalities.

Moreover, UI plays a pivotal role in shaping user perceptions and establishing brand identities. Consistent and visually appealing interfaces not only foster brand recognition but also evoke a sense of trust and reliability in the user. Brands invest considerable resources in crafting distinct visual elements and design languages to ensure a cohesive and memorable user interface across their digital products and services.

In the realm of software development, the concept of User Interface is inexorably linked with User Experience (UX). While UI primarily focuses on the presentation and interactivity of a digital interface, UX encompasses the holistic journey of a user, including their emotions, perceptions, and satisfaction throughout the interaction. A harmonious integration of UI and UX principles results in a compelling and user-centric design that transcends mere functionality, fostering a meaningful and delightful user experience.

Accessibility is another pivotal dimension of UI that underscores its role in inclusivity. A well-designed user interface takes into account the diverse needs of users, including those with disabilities, ensuring that digital interactions are barrier-free and universally accessible. Features like screen readers, voice commands, and customizable font sizes exemplify efforts to make UIs more inclusive and accommodating to a broad spectrum of users.

As technology evolves, the concept of UI continues to undergo transformations, driven by advancements such as artificial intelligence (AI) and machine learning. Intelligent interfaces, empowered by AI algorithms, have the capacity to adapt and personalize user experiences based on individual preferences, behavior patterns, and contextual insights. These interfaces not only enhance efficiency but also contribute to a sense of user empowerment, as the digital systems become more attuned to the unique needs and preferences of each user.

The ubiquity of mobile applications and web-based services underscores the omnipresence of UI in our daily lives. Whether navigating a social media platform, conducting online transactions, or using productivity tools, users are constantly engaging with interfaces that shape their digital interactions. Consequently, the effectiveness of UI directly influences user productivity, satisfaction, and the overall success of digital products and services.

In conclusion, the User Interface stands as a linchpin in the digital ecosystem, acting as the conduit through which users navigate and interact with the expansive world of technology. Its multifaceted role encompasses not only visual and interactive design but also extends to usability, accessibility, and user experience. As technology advances, the evolving landscape of UI continues to shape and redefine our digital experiences, playing a pivotal role in the convergence of technology and human interaction. The seamless fusion of functionality, aesthetics, and user-centric design principles epitomizes the essence of an effective and impactful User Interface in the ever-evolving digital world.

Discuss the impact of UI on user experience and the overall interaction with operating systems.

The impact of User Interface (UI) on user experience within operating systems is profound, shaping the way individuals interact with and perceive the digital realm. Operating systems serve as the foundational layer of computing environments, orchestrating hardware and software interactions, and the UI acts as the primary conduit through which users engage with these systems. A well-crafted UI significantly influences user experience, determining the efficiency, satisfaction, and overall usability of an operating system.

At the heart of the UI's impact is its role in facilitating seamless navigation and interaction. The design elements, such as menus, icons, and navigation structures, are instrumental in guiding users through the complexities of the operating system. Intuitive UI design reduces cognitive load, enabling users to effortlessly locate and execute tasks, whether it be opening applications, managing files, or adjusting system settings. Conversely, a poorly designed or cluttered UI can lead to frustration and hinder the overall user experience.

Consistency is a key aspect of UI design that directly impacts the user's ability to understand and predict interactions within an operating system. A consistent UI across different components and functionalities fosters a sense of familiarity, allowing users to transfer their knowledge and skills seamlessly between various aspects of the system. This uniformity contributes to a cohesive user experience, minimizing the learning curve and enhancing overall usability.

Accessibility is another critical dimension of UI that profoundly influences the inclusivity of operating systems. A well-designed UI considers diverse user needs, ensuring that individuals with disabilities can navigate and interact with the operating system effectively. Features like screen readers, high-contrast modes, and keyboard shortcuts contribute to a more accessible UI, enabling users with different abilities to engage with the system on equal footing.

The visual aesthetics of the UI also play a pivotal role in shaping user perceptions of the operating system. A visually pleasing and well-organized interface not only enhances the user experience but also contributes to a positive brand image for the operating system. Conversely, a dated or visually unappealing UI can create a negative impression, potentially influencing users to perceive the entire operating system as outdated or less sophisticated.

As operating systems evolve, the integration of modern UI design principles becomes increasingly important. The rise of graphical user interfaces (GUIs) marked a significant departure from command-line interfaces, democratizing computing by making it more accessible to non-technical users. Subsequent advancements, such as the introduction of touch interfaces in mobile operating systems, further revolutionized the way users interact with devices, emphasizing the importance of responsive and touch-friendly UI elements.

The advent of flat design and minimalist aesthetics in UI design has become a prevailing trend, characterized by clean lines, simplicity, and a focus on usability. This design philosophy prioritizes the elimination of unnecessary visual elements, enhancing clarity and streamlining the user interface. Operating systems that embrace these design trends often provide users with a more visually coherent and uncluttered experience.

The role of UI extends beyond mere visual design to include interactive elements that enhance user engagement. Animations, transitions, and feedback mechanisms contribute to a more dynamic and responsive user experience within operating systems. Well-timed animations can provide visual cues, indicating system responses to user actions and creating a more engaging and immersive interaction.

The advent of voice-activated interfaces and natural language processing has further expanded the horizons of UI design within operating systems. Voice commands and conversational interfaces offer alternative modes of interaction, catering to users who prefer hands-free or voice-driven interactions. The integration of AI-driven voice assistants into operating systems exemplifies the evolving landscape of UI, where natural language understanding enhances the user experience by providing a more intuitive means of interaction.

The impact of UI on user experience is not limited to traditional computing devices but extends to a diverse array of platforms, including smartphones, tablets, wearables, and even smart home devices. Operating systems designed for these platforms must tailor their UI to suit the unique characteristics of each device, considering factors such as screen size, input modalities, and mobility. The adaptability of UI across various form factors contributes to a consistent and harmonious user experience, regardless of the device in use.

Security and privacy considerations also intersect with UI design in operating systems. Transparent and user-friendly security features contribute to a sense of trust and control for users. Interfaces that effectively communicate security measures, such as encryption indicators and permission requests, empower users to make informed decisions regarding their data and system security. Striking a balance between robust security measures and a user-friendly interface is crucial for cultivating a positive overall user experience.

In conclusion, the impact of UI on user experience within operating systems is multifaceted and pivotal. The design choices made in crafting the user interface significantly influence how users perceive, interact with, and navigate the complexities of operating systems. From the visual aesthetics to the responsiveness of interactive elements, UI shapes the overall user experience and plays a crucial role in determining the success and adoption of an operating system in the ever-evolving digital landscape. As technology continues to advance, the ongoing refinement of UI design principles will remain integral to ensuring that operating systems deliver not only functionality but also an enriching and user-centric experience.

Explore various types of UIs, including graphical user interfaces (GUIs), command-line interfaces (CLIs), and touch-based interfaces.

User Interfaces (UIs) come in diverse forms, each tailored to specific user needs and technological contexts. Graphical User Interfaces (GUIs) represent one of the most prevalent and user-friendly types. GUIs utilize graphical elements such as icons, buttons, and menus to enable users to interact with a system. Widely popularized by operating systems like Microsoft Windows, macOS, and Linux desktop environments, GUIs simplify complex operations by providing a visual representation of tasks and options. Users can navigate through the system by pointing and clicking, making GUIs particularly accessible to non-technical users. The intuitive nature of GUIs has been a driving force in making computing more user-friendly, democratizing access to technology.

In contrast, Command-Line Interfaces (CLIs) present a more text-centric and script-driven approach to interacting with systems. Operating primarily through text commands, CLIs have been a staple in computing since the early days of mainframes and minicomputers. While they may seem intimidating to some users, CLIs offer unparalleled efficiency for power users and administrators who appreciate the speed and precision of command-driven interactions. Unix-based systems, including Linux distributions, exemplify the enduring relevance of CLIs in modern computing. CLIs remain a crucial tool for system configuration, automation, and troubleshooting, providing a level of control and customization often favored by experienced users.

Touch-based interfaces have surged in popularity with the proliferation of smartphones and tablets. This intuitive form of interaction relies on gestures, swipes, and taps to control devices. Mobile operating systems like iOS and Android have spearheaded the adoption of touch interfaces, bringing a new dimension to user interactions. The tactile nature of touchscreens enhances the user experience, allowing for direct manipulation of content. Beyond mobile devices, touch interfaces have extended to laptops, interactive kiosks, and even tabletop displays. The evolution of touch technology has reshaped how users engage with digital content, fostering a more natural and immediate connection between the user and the interface.

Voice-activated interfaces represent another transformative type of UI, leveraging natural language processing and voice recognition technologies. Virtual assistants like Apple's Siri, Amazon's Alexa, and Google Assistant exemplify this interface type. Users can issue verbal commands, ask questions, or initiate actions, and the interface responds accordingly. Voice interfaces have found applications not only in smartphones and smart speakers but also in various smart home devices and automotive systems. The hands-free and conversational nature of voice interfaces enhances accessibility and convenience, providing an alternative mode of interaction that resonates with users seeking a more fluid and natural way to engage with technology.

Augmented Reality (AR) and Virtual Reality (VR) interfaces introduce immersive experiences by blending digital elements with the user's physical environment or transporting them to entirely virtual worlds. AR overlays digital information onto the real world, often through devices like smart glasses or smartphone cameras. Applications range from navigation and gaming to industrial training and education. VR, on the other hand, immerses users in entirely simulated environments, often accessed through specialized headsets. These interfaces have implications not only in entertainment and gaming but also in fields such as education, healthcare, and design. The ability to interact with digital content in three-dimensional space adds a layer of depth and engagement that traditional interfaces may lack.

Gesture-based interfaces leverage hand movements and gestures to control devices or interact with digital content. This type of interface gained prominence with devices like Microsoft's Kinect and is now commonly found in smartphones, smart TVs, and interactive displays. Gesture-based interfaces offer a hands-on and intuitive approach to interaction, allowing users to navigate, select, and manipulate content by moving their hands in specific patterns. This type of UI has found applications in gaming, virtual reality, and even in public spaces, where touchless interactions are increasingly desirable for hygiene and convenience.

Biometric interfaces, such as fingerprint scanners, facial recognition, and iris scans, have become integral components of modern devices. These interfaces provide secure and convenient methods for user authentication and identification. Mobile devices, laptops, and even some payment systems utilize biometric data for access control. The seamless integration of biometrics into UIs streamlines authentication processes, enhancing security while reducing reliance on traditional passwords or PINs. The use of biometric interfaces also contributes to a more personalized and user-friendly experience.

Adaptive interfaces represent a dynamic approach to UI design, adjusting and customizing based on user behavior, preferences, and contextual factors. Machine learning algorithms and artificial intelligence power adaptive interfaces, allowing systems to learn from user interactions and optimize the user experience over time. Recommendations in streaming services, personalized content feeds on social media, and adaptive menus in software applications showcase the impact of adaptive interfaces. By tailoring the UI to individual users, adaptive interfaces aim to enhance user satisfaction, engagement, and efficiency, showcasing the potential of AI-driven customization in shaping digital interactions.

Inclusive interfaces prioritize accessibility for users with diverse abilities and needs. These interfaces aim to make digital systems usable for everyone, regardless of physical or cognitive challenges. Features like screen readers, closed captions, and voice commands contribute to the inclusivity of interfaces. Inclusive design recognizes the importance of accommodating a wide range of users, fostering a sense of equity and ensuring that digital experiences are accessible to individuals with disabilities. This approach aligns with the principles of universal design, emphasizing the creation of products and environments that are usable by all people, to the greatest extent possible, without the need for adaptation or specialized design.

In conclusion, the landscape of User Interfaces is expansive and continually evolving to meet the demands of diverse users and emerging technologies. Graphical User Interfaces offer accessibility and visual representation, Command-Line Interfaces provide precision and control, Touch-based Interfaces revolutionize mobile interactions, Voice-activated Interfaces enable hands-free engagement, Augmented and Virtual Reality interfaces immerse users in new realms, Gesture-based Interfaces introduce intuitive control, Biometric Interfaces enhance security, Adaptive Interfaces utilize machine learning for personalization, and Inclusive Interfaces prioritize accessibility for all. As technology advances, the fusion and evolution of these interface types will continue to shape how users interact with digital systems, emphasizing usability, accessibility, and a seamless integration of technology into our daily lives.

Discuss the strengths and weaknesses of each type, highlighting their applications and user demographics.

Graphical User Interfaces (GUIs) stand out for their visual appeal and intuitive nature, making them accessible to a broad user demographic, including those with limited technical expertise. The strengths of GUIs lie in their ability to present information in a visually organized manner, with icons, menus, and buttons guiding users through tasks. This visual representation simplifies complex operations, reducing the learning curve for users interacting with operating systems, applications, and websites. GUIs excel in applications where a graphical representation of data or tasks enhances user understanding, such as design software, multimedia applications, and general-purpose computing. However, their weaknesses may surface in scenarios where speed and efficiency are paramount, as excessive graphical elements can introduce navigation overhead. Power users may also find GUIs limiting in terms of customization and precision compared to command-line dipterfaces.

Command-Line Interfaces (CLIs) cater to a more technically proficient audience, providing efficiency and precision in executing commands and automating tasks. The text-driven nature of CLIs allows for quick and direct communication with the operating system, making them powerful tools for system administrators and developers. The strength of CLIs lies in their scripting capabilities, enabling the automation of repetitive tasks and intricate system configurations. However, the text-based nature of CLIs can be intimidating for users unfamiliar with command syntax, limiting their accessibility. While CLIs excel in scenarios requiring speed, automation, and a high degree of control, they may not be the ideal choice for users who prioritize visual cues or those less experienced in command-driven interactions.

Touch-based interfaces have gained widespread adoption, particularly in mobile devices, due to their intuitive nature and immersive user experience. The strengths of touch interfaces lie in their direct manipulation of digital content, allowing users to interact with devices in a tactile and natural manner. Swipe gestures, taps, and pinches provide a more immediate connection between the user and the interface. Touch interfaces find extensive applications in smartphones and tablets, where portability and simplicity are key. However, they may face challenges in certain professional settings where precise input is crucial, such as graphic design or detailed data entry. Additionally, touch interfaces might not be optimal for users with motor impairments, as they heavily rely on gestures that may pose challenges for some demographics.

Voice-activated interfaces represent a hands-free and convenient means of interaction, particularly suited for scenarios where manual input is impractical or unsafe. Virtual assistants like Siri, Alexa, and Google Assistant exemplify the strengths of voice interfaces, enabling users to perform tasks, get information, and control devices using natural language. The accessibility of voice interfaces is advantageous for users with mobility issues or those in situations where hands-free interaction is preferred, such as driving. However, their weaknesses include potential misinterpretation of commands, limited precision compared to other input methods, and concerns regarding privacy and data security. Voice interfaces have found widespread use in smart speakers, smartphones, and automotive systems, catering to a diverse user demographic.

Augmented Reality (AR) and Virtual Reality (VR) interfaces offer immersive experiences that extend beyond traditional screens. AR overlays digital information onto the real world, enhancing users' perception of their surroundings, while VR transports users to entirely simulated environments. The strengths of AR lie in its applications for navigation, training, and information overlay in real-world contexts. VR, on the other hand, excels in gaming, simulations, and virtual experiences. Both AR and VR provide a heightened sense of engagement but may face challenges related to hardware requirements, potential motion sickness in VR, and the need for specialized devices. While these interfaces have found success in gaming and entertainment, they also hold promise in areas like education, healthcare, and industrial training.

Gesture-based interfaces leverage hand movements to control devices, offering an intuitive and interactive experience. Devices like Microsoft's Kinect and touchless interactions in smartphones exemplify the strengths of gesture-based interfaces. Their hands-on approach provides a natural way to interact with digital content, making them suitable for applications in gaming, interactive displays, and public spaces. However, the technology's accuracy and reliability may pose challenges, and prolonged use can lead to user fatigue. Gesture-based interfaces find applications in scenarios where touchless interaction is desirable, such as interactive kiosks, and they appeal to users who appreciate a more physical and interactive mode of engagement.

Biometric interfaces, including fingerprint scanners, facial recognition, and iris scans, enhance security and streamline user authentication. The strengths of biometric interfaces lie in their convenience and the reduction of reliance on traditional passwords. Fingerprint and facial recognition are commonly found in smartphones, laptops, and other devices, offering a quick and secure means of unlocking. However, concerns about privacy, data security, and the potential for false positives or negatives are challenges associated with biometric authentication. Biometric interfaces cater to users who prioritize ease of access while recognizing the need for secure authentication in various contexts.

Adaptive interfaces leverage machine learning algorithms to personalize user experiences based on individual behavior, preferences, and contextual factors. The strengths of adaptive interfaces lie in their ability to dynamically adjust and optimize the user interface, providing tailored content and recommendations. Applications like personalized content feeds, recommendation algorithms in streaming services, and adaptive menus showcase the strengths of this interface type. However, challenges include potential privacy concerns and the need for sufficient user data to train effective machine learning models. Adaptive interfaces cater to users who appreciate personalized and contextually relevant experiences, contributing to increased user engagement.

Inclusive interfaces prioritize accessibility, ensuring that digital systems are usable by individuals with diverse abilities and needs. The strengths of inclusive interfaces lie in their commitment to providing equitable access to technology. Features such as screen readers, closed captions, and voice commands contribute to a more accessible user experience. The demographic for inclusive interfaces encompasses users with disabilities, making technology more inclusive and user-friendly for a broader audience. The challenge lies in ensuring that accessibility features are comprehensive and well-implemented, addressing various needs across different user demographics.

In summary, each type of User Interface possesses unique strengths and weaknesses, catering to specific user preferences, needs, and contexts. Graphical User Interfaces offer visual simplicity and accessibility but may lack efficiency for power users. Command-Line Interfaces provide precision and automation but require technical expertise. Touch-based interfaces offer an intuitive and tactile experience but may lack precision for certain tasks. Voice-activated interfaces provide hands-free convenience but face challenges in accuracy and privacy. Augmented and Virtual Reality interfaces offer immersive experiences but may require specialized hardware. Gesture-based interfaces offer a physical and interactive experience but may pose accuracy challenges. Biometric interfaces enhance security but raise privacy concerns. Adaptive interfaces provide personalized experiences but rely on user data. Inclusive interfaces prioritize accessibility, making technology more usable for individuals with diverse abilities. The choice of interface type depends on the specific requirements of the task, the preferences of the user demographic, and the technological context in which they are applied. As technology continues to advance, the interplay and evolution of these interface types will shape the future of digital interactions, aiming to provide seamless, engaging, and inclusive user experiences.

Break down the essential elements that constitute a user interface.

A User Interface (UI) is a complex amalgamation of various elements that collectively shape the interaction between users and digital systems. At its core, a UI serves as the intermediary layer through which users engage with software, applications, or devices. Visual design stands out as one of the foundational elements, encompassing the aesthetic aspects that users perceive. This includes the arrangement of elements, color schemes, typography, and overall layout, all working together to create a visually cohesive and appealing interface. The visual design not only contributes to the aesthetics but also plays a crucial role in conveying information hierarchy, guiding user focus, and enhancing overall usability.

Interactivity is another indispensable element of a user interface, defining how users can engage with and manipulate the system. Interactive elements such as buttons, sliders, menus, and input fields provide the means for users to input commands, make selections, and navigate through the interface. The responsiveness of these elements, coupled with smooth transitions and feedback mechanisms, contributes to a dynamic and engaging user experience. Interactivity also extends to the seamless integration of animations and transitions, which not only add a layer of visual interest but also serve functional purposes by indicating system responses to user actions.

Navigation forms a fundamental aspect of UI, dictating how users move through different sections, features, or content within a digital system. The structure and organization of menus, navigation bars, and links determine the ease with which users can locate and access information. Intuitive navigation design reduces cognitive load, ensuring that users can efficiently navigate the interface without confusion. Clear hierarchies, well-defined pathways, and logical grouping of related features contribute to an interface that is both user-friendly and efficient in facilitating user tasks.

Information architecture plays a pivotal role in shaping how information is structured and presented within a user interface. This element focuses on the organization and categorization of content, ensuring that users can easily find what they are looking for. Hierarchical structures, categorization schemes, and the labeling of content contribute to an interface that is intuitive and aligns with users' mental models. A well-thought-out information architecture not only aids navigation but also enhances the overall comprehensibility of the interface, allowing users to quickly grasp the relationships between different pieces of information.

Accessibility is a critical element that underscores the inclusivity of a user interface. A truly effective UI is one that caters to users with diverse abilities and needs. Accessibility features such as screen readers, alternative text for images, keyboard shortcuts, and adjustable font sizes ensure that the interface is usable by individuals with disabilities. Designing for accessibility goes beyond compliance with standards; it embodies a commitment to making digital experiences barrier-free, allowing a broader spectrum of users to engage with the interface.

Consistency serves as a foundational principle in UI design, encompassing visual, interactive, and behavioral aspects. Consistency ensures that similar elements or actions are represented in the same way throughout the interface, promoting a sense of familiarity for users. Consistent design patterns, color schemes, and iconography contribute to a cohesive and unified user experience. This uniformity extends across different sections of an application or website, as well as across various platforms, ensuring a seamless and predictable interaction for users.

Feedback mechanisms are integral to user interfaces, providing users with information about the outcomes of their actions. Whether it's a button press, form submission, or error notification, feedback mechanisms convey the system's response to user input. Visual cues, such as success messages, error alerts, or loading indicators, contribute to a transparent and communicative interface. Effective feedback not only informs users about the status of their interactions but also helps in preventing confusion and frustration.

Typography, often considered a subset of visual design, merits special attention due to its impact on readability and overall user experience. The choice of fonts, font sizes, line spacing, and text alignment contribute to the legibility of textual content within the interface. A well-considered typographic hierarchy aids in emphasizing important information, guiding users through content, and creating a visually balanced layout. Moreover, responsive typography ensures that the text remains readable across various screen sizes and devices, enhancing the overall accessibility of the interface.

Color plays a dual role in UI design, serving both aesthetic and functional purposes. The color scheme contributes to the overall visual appeal of the interface, creating a cohesive and visually pleasing design. Simultaneously, color is used strategically to convey meaning, signify interactive elements, and communicate feedback. Attention to color contrast is crucial for accessibility, ensuring that users with visual impairments can discern different elements within the interface. By leveraging color effectively, UI designers can guide user attention, establish visual hierarchies, and create a harmonious and engaging user experience.

Error handling and messaging constitute a critical aspect of UI design, addressing situations where users encounter issues or make mistakes. Clear and concise error messages guide users in understanding the nature of the problem and provide actionable steps to resolve it. Thoughtful error handling prevents user frustration by offering solutions and alternatives. The language used in error messages also contributes to the overall tone of the interface, influencing the user's perception of the system's reliability and user-friendliness.

In conclusion, a successful user interface is a holistic integration of visual, interactive, and informational elements that collectively shape the user experience. Visual design, interactivity, navigation, information architecture, accessibility, consistency, feedback mechanisms, typography, color, error handling, and messaging each contribute to the overall usability and appeal of the interface. The effective combination of these elements aligns with the overarching goal of creating an interface that is not only aesthetically pleasing but also intuitive, accessible, and capable of facilitating seamless user interactions in the digital landscape.

Explore common UI components such as buttons, menus, icons, and their significance in facilitating user interaction.

Common UI components, including buttons, menus, and icons, serve as fundamental building blocks that significantly contribute to the user's interaction and navigation within digital interfaces. Buttons are ubiquitous elements designed to elicit user actions, serving as clickable entities that initiate specific functions or processes. Their significance lies in providing a tangible and visually recognizable means for users to interact with the system. Whether it's submitting a form, confirming a decision, or triggering a command, buttons embody a call-to-action, guiding users through various tasks with clarity and responsiveness. The visual design of buttons, including shape, color, and size, plays a crucial role in conveying their significance and creating a consistent and intuitive user experience. Well-designed buttons enhance the overall usability of an interface, ensuring that users can effortlessly navigate and engage with the digital environment.

Menus, another integral UI component, offer a structured and organized way to present a range of options or features to users. Menus come in various forms, including dropdown menus, navigation menus, and context menus, each tailored to specific use cases. The significance of menus lies in their ability to streamline information and functionality, preventing interface clutter and cognitive overload. Dropdown menus, for instance, allow for hierarchical categorization, facilitating the grouping of related options. Navigation menus provide a roadmap for users to access different sections of an application or website, contributing to a logical and intuitive flow. Context menus, often activated through right-click actions, offer contextual options based on the user's interaction with specific elements. Effective menu design enhances user navigation, accessibility, and the overall organization of content within the interface.

Icons serve as visual symbols that represent actions, objects, or concepts within a user interface. Their significance is rooted in their ability to convey information quickly and efficiently, transcending language barriers and providing a universal means of communication. Icons contribute to a more visually appealing and streamlined interface by condensing complex ideas or functionalities into simple graphical representations. The use of consistent and recognizable icons fosters a sense of familiarity, aiding users in understanding the purpose of different elements. Icons often accompany textual labels to reinforce meaning, creating a visual language that enhances the overall comprehension of the interface. The scalability of icons makes them versatile across various devices and screen sizes, ensuring a consistent and coherent visual identity.

Input fields, such as textboxes, checkboxes, radio buttons, and dropdown lists, are essential UI components that facilitate user interaction by allowing the input of data or making selections. These components play a crucial role in forms, search bars, and configuration settings. The significance of input fields lies in their role as conduits for user input, enabling users to provide information, make choices, or perform searches. Well-designed input fields consider factors such as labeling, validation, and feedback, ensuring that users can interact seamlessly while avoiding confusion or errors. Clear and concise labels guide users in understanding the expected input, and thoughtful validation mechanisms provide feedback on the accuracy of entered data. The design of input fields directly influences the efficiency and user-friendliness of tasks that involve data entry.

Toggle switches and sliders are interactive UI components that allow users to control binary states or adjust values within a specified range. The significance of toggle switches lies in their ability to represent on/off or enable/disable states in a visually straightforward manner. Users can easily grasp the status of a setting by observing the position of the toggle switch. Sliders, on the other hand, offer a dynamic way to adjust numerical values, such as volume, brightness, or scale. The drag-and-slide interaction allows for precise adjustments, providing users with a tactile and intuitive means of control. Both toggle switches and sliders contribute to a more engaging and user-friendly interface, allowing users to customize their experience and preferences with minimal effort.

Progress indicators and loading spinners are UI components that convey the status of ongoing processes or asynchronous tasks, providing users with visual feedback on the system's activity. The significance of progress indicators lies in their ability to manage user expectations and reduce uncertainty during tasks that require time to complete. Progress indicators can take various forms, including progress bars, spinners, or animated graphics, each designed to visually communicate the progression of a task. Loading spinners, in particular, indicate that the system is actively working on a task, preventing users from perceiving delays as system unresponsiveness. The thoughtful inclusion of progress indicators contributes to a transparent and communicative interface, enhancing the overall user experience.

Cards and tiles are UI components that present discrete units of information or content in a structured and visually appealing manner. The significance of cards and tiles lies in their ability to organize and display information in a digestible format, facilitating content discovery and navigation. Cards often feature a combination of text, images, and interactive elements, making them versatile for presenting various types of content, such as articles, products, or user profiles. The modular nature of cards allows for flexibility in layout, enabling responsive design that adapts to different screen sizes. Whether used in social media feeds, e-commerce platforms, or content management systems, cards and tiles contribute to a visually cohesive and engaging interface that prioritizes content hierarchy and user interaction.

Dialog boxes and modals are UI components that temporarily interrupt the main flow of an interface to prompt users for input, convey information, or confirm actions. The significance of dialog boxes lies in their ability to focus user attention on a specific task or decision, preventing distraction from the surrounding interface. Modals, often used for tasks like form submissions, login prompts, or alerts, provide a layer of context to user interactions. The controlled and contained nature of dialog boxes ensures that users address specific tasks or decisions before returning to the main interface, contributing to a more guided and intentional user experience. Effective design of dialog boxes considers clarity in messaging, appropriate use of visuals, and a seamless transition in and out of the modal state.

Navigation bars and breadcrumbs are UI components designed to aid users in orienting themselves within an interface and navigating between different sections or pages. The significance of navigation bars lies in their role as persistent elements that offer a comprehensive menu of available destinations. Whether placed at the top, bottom, or sides of the interface, navigation bars provide users with a clear pathway to access different sections. Breadcrumbs, on the other hand, display a hierarchical trail of the user's current location, aiding in backtracking or jumping to higher-level pages. The thoughtful implementation of navigation bars and breadcrumbs enhances the overall navigational experience, ensuring that users can seamlessly move through the interface with clarity and ease.

Scrollbar and pagination are UI components that address the challenge of navigating through large sets of content, such as lengthy documents or extensive lists. The significance of scrollbars lies in their ability to facilitate vertical or horizontal scrolling, allowing users to explore content beyond the immediate viewport. Scrollbars provide a visual representation of the user's position within the content, indicating the extent of available information. Pagination, on the other hand, breaks down content into discrete pages, offering a more controlled navigation method. Pagination is often used in scenarios where content is logically segmented, such as search results or articles. Both scrollbar and pagination contribute to a more manageable and user-friendly experience when dealing with sizable amounts of information.

In conclusion, the significance of common UI components such as buttons, menus, icons, input fields, toggle switches, sliders, progress indicators, loading spinners, cards, tiles, dialog boxes, modals, navigation bars, breadcrumbs, scrollbars, and pagination lies in their collective ability to shape the user's interaction, navigation, and overall experience within digital interfaces. These components serve as the tangible elements through which users engage with and manipulate the system, providing visual cues, interactivity, and feedback. The thoughtful design and implementation of these components contribute to an interface that is not only aesthetically pleasing but also intuitive, accessible, and efficient in facilitating seamless user interactions across various platforms and devices.

Trace the historical evolution of user interface design.

The historical evolution of user interface (UI) design spans several decades, reflecting technological advancements, changing user expectations, and the iterative refinement of design principles. The early era of computing, marked by mainframes and early minicomputers in the mid-20th century, featured command-line interfaces (CLIs) as the predominant means of interaction. Users had to input commands through text, often using complex syntax, reflecting the nascent stage of digital interfaces where accessibility and user-friendliness were not the primary considerations.

The introduction of graphical user interfaces (GUIs) in the 1970s and 1980s revolutionized UI design, making computing more accessible to a broader audience. Pioneered by Xerox PARC with the development of the Alto, GUIs replaced text-heavy interfaces with visual elements such as icons, windows, and menus. The iconic Xerox Star, released in 1981, was the first commercial computer to feature a GUI, setting the stage for future innovations. However, it was Apple's Macintosh, launched in 1984, that brought GUIs to the mainstream. The Macintosh showcased a user-friendly interface with a point-and-click system, introducing concepts like the desktop metaphor, file icons, and the trash can, which became standard elements in subsequent UI design.

Simultaneously, Microsoft Windows emerged as a major player in GUI-based computing, initially with Windows 1.0 in 1985. Windows popularized concepts introduced by the Macintosh, embracing the GUI paradigm and contributing to the establishment of a standard graphical interface across personal computers. The rivalry between Apple and Microsoft in the late 20th century fueled innovation in UI design, leading to the refinement of graphical elements, color schemes, and iconography.

The 1990s witnessed a proliferation of personal computers and the rise of the internet, shaping UI design to accommodate evolving user needs. The advent of web browsers brought forth a new frontier, prompting the development of web-based UIs. Websites initially embraced a utilitarian design with static pages, limited interactivity, and basic navigation. However, the late 1990s saw the emergence of Dynamic HTML (DHTML) and cascading style sheets (CSS), allowing for more interactive and visually appealing web interfaces.

The early 2000s marked a significant shift with the advent of Web 2.0, characterized by dynamic content, social media, and the increased interactivity of web applications. UI design became more user-centric, with a focus on responsiveness, fluid interactions, and the integration of multimedia elements. Notable examples include the clean and minimalist interfaces of Google and the introduction of the "card" layout by platforms like Pinterest. The rise of smartphones in the late 2000s further reshaped UI design, with touchscreens introducing new interaction paradigms.

The launch of the iPhone in 2007 by Apple marked a watershed moment in UI design. The touchscreen interface, coupled with gestures like swiping and pinching, redefined user interactions. Apple's iOS introduced the App Store, unleashing a wave of mobile applications with diverse UI designs. Android, Google's mobile operating system, followed suit, contributing to the establishment of common mobile UI patterns. The mobile era emphasized simplicity, intuitive navigation, and touch-friendly interfaces, influencing UI design across various platforms.

As technology progressed, responsive design became a pivotal consideration. With users accessing content on an array of devices, UI design needed to adapt to different screen sizes. Responsive design principles focused on creating interfaces that could seamlessly adjust to various resolutions and orientations, ensuring a consistent and user-friendly experience across devices.

The mid-2010s witnessed a surge in flat design, characterized by minimalist aesthetics, simple color schemes, and the removal of embellishments like gradients and shadows. This design trend, championed by platforms like Microsoft's Windows 8 and Apple's iOS 7, prioritized clarity, legibility, and a focus on content. Flat design also contributed to faster loading times, particularly important in an era where users increasingly accessed content over mobile networks.

The subsequent rise of Material Design by Google introduced a new design language that blended flat design principles with tactile and real-world elements. Material Design emphasized the use of layers, shadows, and responsive animations, creating a visually rich and intuitive experience. This design language aimed to provide a consistent UI across diverse platforms, including web and mobile applications.

In recent years, dark mode has gained prominence as a UI design option, driven by considerations of eye comfort, energy efficiency for OLED displays, and aesthetic preferences. Platforms and applications started offering dark mode settings to allow users to choose their preferred visual experience.

The integration of artificial intelligence (AI) and machine learning (ML) into UI design is another contemporary trend. AI-powered features, such as predictive typing, personalized recommendations, and smart assistants, enhance user experiences by adapting interfaces to individual preferences and behaviors. The use of chatbots and voice-activated interfaces also represents a shift towards more natural and conversational interactions.

The ongoing evolution of UI design continues to be influenced by emerging technologies such as augmented reality (AR) and virtual reality (VR). AR interfaces overlay digital content onto the real world, demanding new design considerations, while VR interfaces immerse users in entirely digital environments, requiring innovative approaches to interaction and navigation.

In conclusion, the historical evolution of user interface design reflects a dynamic interplay between technological advancements, changing user expectations, and design philosophies. From the command-line interfaces of early computing to the graphical user interfaces of desktop computing, the advent of the internet, the mobile revolution, and contemporary trends like responsive design, flat design, and AI integration, UI design has continually adapted to meet the evolving needs of users in the digital age. The journey of UI design showcases a commitment to enhancing user experiences through thoughtful, intuitive, and aesthetically pleasing interfaces. As technology continues to advance, UI design will undoubtedly remain at the forefront of shaping how individuals interact with digital systems.

Highlight key milestones, paradigm shifts, and influential technologies that have shaped the UI landscape over time.

The history of user interface (UI) design is punctuated by key milestones, paradigm shifts, and the introduction of influential technologies that have continually shaped the UI landscape. In the early years of computing during the mid-20th century, command-line interfaces (CLIs) were the dominant means of interaction. This era was marked by the advent of mainframes and early minicomputers, where users had to input commands through text, reflecting a nascent stage in UI design characterized by technical complexity and limited accessibility.

The paradigm shift towards graphical user interfaces (GUIs) in the 1970s and 1980s stands as one of the most transformative milestones in UI history. The Xerox Alto, developed at Xerox PARC in the early 1970s, was a pioneering computer that introduced the concept of GUIs, featuring a graphical display, mouse, and windows. While the Alto was not commercially released, it laid the foundation for future GUI developments. Subsequently, the Xerox Star in 1981 became the first commercial computer to feature a GUI, establishing fundamental elements such as icons, windows, and menus. This marked a departure from the text-heavy interfaces of the past, making computing more accessible and user-friendly.

The release of the Apple Macintosh in 1984 marked a significant milestone in GUI adoption. Apple's Macintosh brought the graphical interface to a wider audience with its iconic desktop metaphor, graphical icons, and point-and-click interaction. The Macintosh showcased a revolutionary approach to UI design, emphasizing visual appeal, simplicity, and intuitive interactions. This shift laid the groundwork for subsequent developments in personal computing and had a profound impact on the expectations of users.

Simultaneously, Microsoft Windows emerged as a major player in the GUI-based computing landscape. Windows 1.0, released in 1985, introduced a multitasking graphical environment for IBM-compatible PCs. The Windows series played a pivotal role in popularizing GUIs on personal computers, creating a standard visual interface across various platforms. The rivalry between Apple and Microsoft during this period spurred innovation and refinement in

GUI design, contributing to the establishment of common graphical elements, color schemes, and iconography.

The 1990s witnessed the advent of the internet, bringing about a paradigm shift in UI design with the introduction of web-based interfaces. Early websites were characterized by static pages, minimal interactivity, and rudimentary navigation. However, the late 1990s saw the emergence of Dynamic HTML (DHTML) and cascading style sheets (CSS), allowing for more interactive and visually appealing web interfaces. This shift towards dynamic and visually engaging web design laid the groundwork for the evolution of user experiences on the internet.

The early 2000s marked the era of Web 2.0, characterized by the rise of dynamic content, social media, and interactive web applications. Websites became more user-centric, emphasizing user-generated content and the integration of multimedia elements. This period saw the transition from utilitarian web design to more visually engaging and interactive interfaces. Platforms like Google Maps and Gmail exemplified the potential of richer, more dynamic web applications.

The introduction of smartphones in the late 2000s initiated another significant paradigm shift in UI design. The release of the iPhone by Apple in 2007 marked the beginning of the mobile era. The touchscreen interface, coupled with gestures like swiping and pinching, redefined user interactions. Apple's iOS introduced the concept of the App Store, unleashing a wave of mobile applications with diverse UI designs. Google's Android platform followed suit, contributing to the establishment of common mobile UI patterns. The mobile era emphasized simplicity, intuitive navigation, and touch-friendly interfaces, influencing UI design across various platforms.

Responsive design became a pivotal consideration in UI design as users began accessing content on an array of devices with different screen sizes. Responsive design principles focused on creating interfaces that could seamlessly adjust to various resolutions and orientations, ensuring a consistent and user-friendly experience across devices. This milestone addressed the challenges posed by the diverse landscape of smartphones, tablets, and desktops.

The mid-2010s witnessed the rise of flat design, characterized by minimalist aesthetics, simple color schemes, and the removal of embellishments like gradients and shadows. This design trend, championed by platforms like Microsoft's Windows 8 and Apple's iOS 7, prioritized clarity, legibility, and a focus on content. Flat design also contributed to faster loading times, particularly important in an era where users increasingly accessed content over mobile networks.

Material Design, introduced by Google in 2014, marked another significant milestone in UI design. Material Design is a design language that blends flat design principles with tactile and real-world elements. It emphasizes the use of layers, shadows, and responsive animations, creating a visually rich and intuitive experience. Material Design was introduced to provide a consistent UI across diverse platforms, including web and mobile applications.

The concept of dark mode gained prominence in UI design in the late 2010s. Driven by considerations of eye comfort, energy efficiency for OLED displays, and aesthetic preferences, dark mode options started becoming prevalent in various platforms and applications. Dark mode provided users with an alternative visual experience, contributing to the ongoing customization and personalization of UI design.

The integration of artificial intelligence (AI) and machine learning (ML) into UI design represents a contemporary trend. AI-powered features, such as predictive typing, personalized recommendations, and smart assistants, enhance user experiences by adapting interfaces to individual preferences and behaviors. The use of chatbots and voice-activated interfaces also represents a shift towards more natural and conversational interactions, further blurring the lines between human and machine interaction.

The ongoing evolution of UI design continues to be influenced by emerging technologies such as augmented reality (AR) and virtual reality (VR). AR interfaces overlay digital content onto the real world, demanding new design considerations, while VR interfaces immerse users in entirely digital environments, requiring innovative approaches to interaction and navigation. These technologies are shaping the UI landscape by introducing new possibilities and challenges for designers.

In conclusion, the historical evolution of user interface design is characterized by a series of transformative milestones, paradigm shifts, and the introduction of influential technologies. From the early command-line interfaces to the graphical user interfaces of desktop computing, the rise of the internet, the mobile revolution, and contemporary trends like responsive design, flat design, dark mode, and AI integration, UI design has continually adapted to meet the evolving needs of users in the digital age. These milestones collectively highlight the dynamic nature of UI design, shaped by advancements in technology, changes in user behavior, and the ongoing pursuit of creating intuitive, accessible, and aesthetically pleasing interfaces across diverse platforms and devices.

Discuss challenges and solutions in designing UIs that work seamlessly across different platforms.

Designing user interfaces (UIs) that work seamlessly across different platforms poses a myriad of challenges stemming from variations in device capabilities, screen sizes, interaction methods, and user expectations. One of the primary challenges is achieving consistency while accommodating the diversity of platforms, including desktops, tablets, and smartphones. Striking a balance between a unified visual identity and tailoring the interface to specific platform conventions is crucial. Maintaining brand consistency while adhering to platform-specific design guidelines requires thoughtful adaptation to ensure that users feel comfortable and familiar regardless of the device they are using.

Another challenge lies in the diversity of screen sizes and resolutions across different platforms. Responsive design has emerged as a solution, allowing UIs to dynamically adjust and optimize layout and content based on the screen size. This approach ensures that the interface remains visually appealing and functional, providing an optimal user experience irrespective of the device. However, implementing responsive design requires careful consideration of content hierarchy, prioritization, and the restructuring of UI elements to maintain clarity and usability on both large desktop monitors and smaller mobile screens.

Navigational structures pose another challenge in cross-platform UI design. The navigation patterns that work well on a desktop might not translate seamlessly to a mobile device. Designers need to consider how users interact with different platforms and tailor navigation accordingly. Hierarchical menu structures might be suitable for desktops, while mobile interfaces may benefit from simplified navigation, such as hamburger menus, swipe gestures, or tab bars. Balancing navigational consistency with platform-specific optimizations is essential to ensure an intuitive and efficient user experience.

Interaction methods vary significantly across platforms, with devices ranging from traditional mouse and keyboard setups to touchscreens, voice commands, and gestures. Designing UIs that seamlessly adapt to these diverse interaction methods requires a deep understanding of each platform's capabilities and limitations. Solutions involve providing alternative interactions based on the device in use, such as touch-friendly buttons for mobile interfaces and keyboard shortcuts for desktop applications. Ensuring that the UI responds intuitively to user inputs on different platforms contributes to a cohesive and user-friendly experience.

Performance optimization presents another challenge, especially when designing for platforms with varying processing power and network conditions. Heavy graphics, complex animations, or data-heavy content might work well on high-performance desktops but could lead to slow loading times and increased data usage on mobile devices. Implementing performance-focused design strategies, such as lazy loading of assets, compressing images, and minimizing unnecessary animations, helps ensure a smooth and efficient experience across different platforms.

Maintaining accessibility is a critical consideration in cross-platform UI design. Different devices cater to users with varying abilities and preferences. Ensuring that UIs are accessible to individuals with disabilities, such as providing alternative text for images, adhering to contrast guidelines, and offering keyboard navigation options, is imperative. Additionally, accommodating the needs of users with different language preferences and cultural contexts adds another layer of complexity to cross-platform design. Solutions involve adopting inclusive design practices that prioritize accessibility and cultural sensitivity, ensuring that the interface caters to a diverse user base.

Consistent branding and visual elements are essential for building a strong and recognizable identity across platforms. However, achieving this consistency while adhering to the design guidelines and aesthetics of each platform can be challenging. Customization options and theming capabilities can offer users a sense of familiarity with their chosen platform while still allowing for brand expression. By leveraging platform-specific design patterns and maintaining a consistent visual language, designers can create UIs that align with both the brand identity and the expectations of users on different platforms.

The ever-evolving nature of platforms, with updates, new features, and changes in design guidelines, presents an ongoing challenge in cross-platform UI design. Designers must stay abreast of updates and modifications to platforms to ensure that their interfaces remain compatible and optimized for the latest technologies. Regular audits and adjustments may be necessary to address changes in platform conventions and maintain a seamless user experience across diverse devices.

Cross-platform development frameworks and tools offer solutions to streamline the process of designing UIs for different platforms. These tools, such as React Native, Xamarin, and Flutter, enable the creation of applications that can run on multiple platforms with a single codebase. While these frameworks offer efficiency, they may come with limitations in terms of platform-specific optimizations and access to native features. Designers and developers must carefully weigh the benefits and trade-offs of using cross-platform development tools based on the project's specific requirements and user experience goals.

User testing and feedback collection play a pivotal role in refining cross-platform UIs. Conducting usability testing across various devices and platforms helps identify potential issues, gather user insights, and validate design decisions. Regularly seeking feedback from users on different devices ensures that the UI remains intuitive, functional, and aligned with user expectations. This iterative approach enables designers to address platform-specific challenges and continually improve the cross-platform user experience.

In conclusion, designing UIs that seamlessly work across different platforms demands a delicate balance between consistency and adaptation. Addressing challenges related to visual identity, screen sizes, navigation, interaction methods, performance, accessibility, branding, platform updates, and development frameworks requires a comprehensive and user-centric approach. By prioritizing user experience, staying informed about platform changes, leveraging responsive design strategies, and embracing user feedback, designers can create cross-platform UIs that offer a harmonious and effective experience across a diverse range of devices.

Explore the importance of responsive design and cross-platform consistency for a unified user experience.

Responsive design and cross-platform consistency play integral roles in achieving a unified user experience, ensuring that interfaces seamlessly adapt to diverse devices and screen sizes while maintaining a cohesive visual identity. In the contemporary digital landscape, users access content across an array of devices, ranging from desktop computers and laptops to tablets and smartphones. The importance of responsive design lies in its ability to address the challenges posed by this diversity, offering a solution that ensures optimal usability and visual appeal across the entire spectrum of devices. By dynamically adjusting layout, content, and functionality based on screen size and orientation, responsive design aims to provide users with a consistent and enjoyable experience, regardless of the device they choose.

One of the primary drivers of responsive design is the necessity to cater to the proliferation of mobile devices. With the advent of smartphones and tablets, the way users interact with digital content has undergone a paradigm shift. Responsive design acknowledges this shift and acknowledges that a one-size-fits-all approach is no longer viable. By embracing responsive design principles, designers and developers can create interfaces that fluidly adapt to the unique characteristics of various devices, optimizing the user experience and eliminating the need for separate mobile and desktop versions.

The significance of responsive design extends beyond mere adaptation to different screen sizes. It involves a fundamental rethinking of user interfaces, focusing on prioritizing content, streamlining navigation, and enhancing usability across a variety of devices. A well-implemented responsive design considers factors such as touch-friendly interactions for mobile devices, intuitive navigation for varying screen sizes, and the optimization of images and media to ensure fast loading times on slower mobile networks. Through these considerations, responsive design contributes to a holistic and user-centric approach that transcends the limitations of traditional fixed layouts.

Cross-platform consistency further reinforces the goal of a unified user experience by ensuring that design elements, branding, and functionality remain coherent across different devices and operating systems. Inconsistencies in visual elements, such as color schemes, typography, and iconography, can create confusion for users transitioning between platforms. Cross-platform consistency addresses this challenge by adhering to a standardized visual language while accommodating platform-specific guidelines. Whether a user interacts with an application on a Windows PC, an iOS device, or an Android tablet, maintaining a consistent look and feel fosters a sense of familiarity and usability.

The importance of cross-platform consistency is amplified in an era where users frequently switch between devices throughout the day. A user might start browsing content on a desktop computer at work, continue on a tablet during a commute, and finish on a smartphone at home. Inconsistencies in the user interface can disrupt this seamless transition, leading to frustration and a disjointed user experience. By prioritizing cross-platform consistency, designers aim to create a sense of continuity, allowing users to effortlessly pick up where they left off, regardless of the device they are using.

The user experience benefits of responsive design and cross-platform consistency are not limited to convenience; they also have a direct impact on user engagement and satisfaction. When users encounter interfaces that adapt effortlessly to their chosen device and consistently adhere to familiar design patterns, they are more likely to stay engaged and explore the content or features offered. A positive user experience fosters a sense of trust and reliability, contributing to increased user satisfaction and loyalty. Conversely, a disjointed or inconsistent experience may lead to frustration, diminishing the likelihood of users returning to the platform.

Search engine optimization (SEO) is another crucial aspect where responsive design plays a pivotal role. Search engines prioritize mobile-friendly websites in their rankings, recognizing the prevalence of mobile device usage. Responsive design ensures that a single version of the website serves both desktop and mobile users, avoiding the need for separate URLs or versions. This not only streamlines the management of content but also enhances the website's visibility in search engine results, positively impacting its reach and accessibility.

Moreover, the need for cross-platform consistency becomes particularly pronounced in the realm of brand identity. Brands invest significant resources in developing a distinct visual identity that resonates with their audience. Inconsistencies in design elements across platforms can dilute this identity, compromising brand recognition and trust. A unified and consistent design language strengthens brand recall, fostering a connection with users who encounter the brand across various touchpoints. Consistent branding reinforces a sense of reliability and professionalism, influencing users' perception of the brand's integrity and commitment to a high-quality user experience.

In the context of application development, achieving cross-platform consistency becomes even more challenging due to the diversity of operating systems and design guidelines. Platforms like iOS, Android, Windows, and macOS each have their unique design principles and user expectations. Cross-platform development frameworks, such as React Native, Xamarin, and Flutter, attempt to bridge this gap by allowing developers to create applications that run on multiple platforms with a single codebase. While these frameworks offer efficiency, designers must collaborate closely with developers to ensure that the user interface aligns with each platform's specific visual and interaction guidelines.

The evolution of technology, especially the advent of new devices and form factors, further emphasizes the ongoing importance of responsive design and cross-platform consistency. With the rise of wearable devices, smart TVs, and other emerging technologies, designers face new challenges in adapting interfaces to unconventional screen sizes and interaction methods. Responsive design principles must evolve to encompass these diverse devices, ensuring that interfaces remain accessible and user-friendly in an ever-expanding digital ecosystem.

In conclusion, responsive design and cross-platform consistency are paramount for delivering a unified user experience that transcends the complexities of the modern digital landscape. Responsive design adapts interfaces to various screen sizes, prioritizing usability and content delivery across devices. Cross-platform consistency ensures that the visual identity, branding, and functionality remain coherent, fostering a seamless transition for users between different platforms. The positive impact extends to user engagement, satisfaction, SEO, brand identity, and the adaptability of applications to emerging technologies. As technology continues to evolve, the principles of responsive design and cross-platform consistency will remain fundamental to creating user interfaces that stand the test of time and cater to the diverse needs of a global audience.

Chapter 2: The Evolution of Operating System Interfaces

Establish the context for the evolution of operating system interfaces.

The evolution of operating system interfaces has been a dynamic and transformative journey, shaped by technological advancements, shifts in user expectations, and the relentless pursuit of improved user experiences. At the dawn of computing in the mid-20th century, operating systems lacked graphical user interfaces (GUIs) and relied heavily on command-line interfaces (CLIs). During this era, mainframes and early minicomputers operated through text-based commands, necessitating a deep understanding of programming syntax and limiting accessibility to those with technical expertise. The interface landscape was starkly utilitarian, devoid of the visual elements and interactive features that characterize contemporary operating systems.

The paradigm shift in operating system interfaces emerged with the introduction of graphical user interfaces (GUIs) in the 1970s and 1980s. Xerox PARC, at the forefront of innovation during this period, developed the Alto, a computer system that introduced the concept of GUIs featuring graphical elements like windows, icons, and menus. Despite the Alto not reaching commercial markets, it laid the groundwork for future GUI development. The Xerox Star, released in 1981, marked the first commercial computer to feature a GUI, bringing an intuitive and visually appealing interface to a broader audience. It introduced the desktop metaphor, allowing users to interact with digital content in a manner analogous to handling physical objects.

Apple's Macintosh, launched in 1984, was a groundbreaking product that played a pivotal role in popularizing GUIs. The Macintosh showcased a user-friendly interface with a graphical desktop, icons, and a pointing device known as the mouse. Apple's emphasis on simplicity, aesthetics, and ease of use set a new standard for operating system interfaces. The graphical elements introduced by the Macintosh became foundational to GUI design, influencing subsequent operating systems and shaping user expectations for years to come.

Simultaneously, Microsoft Windows emerged as a major player in the evolution of operating system interfaces. Windows 1.0, released in 1985, introduced a multitasking graphical environment for IBM-compatible PCs. Windows capitalized on the GUI paradigm, incorporating elements like overlapping windows, icons, and menus. The rivalry between Apple and Microsoft during this era spurred innovation in GUI design, leading to the refinement of graphical elements, color schemes, and iconography. Windows became synonymous with personal computing, and subsequent iterations further solidified the GUI as the standard interface for operating systems.

The 1990s witnessed the advent of the internet, marking a significant contextual shift for operating system interfaces. The rise of the World Wide Web prompted the development of web browsers and the integration of internet-related features into operating systems. Microsoft's Windows 95, released in 1995, included the Internet Explorer browser as a core component, emphasizing the growing importance of online connectivity. Operating systems evolved to accommodate the shift towards digital communication, online information retrieval, and the emerging era of e-commerce.

As computing power increased and hardware capabilities expanded, the graphical richness of operating system interfaces continued to evolve. Windows XP, released in 2001, introduced a more polished and visually appealing interface, incorporating elements like transparencies and a redesigned Start menu. Apple, on the other hand, underwent a significant transition with the release of Mac OS X in 2001. Mac OS X brought a Unix-based foundation, a revamped Aqua user interface, and a commitment to stability and performance.

The mobile revolution, starting in the late 2000s, presented a new contextual landscape for operating system interfaces. The launch of the iPhone by Apple in 2007 marked a watershed moment, introducing a touch-centric interface that redefined user interactions. The iOS operating system featured a grid of colorful icons, intuitive gestures, and a focus on direct manipulation of on-screen elements. Google's Android, released in the same year, embraced a similar touch-centric approach, but with a more open ecosystem and diverse hardware options.

The success of mobile operating systems reshaped user expectations, influencing the design of desktop operating systems as well. Windows 8, released by Microsoft in 2012, featured a radical departure from traditional interfaces with a tile-based Start screen optimized for touch. This marked an attempt to unify the user experience across different device types, from desktops to tablets. However, the shift faced mixed reactions, with some users finding the interface challenging to navigate on non-touch devices.

The concept of convergence became increasingly relevant in the context of operating system interfaces. The idea was to create a seamless experience across various devices, allowing users to transition effortlessly between desktops, laptops, tablets, and smartphones. This led to the development of responsive design principles, adaptive interfaces, and cross-platform consistency to ensure a unified user experience. Operating systems began incorporating features like continuity modes, cloud synchronization, and universal apps to support this vision of seamless device integration.

As operating systems evolved, accessibility became a key focus. Design considerations started encompassing features catering to users with diverse needs, including those with visual or motor impairments. Accessibility settings, screen readers, voice commands, and other inclusive features became integral components of modern operating systems, emphasizing the commitment to making digital experiences accessible to all users.

Security and privacy concerns also became significant contextual factors influencing operating system development. With the increasing frequency and sophistication of cyber threats, operating systems implemented robust security features, such as secure boot processes, encryption, and biometric authentication methods. Privacy settings and user control over data became critical considerations, reflecting the growing awareness of digital privacy in the contemporary landscape.

In recent years, the rise of cloud computing and the widespread adoption of mobile apps have further shaped the context for operating system interfaces. Cloud-based storage, synchronization across devices, and the seamless integration of online services into operating systems have become standard features. The app-centric model, popularized by mobile platforms, has influenced desktop operating systems, leading to the prevalence of app stores, centralized software distribution, and sandboxed application environments.

The future context of operating system interfaces is poised for continued evolution, driven by emerging technologies such as augmented reality (AR), virtual reality (VR), and the Internet of Things (IoT). AR interfaces overlay digital information onto the physical world, introducing new challenges and possibilities for interaction. VR interfaces immerse users in virtual environments, requiring innovative approaches to navigation and input. The integration of IoT devices into operating systems adds another layer of complexity, necessitating seamless connectivity and control over a myriad of smart devices.

In conclusion, the evolution of operating system interfaces is a narrative shaped by the interplay of technological advancements, user expectations, and contextual shifts. From the command-line interfaces of early computing to the graphical richness of contemporary operating systems, each phase reflects the contextual demands and possibilities of its time. The ongoing journey of operating system interfaces continues to be influenced by the pursuit of user-friendly interactions, the impact of mobile and internet technologies, the quest for convergence across devices, and the need to address emerging challenges in security, privacy, accessibility, and the integration of new technologies. As we navigate the digital landscape, the context for operating system interfaces remains a dynamic and ever-evolving story, continually shaped by the changing needs and aspirations of users and the possibilities unlocked by advancing technologies.

Discuss the relationship between hardware advancements, user expectations, and the progression of interface design.

The intricate relationship between hardware advancements, user expectations, and the evolution of interface design has been a driving force shaping the digital landscape. Hardware advancements serve as catalysts, often propelling interface design into new realms of capability and user experience. As hardware capabilities expand, user expectations rise in tandem, demanding interfaces that harness the full potential of cutting-edge technologies. This dynamic interplay has led to a continuous cycle of innovation, where each component influences and reinforces the progression of the others, resulting in an ever-evolving landscape of interface design.

Historically, the early era of computing, marked by mainframes and early minicomputers in the mid-20th century, featured rudimentary interfaces predominantly based on command-line interactions. Hardware during this period was limited in processing power and lacked the graphical capabilities that define contemporary user interfaces. Users interacted with machines through text commands, reflecting the nascent stage of digital interaction where hardware constraints heavily influenced interface design. The expectation was grounded in the novelty of interacting with computers, and the simplicity of command-line interfaces met the user needs of the time.

The advent of graphical user interfaces (GUIs) in the 1970s and 1980s marked a transformative shift in interface design, driven by advancements in hardware capabilities. Pioneered by Xerox PARC, the development of GUIs was made possible by improvements in graphics processing units (GPUs) and display technologies. The Xerox Alto, an early computer featuring a graphical display, mouse, and windows, showcased the potential of GUIs. As hardware advancements enabled richer graphical capabilities, GUIs became more prevalent, introducing visual elements like icons, windows, and menus. Apple's Macintosh and Microsoft Windows played pivotal roles in popularizing GUIs, setting the stage for a new era of user-friendly interfaces.

The progression of interface design in subsequent decades was tightly intertwined with the exponential growth of hardware capabilities. The rise of personal computers in the 1990s was fueled by faster processors, increased memory, and improved graphics capabilities. Operating systems incorporated more sophisticated GUI elements, offering users a more intuitive and visually engaging experience. As users became accustomed to these advancements, their expectations for seamless and aesthetically pleasing interfaces grew.

The internet boom in the late 1990s and early 2000s introduced a new dimension to interface design, driven by both hardware and connectivity advancements. Increased processing power and faster internet speeds facilitated the development of dynamic and interactive web interfaces. Web browsers evolved to support technologies like Dynamic HTML (DHTML) and cascading style sheets (CSS), enabling web designers to create more visually appealing and responsive interfaces. The hardware advancements in networking infrastructure and the proliferation of broadband internet contributed to the rise of web-based applications, transforming user expectations for online interactions.

The mobile revolution, ignited by the introduction of smartphones in the late 2000s, represents a pivotal moment where hardware advancements and user expectations converged to reshape interface design. The integration of powerful processors, high-resolution displays, and touchscreens in handheld devices opened new possibilities for interaction. Users now expected interfaces that were not only visually appealing but also optimized for touch gestures and offered seamless experiences across devices. Mobile operating systems, such as Apple's iOS and Google's Android, emerged with intuitive interfaces tailored for the constraints and capabilities of mobile hardware.

The relationship between hardware and interface design further deepened with the advent of multitouch technology. Capacitive touchscreens, made possible by hardware innovations, allowed users to engage with interfaces through gestures like pinch-to-zoom and swipe. This ushered in a new era of natural and tactile interactions, influencing the design of mobile applications and challenging designers to create interfaces that harnessed the full potential of touch-enabled devices.

Wearable technology introduced another layer to this relationship, demanding innovative interface solutions due to the limited physical space and unique form factors of devices like smartwatches. Hardware advancements in sensors, miniaturization, and energy efficiency facilitated the creation of wearables, while interface designers explored novel ways to present information and facilitate interactions on compact screens.

The advent of augmented reality (AR) and virtual reality (VR) represents a contemporary frontier where hardware advancements and interface design converge to redefine user experiences. AR overlays digital content onto the real world, demanding interfaces that seamlessly integrate with the user's environment. VR immerses users in virtual environments, necessitating interfaces that facilitate natural interactions within these simulated spaces. Advances in GPUs, sensors, and display technologies have been pivotal in enabling these immersive experiences, and interface designers are exploring innovative approaches to create intuitive and immersive AR and VR interfaces.

As users increasingly interact with digital interfaces through voice commands and smart assistants, driven by advancements in natural language processing and machine learning, the relationship between hardware and interface design expands to encompass audio-based interactions. Hardware components such as microphones and speakers play a crucial role in enabling these interfaces, shaping user expectations for seamless voice-controlled interactions across devices.

The contemporary landscape also witnesses the integration of artificial intelligence (AI) into interface design, where machine learning algorithms analyze user behavior, preferences, and context to personalize and optimize the user experience. Hardware advancements in processing power and storage capacities are instrumental in supporting the computational demands of AI-driven interfaces, enabling real-time adaptation and responsiveness.

The ongoing relationship between hardware advancements, user expectations, and interface design extends into considerations of accessibility and inclusivity. As hardware components evolve, interface designers have the opportunity to leverage these advancements to create interfaces that accommodate users with diverse abilities. Features like voice recognition, haptic feedback, and eye-tracking technologies, made possible by hardware innovations, contribute to more inclusive interfaces that cater to a broader audience.

Security and privacy concerns also play a role in shaping the evolution of interface design within the context of hardware advancements. Biometric authentication methods, such as fingerprint scanners and facial recognition, leverage hardware capabilities to enhance security while providing convenient access to users. Interface designers must navigate the delicate balance between usability and privacy, considering the implications of hardware-based security features on user trust and data protection.

Looking ahead, the relationship between hardware advancements, user expectations, and interface design is poised to continue evolving. The integration of 5G technology, the development of flexible and foldable displays, and advancements in edge computing are anticipated to influence the design of interfaces that leverage faster connectivity, novel form factors, and distributed computing capabilities. As emerging technologies like quantum computing and brain-computer interfaces progress, interface designers will face new challenges and opportunities to push the boundaries of user experience.

In conclusion, the evolution of operating system interfaces has been intricately woven into the fabric of hardware advancements and user expectations. Each phase in this dynamic relationship has spurred innovation, driving interface designers to explore new possibilities and redefine user interactions. From the early command-line interfaces shaped by limited computing power to the immersive and adaptive interfaces of the present, the journey reflects the symbiotic nature of hardware capabilities, evolving user expectations, and the relentless pursuit of creating interfaces that seamlessly integrate with the possibilities unlocked by advancing technologies. As technology continues to progress, the unfolding narrative of this relationship promises further exploration, experimentation, and transformation in the realm of interface design.

Explore the early days of computing, focusing on command-line interfaces.

The early days of computing, stretching back to the mid-20th century, were characterized by the emergence of pioneering technologies that laid the foundation for the digital era. During this nascent period, the interface between humans and computers primarily manifested through command-line interfaces (CLIs), a stark departure from the graphical richness of contemporary user interfaces. In an era predating the widespread availability of graphical user interfaces (GUIs), the interaction with computers relied heavily on text-based commands and a deep understanding of programming syntax.

Mainframes and early minicomputers, the technological behemoths of this epoch, were the epicenters of computation, their operations overseen by those with specialized technical expertise. Users interfaced with these early computing systems through command-line interfaces, where every action, from initiating a program to manipulating data, necessitated the manual input of precise textual commands. These commands served as a direct means of communication between the user and the machine, creating an environment where computational tasks were executed through explicit instructions, often written in languages like Fortran or assembly.

The command-line interfaces of this era were austere and utilitarian, reflecting the limited graphical capabilities and processing power of early computing hardware. Instead of the intuitive pointing and clicking associated with modern interfaces, users navigated through directories, executed programs, and managed files by typing commands into a text-based console. The concept of a visual desktop, icons, or windows was yet to materialize, and the user's engagement with the machine was confined to the alphanumeric characters displayed on the screen.

The command-line interface, in essence, encapsulated the fundamental principles of early computing. Users needed to possess a deep understanding of the machine's architecture, the intricacies of programming languages, and the syntax required to communicate their instructions effectively. This reliance on technical proficiency created a barrier to entry, limiting access to computing resources primarily to those with specialized training in computer science or related fields. As a result, the user base of early computing systems was confined to a select group of professionals who could navigate the complexities of command-line interactions.

In this text-dominated computing landscape, users interacted with the machine in a sequential and procedural manner. The command-line interface prompted users to input specific commands, and the computer executed these commands in a linear fashion. The feedback from the system was typically presented as text-based responses, providing information about the success or failure of the executed command and, in some instances, displaying output generated by the program.

Early command-line interfaces were heavily tied to batch processing, where users submitted a sequence of commands to be executed in a predefined order. This approach contrasted with the interactive and real-time nature of modern computing interfaces, as users had to submit their instructions, wait for the system to process the commands, and then review the results. The asynchronous nature of this interaction underscored the deliberate and calculated pace of early computing activities.

Programming during this era was an intricate and meticulous process, often involving the creation of punch cards or paper tapes that contained the program's code. These physical representations of programs were then fed into the computer, and the execution of the program was initiated through the command-line interface. Debugging and troubleshooting were formidable tasks, demanding a keen understanding of the hardware and software interactions.

Despite the apparent limitations and steep learning curve associated with command-line interfaces, they played a pivotal role in shaping the early culture of computing. These interfaces fostered a deep engagement with the inner workings of the machine, cultivating a community of users who embraced the intricacies of programming languages and the direct control offered by text-based commands. The collaborative spirit that emerged within this community laid the groundwork for the sharing of knowledge, code, and expertise that would become a hallmark of the computing culture.

The advent of timesharing systems in the 1960s and 1970s marked a significant evolution in the accessibility of command-line interfaces. Timesharing allowed multiple users to interact with a computer simultaneously, reducing the cost of computing resources and expanding access beyond a select few. Users could now log into a central system from remote terminals and share the computational power, democratizing access to computing resources and fostering a more inclusive computing environment.

The command-line interfaces of early computing also played a pivotal role in the development of the Unix operating system. Created in the late 1960s and refined over subsequent decades, Unix featured a powerful command-line interface that became synonymous with flexibility and efficiency. The Unix philosophy emphasized the idea of small, modular programs that could be chained together through command-line pipes, enabling users to construct sophisticated workflows and manipulate data with concise command sequences.

The emergence of the personal computer in the 1970s and 1980s brought command-line interfaces to a broader audience. Early microcomputers, such as the Altair 8800 and the Apple II, often relied on command-line interactions as the primary mode of operation.

Users interfaced with these machines by typing commands to load programs from storage media, manage files, and perform various computational tasks. The command-line interface served as the gateway for individuals exploring the potential of computing at a personal level.

In conclusion, the early days of computing were marked by the dominance of command-line interfaces, providing users with a direct and text-based means of interacting with the burgeoning world of digital computation. Shaped by the limitations of hardware capabilities and the nascent nature of the field, command-line interfaces laid the groundwork for subsequent developments in user interfaces and computing culture. While the stark simplicity of early command-line interactions may seem antiquated in the context of contemporary interfaces, it was through these text-based exchanges that a foundational understanding of computing principles was established, setting the stage for the dynamic evolution of user interfaces in the digital age.

Discuss the limitations and benefits of CLIs and their influence on subsequent interface developments.

Command-line interfaces (CLIs) have played a crucial role in the history of computing, offering a direct and powerful means of interaction between users and computer systems. However, they come with both limitations and benefits that have significantly influenced the trajectory of interface development over the years.

One of the key limitations of command-line interfaces lies in their steep learning curve. Users are required to memorize and input precise commands, often with specific syntax and parameters, making the interface less accessible to those without a background in programming or computer science. This steep learning curve created a barrier to entry, limiting the user base to individuals with technical expertise. The need for users to understand the internal workings of the system and the intricacies of programming languages made CLIs less user-friendly, especially for novice users who might find the text-based interactions daunting.

Despite these limitations, command-line interfaces offer a level of precision and control that is unparalleled. Users can execute complex tasks by chaining together a series of commands, facilitating automation and scripting. This granular control over the system is particularly advantageous for advanced users and system administrators who need to perform intricate operations efficiently. The ability to manipulate files, manage processes, and configure system settings through text commands provided a depth of control that was not easily achievable through early graphical user interfaces (GUIs).

Another significant limitation of CLIs is their lack of visual representation. Unlike graphical interfaces that present information through images, icons, and windows, CLIs rely solely on text-based output. This limitation can make it challenging to convey complex information or data in a comprehensible manner. Visualizing data structures, file hierarchies, or graphical representations of processes is inherently challenging within the confines of a command-line environment. This limitation becomes increasingly apparent as computing tasks involve more intricate visual elements.

However, the simplicity and efficiency of CLIs contribute to their benefits. With a minimalistic design and absence of graphical clutter, command-line interfaces are lightweight and can be executed on systems with limited resources. This efficiency made CLIs especially relevant during the early days of computing when hardware capabilities were constrained. The lightweight nature of CLIs allowed them to run on machines with modest processing power and memory, enabling users to interact with the system even in resource-constrained environments.

Another benefit of command-line interfaces is their scripting capability. Users can write scripts, sequences of commands stored in a file, to automate repetitive tasks. This scripting functionality significantly enhances the efficiency and productivity of users, allowing them to execute complex operations with a single command. The ability to create and share scripts contributed to the collaborative nature of the computing community, where users could exchange efficient solutions and automate routine tasks.

The lack of a graphical interface in CLIs also contributes to their robustness and reliability. Since command-line interactions are primarily text-based, they are less susceptible to issues related to graphical rendering or display inconsistencies. In server environments or when working with remote systems, where graphical interfaces might not be available, CLIs remain a reliable and consistent means of interaction. This reliability has made CLIs indispensable for system administrators and IT professionals managing remote servers and networks.

The influence of command-line interfaces on subsequent interface developments is profound. While CLIs established the foundations of human-computer interaction, they also laid the groundwork for the evolution towards more user-friendly interfaces. The limitations of CLIs in terms of accessibility and visual representation prompted the exploration of alternatives that could make computing more approachable to a broader audience.

The introduction of graphical user interfaces (GUIs) marked a transformative phase in interface design, addressing many of the limitations associated with CLIs. GUIs replaced the text-heavy commands with visual elements such as icons, buttons, and windows, making interactions more intuitive and user-friendly. The graphical representation of files, folders, and applications eliminated the need for users to remember specific command syntax, fostering a more accessible computing experience.

The shift towards GUIs was epitomized by iconic systems like the Apple Macintosh, released in 1984, which introduced the desktop metaphor and popularized the use of a mouse for navigation.

Microsoft Windows, with its graphical environment and multitasking capabilities, further contributed to the widespread adoption of GUIs. The intuitive nature of GUIs enabled a broader range of users, including those without technical backgrounds, to harness the power of computing.

Despite the rise of GUIs, command-line interfaces persisted and evolved, finding their niche in certain domains where their strengths remained unparalleled. The command-line interface continued to thrive in server environments, programming and development workflows, and system administration tasks. As a result, modern operating systems often provide both GUI and CLI options, recognizing the distinct advantages and preferences of different user groups.

The advent of web-based interfaces in the late 20th century and early 21st century introduced another dimension to the interface landscape. With the proliferation of the internet, users accessed applications and services through web browsers, leading to the development of web-based interfaces. These interfaces, often characterized by a combination of graphical elements and textual interactions, merged aspects of both CLIs and GUIs. The rise of web applications also introduced the concept of asynchronous interactions, where users could input commands or requests through forms, and the system would respond without requiring a continuous connection.

Mobile interfaces, driven by the explosion of smartphones, further diversified the interface ecosystem. Touchscreens, gestures, and intuitive interactions became central to mobile interfaces, departing from the traditional command-line interactions. Mobile operating systems like iOS and Android prioritized simplicity, touch-based interactions, and visual feedback, creating a user experience tailored to the characteristics of handheld devices.

The resurgence of interest in command-line interfaces in contemporary computing culture is noteworthy. Developers and power users appreciate the efficiency and precision offered by CLIs, leading to the development of modern command-line tools and interfaces. Additionally, containerization and virtualization technologies, such as Docker and Kubernetes, rely heavily on command-line interactions for managing and orchestrating containers and services.

In conclusion, command-line interfaces have been integral to the evolution of computing, offering a powerful but initially complex means of interaction. Their limitations, including a steep learning curve and a lack of visual representation, prompted the development of more user-friendly alternatives such as graphical user interfaces (GUIs). However, the efficiency, scripting capabilities, and reliability of command-line interfaces have ensured their enduring relevance, particularly in specific domains and professional workflows. The interplay between command-line interfaces, graphical interfaces, and emerging interface paradigms has enriched the computing experience, creating a diverse landscape that caters to the needs and preferences of a broad spectrum of users.

Examine the emergence of GUIs and their transformative impact on user interactions.

The emergence of graphical user interfaces (GUIs) stands as a transformative milestone in the history of computing, fundamentally reshaping the way users interact with digital systems. The evolution from command-line interfaces to graphical interfaces marked a paradigm shift, democratizing access to computing resources and making computers more accessible to a broader audience. This transformation, which gained momentum in the 1970s and 1980s, introduced a visual and intuitive layer to computing that significantly lowered the entry barrier for users, paving the way for the modern computing experience we take for granted today.

In the early days of computing, command-line interfaces (CLIs) were the predominant means of interaction. However, as computers became more powerful and hardware capabilities expanded, there arose a need for interfaces that could provide a more user-friendly and visually intuitive experience. The pioneering work at Xerox PARC (Palo Alto Research Center) during the 1970s played a pivotal role in the conceptualization and development of GUIs. Xerox PARC researchers, including luminaries such as Alan Kay, Douglas Engelbart, and others, envisioned interfaces that leveraged graphical elements to make computing more accessible and interactive.

The Xerox Alto, developed at PARC in 1973, is widely regarded as the first computer to feature a GUI. It introduced concepts that would become fundamental to GUI design, including windows, icons, menus, and a pointing device known as the mouse. The graphical elements allowed users to interact with the system in a more intuitive manner, breaking away from the command-driven nature of earlier interfaces. Despite its pioneering role, the Xerox Alto did not see widespread commercial success, but its ideas and innovations would be adopted and refined by others in the years to come.

One of the seminal moments in the history of GUIs occurred with the introduction of the Apple Macintosh in 1984. Apple's Macintosh, under the leadership of Steve Jobs, embraced the GUI paradigm and brought it to the masses. The Macintosh featured a graphical desktop environment with a mouse for navigation, and its user-friendly interface was a departure from the text-heavy, command-driven interfaces of the time. The Macintosh showcased a visual metaphor for computing, with icons representing files and folders, and users could manipulate these graphical elements using the mouse.

Microsoft Windows, introduced in 1985 with Windows 1.0, further solidified the influence of GUIs in the computing landscape. While the early versions of Windows were not as sophisticated as the Macintosh interface, they marked the beginning of Microsoft's journey toward graphical computing. With subsequent iterations, Windows evolved to become a dominant force in the personal computer market, offering users a GUI-driven environment that became synonymous with desktop computing.

The transformative impact of GUIs extended beyond the desktop environment to applications and software development. GUIs facilitated the creation of more visually engaging and user-friendly applications. Developers could design interfaces with graphical elements, such as buttons, sliders, and dropdown menus, making applications more intuitive and accessible. This shift in interface design democratized software usage, as users no longer needed to be well-versed in command syntax or programming languages to interact with applications.

The adoption of GUIs was not limited to personal computers; it also extended to workstations and eventually to networked computing environments. The widespread use of GUIs coincided with the growth of networking technologies and the emergence of the internet. GUI-based web browsers, such as Netscape Navigator, played a pivotal role in making the World Wide Web accessible to a global audience. The graphical nature of these browsers simplified navigation, allowing users to explore the internet with point-and-click interactions.

The success of GUIs was driven not only by their visual appeal but also by their ability to enhance productivity. The graphical representation of information, the use of icons for quick identification, and the introduction of drag-and-drop functionality streamlined common tasks. GUI-based applications introduced features like WYSIWYG (What You See Is What You Get) editing, enabling users to manipulate documents on the screen with a visual representation closely resembling the printed output.

The rise of GUIs also impacted the gaming industry, introducing a new level of visual immersion and interactivity. Video games transitioned from text-based and command-driven interfaces to rich graphical environments. The advent of platforms like Microsoft

Windows provided a standardized GUI environment for game developers, making it easier to create visually stunning and user-friendly games.

The educational sector benefited significantly from the introduction of GUIs. The intuitive nature of graphical interfaces made computers more accessible to students and educators, fostering digital literacy. Educational software with graphical elements, interactive simulations, and multimedia content became integral tools in classrooms, contributing to a more engaging learning experience.

The advent of GUIs also had implications for multimedia and creative industries. Graphic design, video editing, and other creative endeavors were revolutionized by software applications that leveraged graphical interfaces. The ability to manipulate visual elements on a screen with precision and ease opened new possibilities for creative expression.

The impact of GUIs on user interactions extended beyond the realm of personal computing to encompass a diverse range of devices. Mobile devices, starting with the introduction of the Apple iPhone in 2007, embraced touch-based GUIs as a primary means of interaction. Touchscreens replaced physical keyboards and mice, ushering in an era where users could directly manipulate on-screen elements with their fingertips. The success of mobile operating systems like iOS and Android demonstrated the widespread acceptance of GUIs on smaller, handheld devices.

The success and ubiquity of GUIs, however, do not negate their own set of challenges and criticisms. One notable critique is the potential for over-reliance on visual metaphors that may not be universally intuitive. Icons and symbols can sometimes be ambiguous, leading to a learning curve for users who need to decipher the meaning of various graphical representations. Additionally, the graphical richness of GUIs can demand significant system resources, potentially leading to slower performance on less powerful hardware.

The graphical nature of GUIs also posed accessibility challenges for users with visual impairments. Screen readers and other assistive technologies have become essential in bridging this gap, providing auditory or tactile feedback to users who may not rely on visual cues. Designing inclusive GUIs that consider diverse user needs has become a focal point in contemporary interface design, reflecting the importance of accessibility and usability for all users.

The ongoing evolution of GUIs is evident in contemporary interface design trends. The integration of design principles such as flat design, minimalist aesthetics, and responsive layouts reflects a desire to balance visual appeal with streamlined functionality. The shift towards dark mode, gesture-based navigation, and immersive user experiences further illustrates the dynamic nature of graphical interfaces as designers respond to changing user expectations and technological advancements.

In conclusion, the emergence of graphical user interfaces represents a pivotal moment in the history of computing, marking a transition from text-driven, command-line interactions to visually intuitive and accessible computing environments. The impact of GUIs extends across personal computing, the internet, education, gaming, and creative industries. GUIs have become synonymous with user-friendly computing experiences, enabling a diverse range of users to interact with digital systems in ways that were once unimaginable. While GUIs have faced criticisms and challenges, their transformative influence on user interactions has left an indelible mark on the world of technology, shaping the way we engage with information, applications, and the digital landscape at large.

Highlight iconic GUI-based operating systems and the shift towards more intuitive and visually oriented interfaces.

The evolution of graphical user interfaces (GUIs) has been synonymous with the development of iconic operating systems that revolutionized user interactions and defined the modern computing experience. One of the earliest pioneers in this transformative journey was the Apple Macintosh, introduced in 1984. Orchestrated by Steve Jobs and his team, the Macintosh marked a departure from command-line interfaces, presenting users with a visually intuitive desktop environment. The Macintosh featured a graphical desktop metaphor, complete with icons representing files and folders, a mouse for navigation, and windows for multitasking. This iconic GUI-based operating system not only set the standard for user-friendly computing but also established Apple as a trailblazer in interface design.

Following in the footsteps of the Macintosh, Microsoft Windows emerged as a dominant force in the realm of GUI-based operating systems. With the release of Windows 3.0 in 1990, Microsoft made significant strides in creating a visually oriented interface for personal computers. Windows introduced a graphical environment that allowed users to navigate through applications using a mouse, featured a taskbar for efficient multitasking, and brought the concept of overlapping windows to the forefront. Subsequent iterations, particularly Windows 95, marked a watershed moment, bringing the Start menu, the taskbar, and the iconic desktop to millions of users worldwide. Windows became synonymous with personal computing, and its GUI design became a blueprint for the industry.

The open-source community also contributed to the GUI revolution with the development of the X Window System in the 1980s. While initially targeted at Unix systems, X Window System laid the foundation for graphical interfaces across various platforms. The flexibility of X Window System allowed for the development of diverse desktop environments, such as KDE and GNOME, providing users with options beyond the proprietary systems. Linux distributions embraced these desktop environments, combining the power of Unix-like systems with visually intuitive interfaces, making Linux accessible to a broader audience.

The late 1990s witnessed the rise of another iconic GUI-based operating system—Apple's Mac OS X. Introduced in 2001, Mac OS X merged the elegance of the Macintosh GUI with the robustness of a Unix-based operating system. This fusion resulted in an operating system that not only appealed to creative professionals but also gained recognition for its stability and performance. Mac OS X introduced the Dock for application shortcuts, a refined Finder for file management, and the Aqua interface that became emblematic of Apple's commitment to visual aesthetics. The success of Mac OS X reinforced Apple's position as an innovator in GUI design.

As the internet became an integral part of daily life, a new wave of GUI-based operating systems emerged with a focus on web-centric computing. Google's Chrome OS, introduced in 2009, represented a departure from traditional desktop computing paradigms. Chrome OS centered around the Chrome web browser and cloud-based applications, offering a lightweight and secure environment. The user interface was streamlined, featuring a taskbar, app launcher, and a simplified desktop, reflecting the shift towards web-centric computing and the rise of cloud services.

The mobile revolution brought GUI-based operating systems to a new frontier with the introduction of iOS and Android. Apple's iOS, launched in 2007 with the iPhone, redefined user interactions on mobile devices. iOS embraced a touch-centric interface, featuring an app grid, a dock for frequently used apps, and intuitive gestures. The success of iOS extended beyond smartphones to tablets with the iPad, showcasing the adaptability of the interface to different form factors. Android, developed by Google and released in 2008, offered a more open and customizable alternative. Android's GUI included a home screen with widgets, a notification bar, and a diverse array of devices from various manufacturers. Both iOS and Android contributed to the ubiquity of touch-based interactions, setting the standard for mobile operating systems.

The evolution of GUI-based operating systems is not solely confined to traditional computing devices; it extends to game consoles. Microsoft's Xbox Dashboard and Sony's PlayStation interface transformed gaming consoles into multimedia hubs. These interfaces incorporated elements of traditional desktop GUIs, offering users an immersive and visually rich experience for accessing games, media, and online services. The convergence of gaming and multimedia further emphasized the importance of intuitive interfaces in enhancing user experiences across diverse platforms.

The advent of Windows 10 in 2015 marked Microsoft's endeavor to unify the user experience across a spectrum of devices, from traditional PCs to tablets and hybrid devices. Windows 10 reintroduced the Start menu, combining the familiarity of previous Windows versions with modern design elements. The operating system embraced a responsive design, adapting to various screen sizes and input methods. Microsoft's focus on creating a cohesive and visually appealing interface reflected the industry's recognition of the need for seamless experiences across different form factors.

In recent years, the rise of smartphones and tablets has fueled the development of new GUI-based operating systems. Apple's iPadOS, a derivative of iOS tailored for the iPad, introduced features like multitasking and a desktop-like file system, emphasizing the tablet's productivity capabilities. Google's efforts extended beyond smartphones with the introduction of Android for tablets, providing a cohesive experience across a wide range of devices. These tablet-centric operating systems highlight the adaptability of GUIs to different form factors and user scenarios.

The trajectory of GUI-based operating systems showcases a continuous quest for more intuitive, visually appealing, and user-friendly interfaces. The design principles introduced by iconic operating systems, such as the use of icons, windows, and graphical elements, have become ingrained in contemporary interface design. The emphasis on touch-based interactions, responsive design, and a seamless transition between devices underscores the industry's commitment to delivering cohesive user experiences.

Looking ahead, the evolution of GUIs is intertwined with emerging technologies such as augmented reality (AR) and virtual reality (VR). Operating systems are exploring interfaces that leverage spatial computing, gesture controls, and immersive environments. Microsoft's Windows Mixed Reality, for example, integrates virtual reality into the Windows ecosystem, presenting new possibilities for interactive and immersive computing experiences.

In conclusion, the evolution of GUI-based operating systems represents a captivating journey that spans decades and encompasses a diverse array of devices. From the iconic Macintosh to the ubiquity of Windows, the openness of Linux, the simplicity of Chrome OS, the mobility of iOS and Android, and the adaptability of tablet-centric operating systems, GUIs have become an integral part of modern computing. These interfaces have not only transformed the way users interact with technology but also influenced the design principles that shape contemporary user experiences. As the digital landscape continues to evolve, the narrative of GUI-based operating systems remains dynamic, driven by innovations that seek to redefine how we engage with information, applications, and the ever-expanding world of computing.

Discuss the evolution of interfaces with the advent of touch-based interactions.

The evolution of interfaces witnessed a profound transformation with the advent of touch-based interactions, ushering in a new era of intuitive and direct engagement between users and digital devices. The catalyst for this paradigm shift can be traced back to the introduction of the Apple iPhone in 2007. Apple's revolutionary device not only redefined the smartphone but also introduced a transformative approach to user interactions. The iPhone's capacitive touchscreen allowed users to navigate through the interface, zoom in on content, and perform gestures with their fingertips. The touch-based interface eliminated the need for physical keyboards and styluses, offering a more natural and tactile way for users to interact with their devices.

Apple's iOS, the operating system powering the iPhone, played a pivotal role in shaping the language of touch-based interactions. The interface featured a grid of colorful icons on a home screen, swiping gestures to navigate between screens, and pinch-to-zoom for manipulating content. The multi-touch capabilities of the iPhone's touchscreen enabled users to perform a variety of gestures, such as tapping, swiping, and rotating, providing a level of interactivity that was unprecedented in the mobile landscape. The success of the iPhone set the stage for the widespread adoption of touch-based interfaces across the industry.

Following Apple's lead, other smartphone manufacturers embraced touch-based interactions, contributing to the proliferation of touchscreen devices running on various operating systems. Google's Android, introduced in 2008, incorporated touch-friendly elements into its interface, fostering competition and innovation in the mobile ecosystem. The rise of touchscreen smartphones not only transformed the way people communicated but also paved the way for a broader integration of touch-based interactions across a spectrum of devices.

The impact of touch-based interactions extended beyond smartphones to tablets, with the introduction of the Apple iPad in 2010. The iPad showcased the versatility of touch interfaces on larger screens, enabling users to interact with content in a more immersive manner. The tablet form factor, characterized by a touch-centric interface, became a popular choice for content consumption, productivity, and creative tasks. Operating systems like Apple's iPadOS and Android for tablets embraced touch-based gestures, multi-window multitasking, and stylus support, enhancing the user experience on larger touch-enabled displays.

The success of touch interfaces was not confined to mobile devices; it permeated various segments of computing, including laptops and desktops. The emergence of convertible laptops and 2-in-1 devices blurred the lines between traditional laptops and tablets, offering users the flexibility to switch between touch-based interactions and more conventional input methods. Microsoft's Windows 8, released in 2012, introduced a touch-focused interface with Live Tiles and a Start screen. While the operating system faced mixed reviews for its departure from the familiar Windows desktop, it underscored the industry's recognition of the transformative potential of touch-based interactions in personal computing.

Touch-based interactions also found their way into the realm of interactive displays and kiosks. Public spaces, retail environments, and educational institutions embraced touchscreen technology to create engaging and user-friendly interfaces. Interactive kiosks allowed users to browse information, place orders, and access services with a simple touch, streamlining interactions and reducing the learning curve associated with more traditional input methods.

The gaming industry witnessed a shift towards touch-based interactions with the popularity of smartphones and tablets as gaming platforms. Touchscreens offered a new dimension to mobile gaming, enabling users to interact directly with on-screen elements. The success of games like Angry Birds, designed around touch gestures, highlighted the potential for touch-based gaming experiences. Touch interfaces also found their way into dedicated gaming devices, such as handheld consoles and gaming laptops, providing an alternative to traditional controllers.

The advent of touch-based interactions was not without its challenges. Designing interfaces for touch required a rethinking of traditional user interface elements, taking into account the precision of touch gestures, finger-friendly button sizes, and responsive feedback. Responsive design principles became essential to accommodate the diversity of screen sizes and resolutions across a myriad of touch-enabled devices. The need for accessible and intuitive interfaces prompted designers to prioritize user experience, leading to the development of user interfaces that were visually engaging, responsive, and tailored to touch interactions.

As the use of touch-based interfaces became more ubiquitous, the concept of gestural interactions gained prominence. Gestures, such as swiping, pinching, and tapping, became integral to navigating and manipulating digital content. Mobile operating systems incorporated gesture-based navigation, allowing users to perform actions with fluid and natural movements. The gesture-based approach not only simplified interactions but also paved the way for more immersive and intuitive user experiences.

The integration of touch interfaces into everyday life extended beyond personal computing to smart home devices, wearables, and automotive infotainment systems. Smartphones became central to the connected ecosystem, serving as remote controls for smart home devices and wearables. Touchscreens in cars transformed infotainment systems, enabling drivers and passengers to interact with navigation, entertainment, and communication features effortlessly. The convergence of touch interfaces with the Internet of Things (IoT) contributed to the creation of seamless and interconnected digital experiences in various aspects of daily life.

In healthcare, touch-based interfaces found applications in medical devices, diagnostics, and patient care. Touchscreens streamlined interactions with electronic health records, diagnostic equipment, and medical imaging systems. The intuitive nature of touch interfaces facilitated communication between healthcare professionals and patients, contributing to a more user-friendly healthcare environment.

The educational sector embraced touch-based interactions as a means of enhancing learning experiences. Interactive whiteboards, tablets, and educational apps enabled students to engage with educational content through touch gestures. The tactile nature of touch interfaces fostered a more hands-on and participatory learning environment, catering to diverse learning styles.

The continuous evolution of touch-based interactions led to advancements in haptic feedback technology. Haptic feedback, such as vibrations or tactile sensations, provided users with a sense of touch in response to their interactions. This technology enhanced the sensory experience of touch interfaces, making virtual interactions more tangible and realistic. Haptic feedback found applications in gaming controllers, smartphones, and virtual reality (VR) systems, adding an additional layer of immersion to digital experiences.

The advent of touch-based interactions has not replaced traditional input methods but has complemented them, creating a diverse and inclusive ecosystem of interface options. The coexistence of touch interfaces with keyboards, mice, styluses, and voice commands reflects the recognition that different contexts and tasks may require distinct input methods. The versatility of touch-based interactions lies in their ability to adapt to the preferences and needs of users in various scenarios.

In conclusion, the advent of touch-based interactions represents a pivotal moment in the evolution of interfaces, reshaping the way users engage with digital devices across diverse platforms. From smartphones to tablets, laptops, interactive displays, and beyond, touch interfaces have become integral to modern computing experiences. The tactile and intuitive nature of touch-based interactions has transcended traditional boundaries, influencing design principles, user expectations, and the way technology integrates into different facets of daily life. As technology continues to advance, the narrative of touch-based interfaces unfolds, promising further innovations that will shape the future of human-computer interactions.

Explore the impact of mobile devices on shaping user expectations and interface design trends.

The impact of mobile devices on shaping user expectations and interface design trends has been nothing short of revolutionary, fundamentally altering the way individuals interact with technology and influencing the broader landscape of digital experiences. The advent of smartphones, starting with the introduction of the Apple iPhone in 2007, marked a paradigm shift in user expectations. Mobile devices, characterized by their portability, touchscreens, and always-connected nature, have not only become ubiquitous but have also set the standard for user-centric design across various platforms.

The rise of mobile devices has deeply influenced user expectations, ushering in an era where immediacy, simplicity, and intuitiveness are paramount. Users now anticipate seamless experiences that transcend device boundaries, allowing them to effortlessly transition from smartphones to tablets, laptops, and other connected devices. The notion of a consistent and coherent user experience across different contexts has become a central tenet of modern interface design. Mobile devices, with their compact form factor and tactile touchscreens, have instilled in users a preference for interactions that are direct, responsive, and tailored to the constraints of smaller screens.

One of the key contributions of mobile devices to interface design trends is the emphasis on touch-based interactions. The touchscreen interface, popularized by smartphones and later adopted by tablets, has become a defining feature of contemporary user interactions. The intuitive gestures associated with touch, such as tapping, swiping, and pinching, have not only become second nature to users but have also influenced interface design across a spectrum of devices. The success of mobile touch interfaces has led to a departure from traditional input methods, shaping a new language of interaction that prioritizes tactile engagement.

The design language introduced by mobile devices is characterized by simplicity, clarity, and a focus on visual elements. The limitations of smaller screens necessitated a reevaluation of interface components, leading to the prominence of minimalist aesthetics. App icons, gestures, and concise textual information are meticulously crafted to optimize screen real estate and ensure a streamlined user experience. This trend towards minimalism has transcended mobile interfaces, influencing design practices across web platforms, desktop applications, and various digital environments.

Mobile devices have also played a pivotal role in popularizing the concept of app ecosystems. The App Store, introduced by Apple in 2008, and subsequently, the Google Play Store, created centralized hubs for users to discover, download, and manage applications. The app-centric model, characterized by standalone applications that serve specific purposes, has become a dominant paradigm. Users now expect a diverse array of apps that cater to their needs, from productivity and communication to entertainment and lifestyle. The success of app ecosystems has prompted designers to prioritize the creation of user-friendly and visually appealing apps that align with the expectations set by mobile platforms.

The advent of mobile devices has propelled the idea of responsive design to the forefront of interface development. Responsive design principles aim to create interfaces that adapt seamlessly to various screen sizes and resolutions, ensuring a consistent and visually pleasing experience across devices. Mobile devices, with their diverse array of screen sizes and form factors, have underscored the importance of flexibility in design. Websites, applications, and digital content are now expected to dynamically adjust to the dimensions of the user's screen, fostering accessibility and usability across a wide range of devices.

User expectations regarding the speed and performance of digital interactions have been significantly shaped by the efficiency of mobile devices. Mobile users demand swift loading times, smooth animations, and instant responsiveness. The constraints of mobile networks and varying degrees of connectivity have compelled designers to prioritize optimization and streamline user interfaces to deliver a seamless experience even in resource-constrained environments. This focus on performance has permeated other digital interfaces, emphasizing the need for speed and efficiency in response to user interactions.

Mobile devices have not only influenced the way interfaces look and behave but have also redefined user expectations regarding accessibility. The touch-based interactions and gesture controls introduced by mobile devices have provided alternative means of engagement for users with disabilities. Accessibility features, such as screen readers, voice commands, and haptic feedback, have become integral components of mobile interfaces, setting a precedent for inclusive design practices across all digital platforms.

The influence of mobile devices extends beyond the digital realm to shape user expectations regarding real-world experiences. The integration of location-based services, augmented reality (AR), and contextual awareness in mobile interfaces has created an expectation for personalized and location-aware interactions. Users now anticipate interfaces that not only understand their preferences but also adapt to the context of their surroundings. This shift has implications for industries ranging from retail and hospitality to navigation and social interactions, where the convergence of digital and physical experiences is increasingly prevalent.

The rise of mobile devices has also fueled the demand for innovative and immersive multimedia experiences. The integration of high-quality cameras, high-resolution displays, and advanced graphics capabilities in smartphones has elevated user expectations for multimedia content. Users now anticipate interfaces that seamlessly integrate photos, videos, and interactive elements, providing a rich and engaging experience. Social media platforms, content streaming services, and multimedia apps have responded to this expectation, pushing the boundaries of interface design to deliver visually captivating and immersive content experiences.

The impact of mobile devices on interface design trends is particularly evident in the evolution of mobile operating systems. Apple's iOS and Google's Android, the two dominant mobile platforms, have continuously iterated on their design languages to stay ahead of user expectations. iOS, with its emphasis on visual clarity, consistent icons, and the cohesive design language of Material Design on Android, have set benchmarks for interface aesthetics and functionality. The competition between these platforms has resulted in a cycle of innovation, with each iteration introducing new features, gestures, and design principles that influence the broader landscape of digital interfaces.

The rise of mobile devices has redefined user expectations regarding security and privacy. With smartphones becoming repositories of personal information, users expect interfaces to prioritize robust security measures, including biometric authentication, encrypted communication, and granular privacy controls. The transparency of privacy practices and the implementation of features like app permissions reflect the heightened awareness and expectations of users regarding the protection of their personal data.

The influence of mobile devices on shaping user expectations has extended to e-commerce and digital transactions. Mobile platforms have popularized the concept of frictionless payments, allowing users to make purchases with a few taps on their devices. Users now expect secure, seamless, and convenient payment experiences, prompting the integration of mobile payment solutions, digital wallets, and contactless transactions across various interfaces beyond mobile devices.

The impact of mobile devices on interface design trends is an ongoing narrative, continually evolving as technology advances and user behaviors adapt. As mobile devices continue to play a central role in daily life, the principles of user-centric design, intuitive interactions, and seamless experiences are likely to remain at the forefront of interface development. The lessons learned from mobile interfaces are not confined to smartphones and tablets but are integral to shaping the future of human-computer interactions across an increasingly interconnected and diverse digital landscape.

Provide insights into the contemporary landscape of OS interfaces.

The contemporary landscape of operating system (OS) interfaces reflects a dynamic and diverse ecosystem shaped by evolving user expectations, technological advancements, and design trends. At the forefront of this landscape are the two major players, Microsoft's Windows and Apple's macOS, each contributing to the rich tapestry of interface design with their unique philosophies and approaches. Windows, with its latest iteration, Windows 11, introduced in 2021, showcases a departure from the familiar Start menu and taskbar, embracing a centered Start menu and a more streamlined taskbar. The design language, characterized by rounded corners, translucent elements, and a focus on simplicity, aligns with the broader industry trend towards minimalism and visual coherence. Windows 11 emphasizes productivity with features like Snap layouts, making multitasking more intuitive, and the Microsoft Store's redesign, offering a curated experience for users. The evolution of Windows interfaces underscores Microsoft's commitment to creating a modern, visually appealing, and user-friendly environment.

On the other side of the spectrum, Apple's macOS, with its latest release Monterey in 2021, continues the trajectory set by macOS Big Sur. The macOS interface epitomizes Apple's dedication to a unified design language across its ecosystem, commonly referred to as the

"Big Sur" design. Featuring a refreshed menu bar, redesigned icons, and a Control Center for quick access to settings, Monterey builds upon the foundation laid by Big Sur. The introduction of Universal Control, allowing seamless movement of the cursor and files across Apple devices, exemplifies Apple's focus on creating a cohesive user experience within its ecosystem. The macOS interface reflects Apple's commitment to harmonizing aesthetics, functionality, and interoperability.

The mobile landscape has significantly influenced contemporary OS interfaces, with the prominence of touch-based interactions and app-centric ecosystems. Google's Android, the leading mobile operating system, has evolved to accommodate larger screens, foldable devices, and diverse form factors. Android 12, released in 2021, introduced Material You, a design paradigm emphasizing personalization through dynamic theming. This approach allows users to customize the look and feel of their interface, reflecting a departure from static design principles. Android's interface continues to prioritize intuitive navigation, notifications, and a consistent experience across a vast array of devices, catering to a diverse user base.

Apple's iOS, synonymous with the iPhone and iPad, has undergone transformative changes with iOS 15. Building on the foundation of iOS 14, the latest iteration refines the interface with features like Focus mode for tailored notifications, redesigned notifications, and improvements to FaceTime. iOS 15 continues Apple's commitment to a clean, intuitive design characterized by the App Library, Control Center, and gestures. The interface leverages vibrant colors, rounded elements, and a focus on accessibility, creating an environment that resonates with a global audience. The integration of widgets on the home screen and App Clips, allowing users to interact with parts of apps without installation, further exemplifies Apple's emphasis on user-centric design.

Beyond traditional computing and mobile devices, the contemporary OS interface landscape extends to emerging platforms. Chrome OS, developed by Google, has gained prominence in the realm of lightweight, web-centric computing. Chrome OS interfaces prioritize simplicity, speed, and cloud-based applications. The integration of the Chromebook interface with Android apps and Linux applications underscores Google's vision of a versatile and accessible computing environment. The interface is designed to provide a seamless experience for users who prioritize web-based applications and cloud-centric workflows.

In the realm of gaming, console interfaces play a pivotal role in shaping the user experience. Microsoft's Xbox dashboard and Sony's PlayStation interface have evolved to become multimedia hubs, offering not only access to games but also streaming services, social interactions, and other entertainment features. The interfaces prioritize visual appeal, ease of navigation, and integration with online services, reflecting the broader trend of converging gaming and multimedia experiences within a unified interface.

The growth of smart home devices and IoT has given rise to new OS interfaces that bridge the gap between physical and digital interactions. Operating systems like Amazon's Alexa and Google's Assistant operate on voice-based interfaces, allowing users to control smart devices, ask questions, and perform tasks through natural language interactions. These interfaces prioritize simplicity and accessibility, enabling users to interact with a diverse array of connected devices seamlessly.

The significance of web browsers in the contemporary OS landscape cannot be understated. While not traditional operating systems, browsers like Google Chrome and Mozilla Firefox serve as gateways to the digital world. Browser interfaces have evolved to incorporate features like minimalist design, omniboxes for search and navigation, and robust security measures. The browser interface, often the first point of contact for users in the digital realm, embodies principles of simplicity and efficiency.

The advent of augmented reality (AR) and virtual reality (VR) has introduced novel challenges and opportunities in interface design. Operating systems for AR glasses, such as those developed by companies like Microsoft (HoloLens) and Google (Google Glass), aim to seamlessly integrate digital information into the user's physical environment. These interfaces prioritize unobtrusive overlays, gesture-based controls, and spatial awareness, enhancing the user's perception of the real world. VR interfaces, exemplified by platforms like Oculus, focus on creating immersive environments with intuitive controls and spatial interactions, redefining how users engage with digital content.

The contemporary OS interface landscape is also characterized by the increasing integration of AI and machine learning. Smart assistants, like Apple's Siri, Google Assistant, and Microsoft's Cortana, are embedded within operating systems to provide users with contextual information, perform tasks, and facilitate natural language interactions. The interface design of these AI-driven features emphasizes conversational interfaces, visual feedback, and integration with other system components.

Security and privacy considerations have become integral to contemporary OS interfaces, reflecting the growing awareness and concerns of users. Both Microsoft and Apple have incorporated features in their interfaces to enhance security, such as biometric authentication, encrypted communication, and granular privacy controls. User interfaces now include prompts and notifications to inform users about privacy settings, app permissions, and potential security risks, empowering users to make informed decisions about their digital footprint.

The contemporary OS interface landscape is characterized by a pursuit of seamlessness and cohesiveness across diverse platforms.

The convergence of design languages, shared design principles, and cross-device interoperability are prominent trends. Operating systems seek to create unified experiences that transcend individual devices, allowing users to seamlessly transition between smartphones, tablets, laptops, and other connected devices. The emphasis on responsive design, consistent visual elements, and streamlined interactions reflects the industry's recognition of the importance of a cohesive user experience in an increasingly interconnected digital ecosystem.

In conclusion, the contemporary OS interface landscape is a dynamic interplay of design philosophies, technological innovations, and user expectations. From the desktop environments of Windows and macOS to the mobile interfaces of Android and iOS, and the specialized interfaces of emerging platforms, each OS interface contributes to the evolving narrative of human-computer interactions. The emphasis on simplicity, personalization, security, and cross-platform consistency underscores the industry's commitment to creating interfaces that cater to the diverse needs of users in an interconnected and digitally immersive world.

Discuss recent developments, such as minimalistic design, voice interfaces, and immersive experiences.

Recent developments in the realm of interface design have witnessed a transformative shift influenced by minimalistic design principles, the integration of voice interfaces, and the exploration of immersive experiences. Minimalism, characterized by simplicity, clarity, and a focus on essential elements, has become a pervasive design philosophy across digital interfaces. The resurgence of minimalistic design is evident in operating systems, web applications, and mobile interfaces. Interfaces now prioritize clean layouts, uncluttered visual elements, and intuitive navigation, reducing visual noise to enhance user focus and comprehension. This approach not only aligns with contemporary aesthetics but also reflects an acknowledgment of the importance of user-centric design, where streamlined experiences cater to diverse user preferences and facilitate efficient interactions.

Voice interfaces represent another noteworthy development that has gained prominence in recent years. The integration of voice-driven interactions into operating systems, smart devices, and applications has transformed how users engage with technology. Platforms like Amazon's Alexa, Google Assistant, and Apple's Siri exemplify the growing influence of voice interfaces. Users can perform tasks, ask questions, and control devices using natural language commands. The emphasis on voice interfaces addresses accessibility concerns and provides an alternative means of interaction, particularly in scenarios where traditional input methods may be impractical. This development marks a departure from traditional graphical interfaces and opens new possibilities for hands-free, context-aware computing experiences.

Immersive experiences, driven by advancements in augmented reality (AR) and virtual reality (VR) technologies, represent a frontier that continues to shape the contemporary landscape of interface design. AR overlays digital information onto the real world, enhancing the user's perception and interaction with their surroundings. Applications like Pokémon GO and Snapchat filters showcase the potential of AR in providing interactive and context-aware experiences. VR, on the other hand, immerses users in virtual environments, offering a transformative and interactive medium for gaming, education, and simulations. The integration of immersive experiences in interface design challenges conventional paradigms, emphasizing spatial interactions, gestural controls, and a sense of presence that transcends traditional screen-based interfaces.

The resurgence of minimalistic design is particularly evident in the evolution of operating system interfaces, web applications, and mobile experiences. Operating systems like Windows 11 and macOS Monterey embrace minimalism by adopting clean lines, simplified icons, and unobtrusive visual elements. The centered Start menu in Windows 11 and the redesigned Control Center in macOS Monterey exemplify the shift towards decluttered interfaces that prioritize essential functionalities. This trend extends to web design, where websites increasingly favor minimalist layouts, generous white spaces, and simplified navigation menus. Mobile interfaces, including those of iOS and Android, emphasize minimalist aesthetics with flat design, vibrant colors, and unambiguous icons, creating visually coherent and user-friendly environments.

The integration of voice interfaces into contemporary digital experiences marks a significant departure from traditional input methods. Voice-activated assistants, such as Amazon's Alexa, have become integral components of smart homes, allowing users to control devices, retrieve information, and perform tasks through voice commands. Google Assistant, with its natural language processing capabilities, offers a conversational interface that understands context and user preferences. Apple's Siri, present across various devices, enables hands-free interactions and leverages machine learning for personalized assistance. The increasing prevalence of voice interfaces acknowledges the convenience and accessibility they bring, addressing scenarios where manual input may be cumbersome or impractical.

The immersive experiences facilitated by AR and VR technologies represent a paradigm shift in interface design, introducing spatial interactions and three-dimensional environments. Augmented reality overlays digital content onto the real world, creating interactive and context-aware experiences. AR applications, such as IKEA Place, allow users to visualize furniture in their living spaces before making a purchase. Snapchat's AR filters enable users to augment their selfies with playful animations. Virtual reality, on the other hand, immerses users in entirely digital environments, offering applications ranging from immersive gaming experiences to virtual meetings and training simulations. VR headsets like Oculus Rift and

HTC Vive provide users with a sense of presence and spatial engagement, reshaping how individuals interact with digital content.

The impact of minimalistic design, voice interfaces, and immersive experiences extends beyond individual platforms to influence a diverse array of industries and applications. E-commerce websites, for instance, increasingly adopt minimalist design principles to create streamlined shopping experiences. Clean interfaces, concise product information, and intuitive navigation contribute to a more focused and enjoyable shopping process. Voice interfaces have found applications in automotive infotainment systems, enabling drivers to control navigation, make calls, and manage entertainment using voice commands. The automotive industry's integration of voice assistants reflects a commitment to hands-free interactions, prioritizing safety and convenience.

The field of healthcare has also witnessed the incorporation of these design trends. Minimalistic interfaces in healthcare applications focus on presenting crucial information clearly and reducing cognitive load for medical professionals. Voice interfaces enhance accessibility in healthcare settings, allowing practitioners to access patient records, dictate notes, and navigate interfaces without the need for physical input. In the context of immersive experiences, AR has been used for medical training, offering simulations for surgeries and procedures. VR finds applications in therapy, creating virtual environments to treat conditions such as anxiety and post-traumatic stress disorder.

Education is another sector where these design trends have made a significant impact. Minimalistic interfaces in e-learning platforms prioritize ease of navigation and engagement, ensuring that learners can focus on content without distraction. Voice interfaces enhance accessibility in educational applications, allowing students to ask questions, seek clarification, and engage with course materials using natural language. Immersive experiences, whether through AR applications for interactive learning or VR simulations for virtual field trips, contribute to a more engaging and experiential educational environment.

The gaming industry has been at the forefront of adopting immersive experiences, leveraging VR technologies to create compelling and realistic gaming environments. Minimalistic design principles are evident in gaming interfaces that prioritize essential information, unobtrusive menus, and intuitive controls. Voice interfaces are increasingly integrated into gaming consoles, allowing players to control gameplay, access information, and communicate with other players using voice commands. The convergence of these design trends in gaming reflects a commitment to enhancing user experiences and pushing the boundaries of interactive entertainment.

As the design landscape continues to evolve, the interplay of minimalistic design, voice interfaces, and immersive experiences is likely to shape the future trajectory of interface design. The emphasis on simplicity, accessibility, and engagement underscores the industry's commitment to creating interfaces that resonate with diverse user preferences and adapt to evolving technological landscapes. Minimalism streamlines interactions, voice interfaces provide new modes of engagement, and immersive experiences redefine the boundaries of digital interaction, collectively contributing to a dynamic and user-centric design ecosystem.

Chapter 3: Design Principles for Intuitive User Interaction

Define the fundamental principles that guide intuitive user interaction.

Intuitive user interaction is guided by a set of fundamental principles that aim to create a seamless and user-friendly experience, allowing individuals to engage with digital systems effortlessly. At the core of these principles lies the concept of simplicity, emphasizing the reduction of complexity in design to make interactions more straightforward and comprehensible. Simplicity encompasses various facets, from the clarity of visual elements to the simplicity of navigation, ensuring that users can easily understand and navigate the interface without unnecessary cognitive load.

Consistency is another foundational principle that underpins intuitive user interaction. Consistency ensures uniformity in design elements, layout, and functionality throughout the interface, promoting predictability and reducing the need for users to learn different patterns for similar actions. Whether it's the placement of navigation menus, the use of icons, or the behavior of interactive elements, maintaining consistency fosters a sense of familiarity that enhances user confidence and reduces the learning curve.

Feedback is a crucial principle in intuitive user interaction, providing users with information about the outcome of their actions. Visual, auditory, or haptic feedback signals users about the system's response, reinforcing the cause-and-effect relationship between their inputs and the system's behavior. Real-time feedback helps users understand the consequences of their actions, providing a sense of control and responsiveness, which is essential for an intuitive experience.

The principle of affordance plays a pivotal role in intuitive design by making the purpose and functionality of interactive elements apparent. Affordances are visual or sensory cues that suggest the possible actions or uses of an object. For instance, buttons should look pressable, and links should appear clickable. By leveraging affordances, designers guide users in understanding the interactive nature of elements, reducing the need for explicit instructions and making the interface more intuitive.

Hierarchy and prioritization contribute significantly to intuitive user interaction, emphasizing the organization of information in a logical and easily digestible manner. Establishing a clear hierarchy ensures that users can quickly grasp the structure of the interface, identifying primary and secondary elements based on their importance. Effective prioritization of content and features aligns with users' expectations and guides them toward the most relevant information or actions, enhancing the overall intuitive nature of the interface.

Progressive disclosure is a principle aimed at revealing information progressively, based on users' needs and context. Instead of overwhelming users with all available options upfront, progressive disclosure presents information gradually, allowing users to explore features as needed. This approach minimizes cognitive overload and supports a more intuitive interaction by presenting complexity only when users express interest or require additional functionality.

Inclusivity is a fundamental principle that recognizes the diversity of users and ensures that the interface accommodates individuals with various abilities, backgrounds, and preferences. Inclusive design involves creating interfaces that are accessible to all users, regardless of their physical abilities, sensory perception, or technological proficiency. Intuitive user interaction considers the broad spectrum of users, incorporating features like text alternatives, keyboard short-cuts, and adjustable font sizes to enhance accessibility.

The principle of predictability aligns with users' expectations, ensuring that the system behaves in a way that users anticipate based on their prior experiences. Predictability involves consistent use of language, the logical placement of elements, and adherence to established design patterns. When users can accurately predict how the interface will respond to their actions, it fosters a sense of control and confidence, contributing to an intuitive user experience.

Discoverability is a key principle aimed at helping users explore and find features within the interface. Designers leverage visual cues, tooltips, and onboarding processes to guide users in discovering functionalities without resorting to trial and error. By making features easily discoverable, users can efficiently navigate the interface and uncover its capabilities, fostering a sense of exploration and mastery.

The principle of flexibility acknowledges the diverse ways users may interact with a system. An intuitive interface accommodates different input methods, such as touch, mouse, or keyboard, and adapts to various device types and screen sizes. A flexible design ensures that users can choose the interaction method that suits their preferences or requirements, contributing to a more personalized and user-centric experience.

Error prevention and recovery are critical principles that contribute to the overall intuitiveness of an interface. By incorporating clear and proactive error prevention mechanisms, designers reduce the likelihood of users making mistakes. Additionally, providing informative error messages and easy-to-follow recovery paths helps users understand and address errors when they occur, fostering a sense of resilience and mitigating potential frustration.

The principle of simplicity extends beyond visual elements to include the language and terminology used within the interface. Clear and concise language promotes understanding, reducing the cognitive load associated with deciphering complex terms or instructions. Simplicity in language ensures that users can easily comprehend the information presented, contributing to a more intuitive and user-friendly experience.

Human-centric design is a foundational principle that emphasizes empathy and understanding of users' needs, behaviors, and motivations. By incorporating user research, personas, and usability testing, designers gain insights into the target audience, enabling them to create interfaces that resonate with users' expectations and preferences. Human-centric design places the user at the center of the design process, ensuring that the interface aligns with their mental models and enhances intuitive interaction.

The principle of user empowerment encourages the design of interfaces that empower users to control their interactions and customize their experiences. Providing users with options for personalization, adjustable settings, and the ability to tailor the interface to their preferences fosters a sense of ownership and control. Empowered users are more likely to engage confidently with the system, contributing to a positive and intuitive interaction.

Aesthetic integrity is a principle that emphasizes the importance of visual coherence and a unified design language. A consistent and aesthetically pleasing interface enhances user satisfaction and contributes to a more intuitive experience. Aesthetic integrity involves harmonizing visual elements, color schemes, and typography to create a cohesive and engaging design that reflects the brand identity and resonates with users.

Iterative design, based on the principle of continuous improvement, involves refining the interface through iterative cycles of testing, feedback, and iteration. The iterative design process allows designers to gather insights from user interactions, identify pain points, and make informed adjustments to enhance the overall intuitiveness of the interface. Continuous refinement ensures that the design aligns with evolving user expectations and technological advancements.

In conclusion, the fundamental principles guiding intuitive user interaction are intertwined with the overarching goal of creating interfaces that prioritize user understanding, engagement, and satisfaction. Simplicity, consistency, feedback, affordance, hierarchy, and the other principles collectively contribute to a design philosophy that places users at the forefront. By aligning with users' expectations, leveraging affordances, and accommodating diverse needs, designers create interfaces that seamlessly integrate with users' mental models, ultimately fostering intuitive and enjoyable interactions.

Emphasize the importance of a user-centric approach in UI design.

The importance of a user-centric approach in UI (User Interface) design cannot be overstated, as it forms the bedrock upon which successful and impactful digital experiences are built. At its core, a user-centric approach revolves around understanding and prioritizing the needs, preferences, and behaviors of the end users throughout the design process. This methodology fundamentally shifts the focus from a system-centric viewpoint, where design decisions are driven solely by technical considerations, to a human-centric perspective that places the user's experience and satisfaction at the forefront. By adopting this approach, designers recognize that the effectiveness of an interface is intrinsically tied to its ability to resonate with and cater to the diverse expectations of the users who interact with it.

One of the primary pillars of a user-centric approach is the emphasis on thorough user research. Understanding the target audience involves delving into their demographics, behaviors, motivations, and pain points. This research provides valuable insights that inform design decisions, ensuring that the resulting interface aligns with the user's mental models and expectations. Through techniques such as user interviews, surveys, and usability testing, designers gain a nuanced understanding of user preferences, allowing for the creation of interfaces that not only meet functional requirements but also resonate emotionally and cognitively with the users.

The iterative nature of a user-centric design process is paramount in ensuring continuous improvement and refinement. Unlike a one-size-fits-all approach, iteration involves gathering feedback from users at various stages of development and using that feedback to make informed adjustments. This cyclical process not only allows designers to catch and rectify issues early on but also ensures that the evolving design aligns with the changing needs and expectations of the user base. By incorporating feedback loops, UI designers can create interfaces that evolve organically, adapting to user preferences and technological advancements over time.

The user-centric approach extends beyond the initial design phase to encompass usability testing and validation. Usability testing involves observing real users interacting with the interface to identify pain points, areas of confusion, and opportunities for improvement. This hands-on evaluation provides designers with actionable insights into how users navigate the interface, interpret visual elements, and accomplish tasks. The iterative loop of testing and refinement ensures that the interface is not only user-friendly but also aligned with the actual behaviors and needs of the intended audience.

Personalization and customization are key tenets of a user-centric approach. Recognizing that users are diverse and have unique preferences, a user-centric design philosophy accommodates personalization features. This can range from simple preferences, such as customizable themes or language settings, to more complex personalization based on user behavior and history. By allowing users to tailor their experience, the interface becomes more adaptable, fostering a sense of ownership and enhancing overall satisfaction. Customization options empower users to shape their interaction with the interface according to their individual needs, creating a more engaging and personalized experience.

Accessibility is a critical aspect of user-centric design that emphasizes inclusivity. A user-centric approach recognizes the diversity of users, including those with different abilities and needs. Designing interfaces that are accessible to individuals with disabilities ensures that everyone, regardless of physical or cognitive limitations, can engage with digital content. This involves considerations such as providing alternative text for images, ensuring keyboard navigation, and accommodating screen readers. By prioritizing accessibility, designers contribute to a more inclusive digital landscape, where everyone can participate in and benefit from the designed experiences.

The concept of empathy is intrinsic to a user-centric approach. Designers actively seek to understand the emotions, motivations, and challenges of the users for whom they are designing. By adopting an empathetic mindset, designers can anticipate user needs and design interfaces that not only fulfill functional requirements but also resonate emotionally. This emotional resonance contributes to user satisfaction and loyalty, fostering a positive perception of the interface and the brand it represents. Empathy ensures that design decisions are not made in isolation but are informed by a deep understanding of the user's context and experiences.

A user-centric approach also prioritizes the visual and interactive aesthetics of an interface. The visual appeal of an interface contributes significantly to the overall user experience. Designers focus on creating visually pleasing layouts, employing consistent color schemes, and using clear typography to enhance readability. Visual hierarchy is carefully considered to guide users through the interface in an intuitive manner. Interactive elements, such as buttons and navigation menus, are designed with affordances that make their purpose clear. The aesthetic aspect of user-centric design goes beyond mere aesthetics; it enhances usability, creates a positive first impression, and contributes to a cohesive and memorable user experience.

User personas play a crucial role in a user-centric approach, helping to personify and understand the diverse user base. User personas are fictional characters created based on the characteristics and behaviors of the target audience. They represent archetypal users with distinct needs, goals, and pain points. Design decisions are informed by the needs of these personas, ensuring that the interface addresses the real-world challenges and expectations of the user base. Personas provide a reference point throughout the design process, keeping the focus on designing for the actual users rather than hypothetical scenarios.

User journeys, mapping out the steps users take to accomplish tasks, are integral to a user-centric approach. By understanding the user journey, designers can identify touchpoints, pain points, and moments of delight or frustration. This comprehensive view allows designers to optimize the interface to streamline user journeys, making interactions more efficient and enjoyable. User journeys also help designers anticipate user expectations at different stages, facilitating the creation of interfaces that align with the natural flow of user interactions.

In the context of a user-centric approach, the concept of usability and learnability takes precedence. Usability focuses on the ease with which users can accomplish tasks within the interface. A user-centric design ensures that interactions are intuitive, minimizing the need for extensive training or guidance. Learnability refers to the user's ability to quickly understand and master the interface. By prioritizing both usability and learnability, designers create interfaces that are not only accessible to new users but also efficient for experienced users, fostering a positive and consistent experience over time.

The principles of transparency and honesty are vital components of a user-centric approach. Users appreciate interfaces that communicate openly about the system's capabilities, limitations, and any potential consequences of their actions. Transparent design involves providing clear information about data usage, privacy policies, and any changes that may impact the user's experience. Honest communication builds trust and ensures that users have a realistic understanding of what to expect, fostering a positive relationship between users and the interface.

The collaborative nature of a user-centric approach encourages multidisciplinary collaboration. Designers work closely with stakeholders, developers, and other team members to ensure that diverse perspectives are considered throughout the design process. This collaborative ethos promotes a holistic understanding of the interface's purpose, functionality, and impact. By integrating various perspectives, designers can create interfaces that not only meet technical requirements but also align with business goals and user expectations.

The continuous evolution of technology and user behaviors underscores the dynamic nature of a user-centric approach. Designers must remain adaptable and responsive to changing user needs, emerging technologies, and industry trends. Regularly updating and refining the interface based on user feedback, analytics, and technological advancements ensures that the design remains relevant and effective over time. A user-centric approach embraces the iterative nature of design, recognizing that the interface is an evolving entity that should continuously align with the evolving landscape of user expectations.

In conclusion, the importance of a user-centric approach in UI design is a cornerstone of creating digital experiences that resonate with users, fostering engagement, satisfaction, and loyalty. By prioritizing user needs, preferences, and behaviors, designers create interfaces that are not only functional but also emotionally resonant. The holistic consideration of user research, empathy, accessibility, personalization, and iterative refinement ensures that the resulting interfaces are not only user-friendly but also adaptable to the dynamic nature of the digital landscape. Ultimately, a user-centric approach is not just a design methodology; it is a commitment to creating interfaces that enrich the lives and experiences of the individuals who interact with them.

Discuss the significance of maintaining consistency in UI elements and layout.

The significance of maintaining consistency in UI (User Interface) elements and layout is fundamental to creating a seamless, intuitive, and user-friendly digital experience. Consistency is a design principle that encompasses various aspects of the user interface, including visual elements, interactions, and layout structures. It plays a pivotal role in shaping user expectations, fostering familiarity, and ultimately enhancing the overall usability of a digital product.

Visual consistency is one of the key dimensions of maintaining a cohesive UI. Consistent use of colors, typography, icons, and other visual elements establishes a unified and recognizable visual identity. When users encounter a consistent visual language throughout an interface, they are better able to understand the hierarchy of information, navigate effortlessly, and associate specific visual cues with certain actions or meanings. Consistency in visual elements creates a harmonious and polished look, contributing to a positive first impression and reinforcing brand identity.

Iconography, in particular, benefits greatly from visual consistency. Icons serve as visual metaphors, representing specific actions or concepts within the interface. Consistent use of icons across different parts of the application or website ensures that users can quickly interpret and understand their meaning. When icons maintain a consistent design language, users don't have to relearn their interpretations, leading to a more intuitive and efficient user experience.

Maintaining consistency in interaction patterns is equally crucial. Users develop mental models of how the interface behaves based on their interactions. When these interactions are consistent, users can confidently predict the outcome of their actions. For example, if clicking on a button consistently leads to a certain action, users will naturally expect the same behavior elsewhere in the interface. This predictability reduces cognitive load, enhances user confidence, and contributes to a smoother and more enjoyable user experience.

Layout consistency is paramount in creating a visually coherent and navigable interface. Consistent placement of navigation menus, buttons, and other interactive elements across different screens or pages contributes to a sense of familiarity. Users quickly learn where to find essential features, leading to increased efficiency and a more seamless navigation experience. A consistent layout also aids in establishing a visual hierarchy, guiding users through the interface in a logical and intuitive manner.

In web design, maintaining consistency in navigation patterns is particularly vital. Users expect to find common navigation elements, such as menus and links, in predictable locations. Consistent navigation patterns contribute to a sense of continuity, making it easier for users to explore different sections of a website without feeling disoriented. Whether it's a header menu, a sidebar navigation, or a footer menu, maintaining consistency in the placement and styling of these elements contributes to a cohesive and user-friendly browsing experience.

Consistency becomes even more critical in the context of multi-platform experiences. With users accessing digital products across various devices, including desktops, tablets, and smartphones, maintaining a consistent experience across different screen sizes and resolutions is imperative. A responsive design that adapts to different devices while preserving the same visual and interaction patterns ensures that users can seamlessly transition between platforms without experiencing a jarring shift in the interface.

The significance of consistency extends beyond the immediate user experience; it also influences brand perception. A consistent and well-designed interface conveys a sense of professionalism and attention to detail. When users perceive a brand as reliable and trustworthy through a consistently designed interface, they are more likely to form positive associations and build a sense of loyalty. Consistency in UI design contributes to brand recognition and establishes a strong visual identity that users can easily associate with a particular product or service.

In e-commerce platforms, where users often engage in a series of actions such as browsing, selecting products, and completing transactions, maintaining consistency is paramount. Users expect a coherent and predictable flow throughout their journey, from the product pages to the checkout process. Consistent design elements, such as buttons, forms, and progress indicators, help users understand where they are in the process, reducing anxiety and increasing the likelihood of completing the desired actions.

Accessibility is another area where consistency plays a crucial role. Users with disabilities, such as visual impairments, rely on consistent design patterns to navigate and interact with digital interfaces. When interactive elements have consistent labels, sizes, and positions, users utilizing assistive technologies can more effectively understand and engage with the content. Consistency in accessibility features ensures that the interface remains inclusive, catering to a diverse user base with varying needs and abilities.

Consistency also facilitates efficient collaboration among design and development teams. When design patterns, components, and guidelines remain consistent, it streamlines the implementation process. Developers can reuse code, reducing redundancy and minimizing the likelihood of introducing errors. Consistency in design documentation and assets ensures that everyone involved in the project shares a common understanding of the intended visual and interaction patterns, fostering a collaborative and efficient development process.

While consistency is undeniably beneficial, it's essential to strike a balance to avoid monotony. Introducing subtle variations within a consistent framework can help maintain visual interest and prevent user fatigue. For example, using different colors or styles for interactive elements to indicate states like hover or click adds a layer of dynamism without compromising overall consistency. Striking this balance allows designers to provide a visually engaging experience while preserving the predictability and familiarity that consistency brings.

In conclusion, the significance of maintaining consistency in UI elements and layout lies in its ability to create a harmonious, predictable, and user-friendly digital experience. Consistency in visual elements, interactions, and layout patterns contributes to user confidence, efficiency, and a positive perception of the brand. It fosters a sense of familiarity, reduces cognitive load, and supports seamless navigation across various screens and devices. As a guiding principle in UI design, consistency not only enhances the immediate user experience but also plays a crucial role in shaping brand identity, fostering trust, and facilitating collaborative development processes.

Explore how consistent design fosters familiarity and ease of use.

Consistent design is a cornerstone in fostering familiarity and ease of use within digital interfaces, creating an environment where users can effortlessly navigate, comprehend, and engage with the elements of a system. At its core, consistency in design establishes a visual language that users can quickly understand, providing them with a familiar framework that extends across various screens, pages, and interactions. This visual cohesion reduces the cognitive load on users, allowing them to focus on their tasks rather than deciphering unfamiliar elements. The familiarity derived from consistent design empowers users with a sense of confidence, enabling them to predict how the interface will behave and making their overall experience more intuitive.

Visual consistency is instrumental in cultivating familiarity within a digital interface. When users encounter a consistent application of colors, typography, and visual hierarchy, they develop a mental model of the interface's visual language. This uniformity creates a predictable and recognizable design language, guiding users through different sections and functionalities without the need for explicit instruction. Visual elements, such as buttons, icons, and navigation menus, become reliable cues that users can interpret consistently across the interface, contributing to a seamless and cohesive visual experience.

Consistency in the application of design patterns across various screens and sections contributes to a coherent and navigable interface. Users often traverse different parts of a website or application during their interaction. Maintaining consistent design patterns in elements like navigation menus, buttons, and layout structures ensures that users encounter a similar visual and interactive language regardless of their location within the system. This predictability fosters a sense of continuity and reduces the learning curve, allowing users to transfer their knowledge and experience seamlessly from one part of the interface to another.

The familiarity engendered by consistent design extends beyond the visual realm to include interaction patterns. When users consistently encounter similar actions associated with specific elements, they develop a clear understanding of how to navigate and engage with the interface. For instance, if clicking on a button consistently leads to a specific outcome or if swiping gestures consistently navigate between pages, users internalize these patterns. This predictability not only enhances ease of use but also establishes a trust in the system's behavior, making the overall interaction more fluid and user-friendly.

In e-commerce platforms, where users engage in a series of actions such as product browsing, selection, and checkout, maintaining consistency in design patterns is particularly crucial. Users expect a coherent flow that aligns with their mental model of online shopping. Consistent placement and styling of elements such as add-to-cart buttons, product images, and checkout forms contribute to a seamless and intuitive shopping experience. The familiarity derived from consistent design patterns reduces friction, making it easier for users to progress through their journey and complete transactions with confidence.

Consistency plays a pivotal role in navigation, ensuring that users can find their way through the interface effortlessly. Whether it's a website with multiple pages or an application with various sections, users rely on consistent navigation patterns to orient themselves. Consistent placement of navigation menus, search bars, and links creates a sense of predictability, empowering users to explore different parts of the interface without feeling disoriented. The navigation elements become reliable signposts, guiding users through the digital space with ease and contributing to an overall sense of familiarity.

In the context of mobile applications, where screen real estate is limited, maintaining consistent design becomes even more critical. Users interact with a myriad of apps on their mobile devices, each with its own unique features and functionalities. Consistency in design patterns, such as the placement of navigation controls, gestures for interaction, and the overall visual language, ensures that users can quickly adapt to new applications. This consistency becomes particularly beneficial when users switch between apps, as they can leverage their existing knowledge of design patterns, reducing the learning curve and enhancing ease of use.

Consistent design fosters familiarity not only within individual interfaces but also across different platforms and devices. With users accessing digital products on desktops, tablets, and smartphones, a consistent cross-platform experience becomes imperative. Responsive design that adapts to various screen sizes and resolutions while maintaining consistent visual and interaction patterns ensures a cohesive experience. Users can seamlessly transition between devices without encountering significant changes in the interface, preserving the learned behaviors and reducing the need for reorientation.

The familiarity derived from consistent design principles contributes significantly to the overall learnability of a digital interface. Learnability refers to the ease with which users can understand and master a system. Consistent design patterns reduce the cognitive effort required for users to grasp the workings of an interface. Once users learn how to perform a particular action or understand the meaning behind a visual cue, that knowledge carries over consistently to other parts of the interface. This interconnected familiarity accelerates the learning process, making it more efficient for users to become proficient in using the digital product.

Consistent design also plays a crucial role in user onboarding and orientation. When users encounter a new interface that aligns with familiar design patterns, they can quickly navigate and understand its features. The visual and interaction cues that users have learned from other contexts become guiding principles, facilitating a smooth onboarding process. Consistency in design patterns ensures that users feel at ease when exploring new interfaces, minimizing the barriers to entry and enhancing the overall ease of use.

In the context of software applications with frequent updates and feature additions, maintaining design consistency becomes a strategic consideration. While innovation and evolution are essential, abrupt changes in design can disrupt user familiarity and lead to confusion. Introducing new features within the context of established design patterns helps users seamlessly incorporate these additions into their existing mental model. This phased approach to innovation balances the need for progress with the importance of preserving user familiarity and ease of use.

Consistent design principles are particularly beneficial in accessibility considerations. Users with disabilities, relying on assistive technologies, often navigate interfaces by recognizing consistent patterns. Consistency in the labeling of interactive elements, the use of descriptive alt text for images, and the placement of navigation controls enables users with disabilities to effectively engage with the content. By maintaining a consistent design language, digital interfaces become more inclusive, ensuring that all users, regardless of their abilities, can navigate and comprehend the interface with ease.

The psychological aspect of consistent design is noteworthy. Familiarity instills a sense of comfort and confidence in users. When users encounter a consistent interface, they feel more in control, as they can anticipate the outcome of their interactions based on learned patterns. This sense of control contributes to a positive user experience, making users more inclined to explore and engage with the interface. The psychological comfort derived from familiarity enhances the overall perception of ease of use and satisfaction.

In conclusion, the significance of maintaining consistency in UI elements and layout is evident in its ability to foster familiarity and ease of use. Consistent design principles, whether applied to visual elements, interaction patterns, or cross-platform experiences, create a predictable and recognizable environment for users. This predictability reduces cognitive load, accelerates the learning process, and instills confidence in users, contributing to a positive and user-friendly experience. Whether in e-commerce, navigation, mobile applications, or accessibility considerations, the benefits of consistent design extend across diverse contexts, shaping interfaces that users can engage with effortlessly and intuitively.

Explore the principles of organizing information hierarchically for optimal user comprehension.

Organizing information hierarchically is a fundamental principle in user interface design, serving as a strategic framework to optimize user comprehension and engagement. At its core, hierarchical organization structures information in a way that reflects its importance and relationships, ensuring that users can navigate and understand content intuitively. This hierarchical approach aligns with human cognitive processes, facilitating the efficient processing of information and contributing to a more seamless user experience.

One of the key principles in hierarchical organization is the establishment of a clear and discernible visual hierarchy. Visual hierarchy guides users through the interface by prioritizing information based on its significance. This involves strategically using design elements such as size, color, contrast, and typography to emphasize certain elements over others. For example, larger font sizes or bold typography may be employed for headings to signal their importance, while subordinate information might be presented in smaller or lighter text. A well-crafted visual hierarchy directs users' attention, allowing them to quickly discern the relative importance of different elements within the interface.

Heading structures play a crucial role in creating a hierarchical flow of information. By using consistent and logically structured headings, designers provide users with a roadmap for understanding content. Headings not only break up the content into digestible sections but also convey the relationships between different pieces of information. This use of headings allows users to scan and navigate the content efficiently, accessing the information they need without feeling overwhelmed. Clear and descriptive headings contribute to the overall coherence of the interface, aiding users in comprehending the underlying structure of the information.

Organizing information hierarchically involves thoughtful categorization and grouping of related content. Grouping similar elements helps users make sense of the information by presenting it in meaningful clusters. This grouping may involve categorizing content based on topics, themes, or functionalities. For instance, in an e-commerce website, products can be grouped by categories such as electronics, clothing, or home goods. This categorization simplifies the user's mental model, allowing them to anticipate the location of specific information and promoting efficient navigation.

Consistent use of layout and alignment principles contributes to the hierarchical organization of information. Aligning elements consistently and employing grid-based layouts creates a sense of order, making it easier for users to follow the flow of information. A well-structured layout reinforces the visual hierarchy, guiding users from broader sections to more detailed content. Grid-based layouts also contribute to the overall aesthetic coherence of the interface, fostering a visually pleasing and organized user experience.

Navigational elements, such as menus and navigation bars, play a pivotal role in hierarchical organization. By presenting a structured set of options, these elements guide users through different levels of information. Drop-down menus, for example, provide a hierarchical structure that allows users to explore subcategories and specific pages within a broader category. Navigation bars with clear labels contribute to the intuitive organization of information, offering users a straightforward means of accessing different sections of the interface.

The principles of progressive disclosure align closely with hierarchical organization, emphasizing the presentation of information in a gradual and layered manner. Instead of overwhelming users with an abundance of information all at once, progressive disclosure involves revealing content progressively as users navigate through the interface. This approach respects users' cognitive load, allowing them to focus on relevant information without feeling inundated. Features like accordions, where information is hidden until a user chooses to expand it, exemplify the application of progressive disclosure to optimize user comprehension.

Strategic use of color can further enhance hierarchical organization by helping users distinguish between different levels of information. Color coding can be employed to indicate categories, importance, or relationships within the content. For example, using a distinct color for headings or category labels allows users to quickly identify and comprehend the structure of the information. However, it's essential to ensure that the color scheme remains accessible and does not rely solely on color distinctions for understanding, considering users with color vision deficiencies.

In the context of information-heavy interfaces, the principle of chunking information aids in optimal user comprehension. Chunking involves breaking down large amounts of information into smaller, manageable units. By organizing content into meaningful chunks, users can process and retain information more effectively. This principle aligns with human cognitive limitations, recognizing that individuals have a finite capacity for processing information at any given time. Well-organized chunks of information make it easier for users to absorb and remember key details, contributing to a more comprehensible user experience.

Incorporating a well-defined information architecture is pivotal in hierarchical organization. Information architecture involves the structuring and labeling of content to facilitate navigation and understanding. A clear information architecture establishes the relationships between different sections and ensures that users can locate information intuitively. Techniques such as card sorting, user testing, and wireframing contribute to the development of a robust information architecture that aligns with user mental models and optimizes comprehension.

The concept of breadcrumbs, a navigational aid that displays the user's current location within the hierarchical structure, enhances user comprehension and orientation. Breadcrumbs provide users with a visual trail, indicating the path they have taken to arrive at the current page. This not only aids in navigation but also helps users understand the broader context of their interactions within the interface. Breadcrumbs are particularly useful in interfaces with deep hierarchies or multi-step processes, providing users with a sense of control and awareness.

A well-designed search functionality complements hierarchical organization by offering users an alternative means of accessing information. When users have a specific query or are looking for a particular item, a robust search feature allows them to bypass the hierarchical structure and directly retrieve the relevant information. Integrating features like auto-suggestions and filters further enhances the search experience, ensuring that users can quickly narrow down their search and locate the desired information with minimal effort.

Icons and visual cues contribute to the hierarchical organization of information by providing users with additional context and guidance. Icons can represent categories, actions, or relationships, serving as visual signifiers within the interface. Well-designed icons help users quickly identify the nature of different elements, reinforcing the visual hierarchy. However, it's crucial to ensure that icons are universally understood and accompanied by text labels or tooltips to prevent ambiguity and enhance user comprehension.

Whitespace, or negative space, is a powerful tool in hierarchical organization, contributing to a clean and uncluttered interface. Whitespace helps separate different elements, preventing visual overload and creating a sense of visual hierarchy. Adequate spacing between elements enhances readability and allows users to focus on individual pieces of information without distraction. Whitespace serves as a visual cue, guiding users through the interface and reinforcing the hierarchical relationships between different sections.

Feedback mechanisms, such as hover effects and click animations, play a subtle yet significant role in hierarchical organization. Providing feedback when users interact with elements reinforces the cause-and-effect relationship, helping users understand the consequences of their actions within the interface. For example, changing the color or adding a subtle animation when a user hovers over a clickable element provides visual feedback that reinforces the hierarchical importance of that element.

The principles of organizing information hierarchically extend beyond individual interfaces to encompass the broader context of a user's journey. Considering the user's flow and sequencing content in a logical order contributes to a cohesive and comprehensible experience. Whether guiding users through a multi-step process or presenting information in a chronological order, aligning the information hierarchy with the user's natural progression enhances overall comprehension and engagement.

In the realm of responsive design, where interfaces must adapt to various screen sizes and orientations, maintaining a consistent hierarchical organization is paramount. The principles of responsive design involve thoughtful consideration of how the hierarchical structure adjusts to different contexts. Elements like collapsible menus, reordering content based on screen size, and maintaining visual hierarchy across devices contribute to a seamless and comprehensible experience for users interacting with the interface on diverse platforms.

The iterative nature of user testing and feedback loops is integral to refining hierarchical organization. Conducting usability tests allows designers to observe how users interact with the hierarchical structure and identify areas for improvement. User feedback provides valuable insights into whether the information is organized intuitively and whether users can comprehend the hierarchy effectively. Iterative refinement based on user input ensures that the hierarchical organization aligns with user expectations and mental models.

In conclusion, the principles of organizing information hierarchically are foundational to creating interfaces that optimize user comprehension. From visual hierarchy and layout consistency to navigation aids and feedback mechanisms, each element contributes to a coherent and intuitive structure. The hierarchical organization not only aligns with human cognitive processes but also reflects an understanding of user behavior and expectations. By implementing these principles, designers can create interfaces that guide users seamlessly through information, fostering a sense of familiarity, efficiency, and overall ease of use.

Discuss how a well-structured information hierarchy enhances the user's ability to navigate.

A well-structured information hierarchy is a linchpin in enhancing the user's ability to navigate through digital interfaces, providing a roadmap that guides users with clarity and efficiency. Navigability, a cornerstone of user experience, hinges on the organization and presentation of information in a manner that aligns with users' mental models and expectations. From visual cues to logical groupings, the components of a robust information hierarchy work synergistically to empower users, allowing them to traverse digital spaces with ease and confidence.

At the forefront of enhancing navigation is the establishment of a clear visual hierarchy. Visual hierarchy employs design principles such as size, color, contrast, and typography to emphasize the importance of different elements within the interface. By strategically arranging visual elements, designers create a roadmap that directs users' attention and guides them through the content. For instance, larger and bolder text may signify headings or key information, providing users with immediate visual cues about the significance of certain elements. This visual guidance fosters a sense of direction, enabling users to navigate with intentionality.

Headings, a fundamental element of information hierarchy, play a pivotal role in aiding navigation by breaking down content into digestible sections. Well-structured and logically labeled headings act as signposts, giving users insights into the organization of information and helping them orient themselves within the interface. The use of descriptive headings not only aids in navigation but also contributes to the overall comprehensibility of the content. Users can quickly scan headings to identify relevant sections, streamlining their navigation process and enabling them to access specific information efficiently.

Grouping related content is a fundamental principle that enhances navigation by presenting information in cohesive clusters. Logical categorization and grouping contribute to a sense of order within the interface, making it easier for users to locate specific information. Whether content is grouped by topics, themes, or functionalities, this organizational strategy simplifies users' mental models and aids in predicting the location of relevant information. Grouping aligns with users' expectations, allowing them to navigate more intuitively and find content that aligns with their interests or goals.

The consistent use of layout and alignment principles is instrumental in shaping a well-structured information hierarchy that aids navigation. A visually cohesive layout, characterized by consistent spacing, alignment, and grid-based structures, contributes to a sense of order. Users rely on a visually organized layout to understand the relationships between different elements and navigate seamlessly. A well-structured layout not only enhances the aesthetic appeal but also ensures that users can follow a logical flow as they move through the interface, reinforcing their ability to navigate with ease.

Navigational elements, such as menus and navigation bars, serve as interactive tools within the information hierarchy, providing users with tangible pathways to explore the interface. Clear and well-organized menus present users with a structured set of options, allowing them to choose their desired destinations. Navigation bars, often placed prominently, offer users a consistent means of accessing key sections or features within the interface. These navigational aids act as guideposts, empowering users to move between different sections of the interface with confidence and minimizing the cognitive load associated with navigation.

Drop-down menus, a common navigational element, contribute to hierarchical organization by offering users access to subcategories or additional options within a broader category. This hierarchical presentation allows users to delve deeper into specific areas of interest without cluttering the main interface. By organizing options in a nested manner, drop-down menus facilitate a streamlined navigation experience, providing users with a clear and structured pathway to explore content based on their preferences.

Progressive disclosure, a principle closely aligned with information hierarchy, complements navigation by presenting information gradually as users interact with the interface. Rather than overwhelming users with a barrage of information, progressive disclosure ensures that content is revealed in a layered manner, aligning with users' navigation choices. Features such as accordions, which hide or reveal information based on user interactions, exemplify how progressive disclosure aids navigation by allowing users to focus on the information relevant to their current context without unnecessary distractions.

Strategic use of color within the information hierarchy enhances navigation by aiding users in distinguishing between different levels of information or categories. Color coding, when applied judiciously, can serve as a visual cue that guides users through the hierarchy. For instance, using a consistent color scheme for category labels or headings helps users quickly identify the nature of the content and understand the relationships within the hierarchy. However, it's essential to ensure that color distinctions are not the sole means of conveying information, considering users with color vision deficiencies.

In the context of responsive design, where interfaces must adapt to various screen sizes and orientations, maintaining a consistent information hierarchy is paramount for effective navigation. Responsive design principles involve thoughtful adjustments to the layout, navigational elements, and visual hierarchy to ensure a seamless experience across devices. Elements like collapsible menus, which adapt to smaller screens, and the reordering of content based on screen size contribute to a cohesive and navigable interface. Consistency in the information hierarchy across different devices ensures that users can navigate with familiarity, regardless of the platform they are using.

Breadcrumbs, a navigational aid that displays the user's current location within the hierarchical structure, significantly enhances navigation by providing users with a visual trail. Breadcrumbs not only help users understand their position within the interface but also offer a quick means of retracing their steps. This navigational feature is particularly beneficial in interfaces with deep hierarchies or multi-step processes, providing users with a sense of control and awareness as they move through different levels

of content.

Search functionality, when well-implemented, is a powerful tool that complements the information hierarchy by offering users an alternative means of navigation. Users with specific queries or those seeking particular content can leverage search features to bypass the hierarchical structure and directly access relevant information. Auto-suggestions, filters, and advanced search capabilities further enhance the search experience, ensuring that users can efficiently narrow down their queries and locate the desired information with minimal effort.

Icons and visual cues play a crucial role in aiding navigation within the information hierarchy by providing additional context and recognition. Icons, when thoughtfully designed and universally understood, serve as visual signifiers that help users quickly identify different elements or actions within the interface. Visual cues, such as hover effects or subtle animations, provide feedback that reinforces the cause-and-effect relationship, enhancing users' understanding of the navigational pathways. However, it's essential to ensure that icons are accompanied by text labels or tooltips to prevent ambiguity and support users with diverse levels of familiarity.

Whitespace, or negative space, contributes significantly to the user's ability to navigate by preventing visual clutter and fostering a sense of clarity. Adequate spacing between elements enhances readability and allows users to focus on individual pieces of information without distraction. Whitespace serves as a visual separator, guiding users through the interface and reinforcing the hierarchical relationships between different sections. A clean and uncluttered interface, facilitated by effective use of whitespace, contributes to a more pleasant and navigable user experience.

Feedback mechanisms, such as hover effects and click animations, are subtle yet impactful elements within the information hierarchy that aid navigation. Providing feedback when users interact with elements reinforces the cause-and-effect relationship, helping them understand the consequences of their actions within the interface. For example, changing the color or adding a subtle animation when a user hovers over a clickable element provides visual feedback that reinforces the hierarchical importance of that element. These feedback mechanisms contribute to a more intuitive and user-friendly navigation experience.

The iterative process of user testing and feedback loops is integral to refining the information hierarchy for optimal navigation. Usability tests allow designers to observe how users interact with the information structure and identify areas for improvement. User feedback provides valuable insights into whether the hierarchy aligns with user expectations and whether users can navigate seamlessly. Iterative refinement based on user input ensures that the information hierarchy evolves in response to user needs, enhancing the overall navigational experience.

In conclusion, a well-structured information hierarchy serves as the backbone for enhancing the user's ability to navigate through digital interfaces. From visual hierarchy and logical groupings to navigational aids and feedback mechanisms, each component plays a crucial role in guiding users with clarity and efficiency. The information hierarchy not only aligns with human cognitive processes but also reflects a deep understanding of user behavior and expectations. By implementing these principles, designers can create interfaces that empower users to navigate seamlessly, fostering a sense of familiarity, confidence, and overall ease of use.

Highlight the role of feedback mechanisms in user interfaces.

Feedback mechanisms in user interfaces play a multifaceted and pivotal role, acting as the dynamic bridge of communication between users and the digital environment. These mechanisms encompass a variety of visual, auditory, and tactile cues that inform users about the outcomes of their actions, guide them through the interface, and create a responsive, interactive, and user-centric experience. At its core, feedback mechanisms are integral in establishing a dialogue, enhancing user understanding, and fostering engagement within the interface.

Visual feedback is a cornerstone of user interfaces, providing users with immediate and tangible responses to their interactions. It includes a spectrum of cues such as color changes, animations, and visual highlights that signify the success or status of an action. For instance, when a user hovers over a clickable button and the color changes, it serves as an anticipatory cue, informing the user that the element is interactive. Visual feedback is crucial in reinforcing the cause-and-effect relationship between user actions and system responses, creating a more intuitive and visually coherent experience.

Auditory feedback, though often overlooked, adds an additional layer to the user experience by utilizing sound cues to communicate information or confirm user actions. Beep sounds, clicks, or subtle tones can indicate successful submissions, errors, or even the completion of background processes. Auditory feedback is particularly valuable in scenarios where visual feedback might be limited or when users benefit from an additional sensory dimension. However, it's essential to strike a balance, ensuring that sounds are unobtrusive, clear, and contextually relevant to prevent user frustration.

Tactile feedback, commonly known as haptic feedback, leverages the sense of touch to enhance user interactions. Devices equipped with haptic technology, such as smartphones with vibration capabilities, provide users with physical sensations that correspond to specific actions. This tactile dimension enhances the user's perception of responsiveness, adding a tangible and immersive element to their interactions. Tactile feedback is especially beneficial in touchscreen interfaces, where users can feel a confirmation vibration upon pressing a button or receive haptic cues to simulate physical interactions.

Feedback mechanisms are instrumental in guiding users through form interactions, where clarity about the correctness of input is crucial. Real-time validation, a form of visual feedback, instantly communicates whether the information entered is valid or requires correction. For instance, as users type their email address, a checkmark or warning icon may appear to signify its validity. This immediate response aids users in identifying and rectifying errors promptly, reducing frustration and contributing to a more efficient and error-resistant form-filling experience.

In the realm of navigation, feedback mechanisms provide users with clear signals about the state of the interface, helping them understand their location, available options, and potential actions. Breadcrumbs, a navigational aid, visually communicates the user's current position within the hierarchy of the interface, enabling them to retrace their steps or navigate to higher-level sections. Visual indicators on buttons or links, such as highlighting the active tab, communicate to users which section they are currently engaged with, promoting orientation and a sense of control.

Microinteractions, subtle and purposeful animations triggered by user actions, are an expressive form of feedback that enriches the user experience. These animations provide visual continuity, indicating the cause and effect of actions. For instance, when a user adds an item to a shopping cart, a smooth animation can visually connect the action to the cart icon, creating a seamless and delightful transition. Microinteractions contribute to a more engaging and human-centered interface, adding finesse to the overall user experience.

In feedback-rich interfaces, error messages play a crucial role in communicating issues, guiding users towards resolution, and preventing frustration. Clear and concise error messages, accompanied by suggestions or corrective actions, provide users with information about what went wrong and how to rectify it. Additionally, incorporating visual cues, such as highlighting the erroneous fields or using color-coded indicators, enhances the visibility of errors and aids users in swiftly addressing issues without unnecessary confusion.

Feedback mechanisms contribute significantly to the user onboarding process, where users are introduced to the features and functionalities of an interface. Guided tours or tooltips, often accompanied by visual highlights, offer users contextual information about specific elements or actions, reducing the learning curve. This proactive feedback not only aids in familiarizing users with the interface but also instills confidence, encouraging exploration and engagement with different features.

In the context of e-commerce and transactional interfaces, feedback mechanisms during the checkout process are paramount. Confirmations of successful transactions, order placements, or updates on the shipping status provide users with reassurance and transparency. Visual and auditory cues, such as a green checkmark or a subtle ping sound, confirm the completion of critical actions, instilling trust in users and enhancing the overall reliability of the transactional experience.

In complex software applications or content-rich platforms, feedback mechanisms assist users in understanding the outcomes of their interactions with data. Sorting, filtering, or searching functionalities often produce immediate feedback, updating the displayed content dynamically based on user preferences. These real-time updates create a responsive and interactive environment, allowing users to refine their interactions iteratively without the need for page reloads, thereby improving efficiency and user satisfaction.

User feedback, obtained through surveys, ratings, or comment sections, is a reciprocal aspect of feedback mechanisms that facilitates continuous improvement. Soliciting user opinions provides valuable insights into their preferences, pain points, and overall satisfaction with the interface. Responsiveness to user feedback demonstrates a commitment to user-centric design, fostering a collaborative relationship between designers and users. Iterative design based on user input allows interfaces to evolve in tandem with user expectations and preferences.

The role of feedback mechanisms extends to the realm of accessibility, where they play a crucial role in catering to users with diverse needs and abilities. Providing alternative text for images, descriptive labels for form fields, and ensuring compatibility with screen readers are forms of feedback that enhance accessibility. Well-designed interfaces consider accessibility as an integral aspect of feedback, ensuring that users with disabilities receive information through multiple modalities, creating a more inclusive user experience.

In the era of touch-based interactions, tactile feedback gains prominence through technologies like haptic feedback and force touch. Devices equipped with haptic capabilities respond to touch with subtle vibrations, providing users with a sense of confirmation or acknowledgment. Tactile feedback in touch interfaces enhances the perceived responsiveness of the system, creating a more immersive and engaging interaction. Force touch, employed in devices like smartphones and smartwatches, responds to the varying levels of pressure applied by users, offering additional layers of interaction and feedback.

User engagement is inherently tied to the emotional impact of the interface, and feedback mechanisms contribute to shaping this emotional resonance. Delightful animations, celebratory sounds upon completing a task, or personalized interactions create positive emotional experiences. Conversely, well-crafted error messages that guide users through challenges with empathy contribute to a more supportive and less frustrating emotional journey. The emotional dimension of feedback mechanisms adds a human touch to the interface, creating memorable and positive user experiences.

In conclusion, feedback mechanisms serve as the vital communication channels within user interfaces, facilitating a dynamic dialogue between users and digital systems. Whether through visual, auditory, or tactile cues, feedback mechanisms guide users through interactions, communicate outcomes, and enhance the overall user experience. From microinteractions and error messages to navigational aids and accessibility considerations, these mechanisms contribute to a responsive, engaging, and user-centric interface. As technology continues to evolve, the role of feedback mechanisms will remain central in creating interfaces that not only meet functional requirements but also resonate emotionally with users, fostering a lasting and positive connection.

Discuss how providing timely feedback enhances the user's understanding of their interactions.

The provision of timely feedback within user interfaces stands as a cornerstone in enriching the user experience by enhancing the user's understanding of their interactions. Timely feedback refers to the swift and relevant responses the system provides to user actions, creating a seamless and dynamic dialogue between the user and the interface. This instantaneous communication not only confirms the success or status of an action but also contributes to a more intuitive, transparent, and user-centric environment. Through various modalities such as visual, auditory, and tactile cues, timely feedback serves as an informational bridge, empowering users with a deeper comprehension of their interactions and fostering a sense of control within the digital space.

In the visual realm, the immediacy of visual feedback plays a pivotal role in signaling the outcomes of user actions. Whether it's the color change of a button upon hover, the smooth transition of a page element, or the appearance of an animated loading spinner, these visual cues offer users real-time insights into the state of the interface. Visual feedback is particularly effective in confirming the successful execution of an action, such as submitting a form or completing a transaction. The rapid response time of these visual cues not only reinforces the cause-and-effect relationship between user inputs and system responses but also contributes to a visually cohesive and engaging user experience.

The role of timely feedback becomes evident in scenarios where users navigate through complex interfaces, such as websites or applications with multiple interactive elements. As users explore various functionalities or features, instant visual feedback guides them through the interface, helping them understand the consequences of their actions. For instance, when users click a link, the immediate change in color or underlining provides a clear indicator that the link has been activated. In the absence of such timely visual cues, users might experience uncertainty and hesitation, potentially leading to a less confident and less enjoyable interaction.

Real-time validation within form interactions is a quintessential example of how timely visual feedback enhances the user's understanding. As users input information, such as an email address or a password, instantaneous visual cues indicate whether the entered data is valid or requires correction. For instance, the appearance of a checkmark or a warning icon beside the form field provides immediate feedback on the correctness of the input. This not only aids users in rectifying errors promptly but also prevents them from submitting a form with invalid information, creating a more efficient and error-resistant form-filling experience.

In the context of navigation, where users move through different sections or pages, timely visual feedback contributes to a heightened sense of orientation. Navigational elements, such as highlighted buttons, color-coded active tabs, or breadcrumbs, provide users with immediate visual clues about their location within the interface. When users click on a menu item, the instantaneous change in appearance signals that their selection has been recognized, offering reassurance and clarity. This form of feedback aids users in understanding the hierarchy of the interface, promoting a more streamlined and confident navigation experience.

Microinteractions, a subset of visual feedback, are subtle animations triggered by user actions, creating a responsive and delightful user experience. These microinteractions, whether it's a heart icon animation when users 'like' a post or a smooth transition when they add an item to a shopping cart, contribute to a more engaging and emotionally resonant interface. The immediacy of these animations not only adds finesse to the interaction but also reinforces the connection between user inputs and system responses. Timely visual feedback through microinteractions creates a sense of liveliness within the interface, fostering a positive and memorable user experience.

The significance of visual feedback amplifies in scenarios where users engage in transactional interactions, such as making a purchase or submitting a form. Timely visual cues confirm the successful completion of these critical actions, instilling confidence and trust in users. For instance, a green checkmark or a brief animation can signify that an order has been successfully placed, providing users with immediate confirmation. The absence of this feedback, or any delay in its provision, may lead to user anxiety and uncertainty, negatively impacting the perceived reliability of the interface.

Error messages, as a form of visual feedback, are crucial in guiding users through challenges and enhancing their understanding of issues. Timely and clear error messages, accompanied by suggestions for correction, inform users about what went wrong and how to rectify it. When users encounter errors, immediate visual cues, such as highlighting the problematic fields or presenting a concise error message, help them pinpoint and address issues promptly. The rapid provision of error feedback reduces user frustration, prevents confusion, and contributes to an overall positive user experience.

Timely auditory feedback, often operating in tandem with visual elements, adds an additional layer to the user experience by leveraging sound cues to communicate information or confirm user actions. For instance, a subtle chime or beep sound upon successfully submitting a form or completing a task provides users with an additional dimension of confirmation. Auditory feedback is particularly valuable in scenarios where visual feedback might be limited or when users benefit from an additional sensory dimension. Striking the right balance in sound design ensures that auditory cues are unobtrusive, clear, and contextually relevant to prevent user annoyance.

In tactile interactions, especially in touch-based interfaces, timely haptic or tactile feedback enhances the user's understanding of their interactions. Haptic feedback, such as a subtle vibration or a tactile response upon tapping a button, creates a tangible and immersive dimension to the interaction. When users feel a confirmation vibration upon pressing a virtual button or receive haptic cues to simulate physical interactions, it provides an immediate and tactile confirmation of their actions. Tactile feedback contributes to the perceived responsiveness of the system, creating a more engaging and sensorially rich user experience.

The provision of timely feedback is particularly instrumental during the onboarding process, where users are introduced to the features and functionalities of an interface. Guided tours or tooltips, often accompanied by visual highlights or auditory cues, offer users contextual information about specific elements or actions. The immediacy of this feedback reduces the learning curve, empowering users with knowledge about the interface's capabilities. Timely feedback during onboarding not only aids in familiarizing users with the interface but also instills confidence, encouraging exploration and engagement with different features.

In the context of e-commerce and transactional interfaces, timely feedback during the checkout process is paramount. Confirmations of successful transactions, order placements, or updates on the shipping status provide users with reassurance and transparency. Visual and auditory cues, such as a green checkmark or a subtle ping sound, confirm the completion of critical actions, instilling trust in users and enhancing the overall reliability of the transactional experience. The immediate feedback during transactional interactions contributes to a seamless and user-friendly process.

Real-time updates and feedback in content-heavy interfaces contribute to a more responsive and user-centric experience. As users interact with data, such as sorting, filtering, or searching, instantaneous visual updates dynamically reflect their preferences. These timely responses create an interactive environment, allowing users to refine their interactions iteratively without the need for page reloads. Real-time feedback in content-heavy interfaces enhances user comprehension by providing instant insights into the consequences of their actions, fostering efficiency and user satisfaction.

In the context of accessibility, timely feedback is integral to catering to users with diverse needs and abilities. Providing alternative text for images, descriptive labels for form fields, and ensuring compatibility with screen readers are forms of feedback that enhance accessibility. Immediate responses to user inputs ensure that users with disabilities receive information through multiple modalities, creating a more inclusive user experience. Timely accessibility feedback contributes to a digital environment where all users, regardless of their abilities, can navigate and interact with confidence.

The emotional impact of timely feedback is a crucial aspect of the user experience. Delightful animations, celebratory sounds upon completing a task, or personalized interactions create positive emotional experiences. The immediacy of these emotional feedback mechanisms adds a human touch to the interface, creating memorable and enjoyable interactions. Conversely, well-crafted error messages that guide users through challenges with empathy contribute to a more supportive and less frustrating emotional journey. Timely emotional feedback contributes to a user experience that goes beyond mere functionality, resonating with users on a deeper and more meaningful level.

In the era of touch-based interactions, timely tactile feedback gains prominence through technologies like haptic feedback and force touch. Devices equipped with haptic capabilities respond to touch with subtle vibrations, providing users with a sense of confirmation or acknowledgment. Timely tactile feedback enhances the perceived responsiveness of the system, creating a more immersive and engaging interaction. Force touch, employed in devices like smartphones and smartwatches, responds to the varying levels of pressure applied by users, offering additional layers of interaction and feedback. The immediacy of these tactile cues enriches the user's understanding of their physical interactions with the interface.

User engagement is inherently tied to the immediacy of feedback, and the emotional impact of timely responses contributes to a positive and memorable user experience. Delightful animations, celebratory sounds upon completing a task, or personalized interactions create positive emotional experiences. The immediacy of these emotional feedback mechanisms adds a human touch to the interface, creating memorable and enjoyable interactions. Conversely, well-crafted error messages that guide users through challenges with empathy contribute to a more supportive and less frustrating emotional journey. Timely emotional feedback contributes to a user experience that goes beyond mere functionality, resonating with users on a deeper and more meaningful level.

In conclusion, providing timely feedback within user interfaces is instrumental in enriching the user's understanding of their interactions. Through visual, auditory, and tactile cues, timely feedback creates a dynamic and responsive dialogue between users and interfaces. Whether confirming successful actions, guiding users through errors, or contributing to an emotionally resonant experience, the immediacy of feedback enhances the user's comprehension, fosters a sense of control, and ultimately contributes to a positive and user-centric interface. As technology continues to evolve, the role of timely feedback will remain central in creating interfaces that not only meet functional requirements but also resonate emotionally with users, forging a lasting and meaningful connection.

Emphasize the importance of simplicity and clarity in UI design.

The importance of simplicity and clarity in UI design transcends aesthetics; it is a fundamental principle that underpins the very essence of user experience, ensuring that digital interfaces are intuitive, accessible, and user-friendly. Simplicity in UI design involves the deliberate elimination of unnecessary complexities, focusing on delivering a straightforward and easily comprehensible interaction for users. Clarity, on the other hand, encompasses the explicit presentation of information, functionality, and navigation, leaving no room for ambiguity. Together, simplicity and clarity form a powerful symbiosis, streamlining the user's journey, reducing cognitive load, and fostering a sense of familiarity that is essential for creating interfaces that resonate with a diverse user base.

Simplicity in UI design manifests in the removal of extraneous elements, decluttering the interface to present users with a clean and unambiguous visual landscape. By prioritizing essential features and content, designers create an environment where users can quickly discern the purpose and functionality of each element. Unnecessary embellishments or visual noise are stripped away, allowing users to focus on their primary objectives without distraction. This intentional simplicity aligns with the principle of "less is more," recognizing that an uncluttered interface contributes to a more seamless and enjoyable user experience.

Clarity in UI design is about transparency and effective communication. It involves presenting information, feedback, and navigational elements in a way that leaves no room for misinterpretation. Clear typography, well-defined color schemes, and intuitive iconography all contribute to a visual language that users can easily understand. Consistency in the use of these design elements ensures that users can predict the meaning of certain visual cues, enhancing the overall predictability and usability of the interface. Clarity is not just about making things visible; it's about making them understandable, reducing the cognitive effort required from users to interpret and interact with the interface.

The significance of simplicity and clarity becomes particularly evident in the context of user onboarding, where first impressions can shape the entire user experience. A simple and clear onboarding process guides users through the initial steps of interacting with an interface, minimizing friction and promoting engagement. Whether through informative tooltips, guided tours, or concise tutorials, the onboarding experience should be designed with simplicity and clarity in mind. Users should be able to grasp the core functionalities effortlessly, setting the stage for a positive and productive ongoing interaction with the interface.

Navigation is a critical aspect where simplicity and clarity shine as beacons for user guidance. Well-designed navigation menus, whether in the form of traditional menus, sidebars, or tabs, should provide users with a clear map of the interface's structure. Labels should be straightforward and indicative of the content they lead to, eliminating any guesswork for users. Consistent placement and styling of navigation elements across the interface contribute to a cohesive and predictable navigation experience. By ensuring that users can effortlessly find their way around, designers enhance the overall accessibility and usability of the interface.

In the design of forms, simplicity and clarity are paramount for reducing friction during data input. Clear and concise labels, well-organized input fields, and contextually relevant placeholders contribute to an intuitive form-filling experience. Visual cues such as checkmarks or error indicators provide immediate feedback, aiding users in understanding the correctness of their inputs. By simplifying the form structure and presenting information in a clear hierarchy, designers facilitate a seamless interaction that minimizes user effort and potential errors.

The role of simplicity and clarity extends to the presentation of content, ensuring that users can easily consume and understand the information provided. Thoughtful use of whitespace helps prevent visual clutter, allowing users to focus on the core content without feeling overwhelmed. A well-defined typographic hierarchy, where headings, subheadings, and body text are clearly differentiated, aids users in scanning and comprehending the information. The use of clear and legible fonts, coupled with appropriate line spacing, contributes to a reading experience that is both comfortable and accessible.

Visual consistency, a key principle in UI design, is closely tied to simplicity and clarity. Consistent use of colors, fonts, and visual elements establishes a visual language that users can quickly learn and adapt to. This consistency fosters a sense of familiarity, reducing the cognitive load associated with interpreting different design patterns throughout the interface. When users encounter a consistent visual language, they can confidently predict the meaning and functionality of various elements, reinforcing a clear and comprehensible user experience.

Mobile UI design, with its constrained screen real estate, places an even greater emphasis on simplicity and clarity. In the mobile context, every pixel counts, and designers must prioritize essential elements while maintaining a visually uncluttered interface. Simplified navigation, touch-friendly buttons, and clear calls to action become paramount. Additionally, responsive design principles ensure that the interface adapts seamlessly to various screen sizes, preserving both simplicity and clarity across different devices. Mobile UI design exemplifies the importance of distilling the user experience to its most essential and understandable elements.

Accessibility, a cornerstone of inclusive design, aligns closely with the principles of simplicity and clarity. A simplified and clear interface is inherently more accessible, catering to users with diverse needs and abilities. Clear labeling, descriptive alt text for images, and an overall reduction of complexity contribute to an interface that is navigable by users with varying levels of digital literacy and different abilities. By embracing simplicity and clarity, designers create interfaces that prioritize universal usability, ensuring that everyone, regardless of their background or abilities, can interact with the digital environment effectively.

In the realm of e-commerce, where user interactions often involve complex decision-making processes, simplicity and clarity become instrumental in guiding users towards successful outcomes. Clear product information, concise descriptions, and intuitive navigation through the shopping journey contribute to an interface that supports users in making informed decisions. Streamlined checkout processes, with clear steps and transparent feedback, minimize friction during the transactional phase. Simplicity and clarity in e-commerce design not only enhance the user experience but also contribute to increased conversions and customer satisfaction.

The realm of visual feedback, encompassing elements like hover effects, transitions, and animations, is another area where simplicity and clarity play a crucial role. These visual cues should be employed judiciously, providing users with additional information about the interactive nature of elements without introducing unnecessary complexity. For instance, a subtle color change when hovering over a clickable button can serve as a clear and simple indicator of interactivity. Well-designed visual feedback enhances the user's understanding of the interface's dynamics, contributing to a more engaging and responsive user experience.

In the context of data visualization, simplicity and clarity are essential for presenting complex information in an understandable manner. Whether designing charts, graphs, or dashboards, the visual representation of data should prioritize simplicity without sacrificing accuracy. Clear labeling, straightforward color coding, and concise legends help users interpret and derive insights from the visualized data. By simplifying the complexity of information, designers create interfaces that empower users to grasp the significance of data effortlessly.

The iterative process of user testing and feedback loops is integral to refining simplicity and clarity in UI design. Observing how users interact with the interface, understanding their pain points, and gathering insights through feedback mechanisms contribute to continuous improvement. User testing helps designers identify areas where simplicity and clarity can be enhanced, ensuring that the interface evolves in response to user needs and preferences. The collaborative relationship between designers and users, facilitated by iterative design processes, leads to interfaces that are not only visually appealing but also highly functional and user-centric.

The emotional dimension of user experience is also influenced by simplicity and clarity. Interfaces that are straightforward, predictable, and easy to navigate contribute to a positive emotional resonance. Users appreciate interfaces that respect their time and intelligence by presenting information in a clear and straightforward manner. On the contrary, interfaces that introduce unnecessary complexities or create confusion may evoke frustration and negative emotions. Simplicity and clarity, therefore, contribute not only to the functional success of an interface but also to the emotional satisfaction of users.

In conclusion, the importance of simplicity and clarity in UI design cannot be overstated. These principles form the bedrock of a positive user experience, guiding users through digital interfaces with ease and confidence. Simplicity, achieved through the elimination of unnecessary elements, reduces cognitive load and fosters an uncluttered visual landscape. Clarity, achieved through transparent communication and visual consistency, ensures that users can readily understand and navigate the interface. Together, simplicity and clarity create interfaces that are not only aesthetically pleasing but also highly functional, accessible, and emotionally resonant. As technology continues to evolve, the enduring relevance of simplicity and clarity will remain crucial in shaping interfaces that cater to the diverse needs of users in an ever-changing digital landscape.

Discuss strategies for avoiding unnecessary complexity and promoting a straightforward user experience.

Avoiding unnecessary complexity and fostering a straightforward user experience is a multifaceted challenge that requires a strategic approach encompassing various aspects of design, functionality, and user interaction. Designers must prioritize simplicity at every stage of the UI development process, from conceptualization to implementation, in order to create interfaces that are intuitive, accessible, and user-friendly. Strategies for achieving this goal involve thoughtful consideration of information architecture, visual design, interaction patterns, and user feedback, all aimed at minimizing cognitive load and enhancing usability.

One foundational strategy for steering clear of unnecessary complexity is to start with a well-structured information architecture. The organization of content and features should align with users' mental models, making it easy for them to predict where to find information or functionality. Employing principles such as card sorting or tree testing during the design phase helps ensure that the structure of the interface reflects user expectations. By establishing a clear hierarchy and grouping related elements together, designers lay the groundwork for an interface that is inherently logical and straightforward.

Streamlining navigation is a key tactic in avoiding unnecessary complexity. Designers should prioritize creating navigation menus that are concise, well-labeled, and reflect the hierarchy of the content. A clear and consistent navigation system allows users to move seamlessly through the interface, reducing the cognitive effort required to find information or perform actions. Progressive disclosure, where information is revealed progressively as needed, is an effective strategy to prevent overwhelming users with a plethora of options at once, maintaining a clean and straightforward navigation experience.

Visual simplicity is a powerful tool in avoiding unnecessary complexity. Clean and uncluttered visual design contributes to a more digestible user interface. Extraneous elements, such as excessive graphics, animations, or decorative features, should be omitted if they don't contribute to the user's understanding or task completion. By adhering to a minimalist design philosophy, designers reduce visual noise and guide users' focus to the essential elements, creating an environment where users can navigate and interact without distractions.

Consistent and intuitive use of visual elements is paramount in promoting a straightforward user experience. Users should encounter a visual language that remains consistent across the interface, employing standardized buttons, icons, and color schemes. This consistency not only aids in creating a cohesive aesthetic but also ensures that users can easily interpret and predict the meaning of different visual cues. Clarity in visual communication promotes a sense of familiarity, contributing to a more intuitive and user-friendly experience.

Employing a responsive design approach is crucial for avoiding unnecessary complexity, especially in the era of diverse devices and screen sizes. A responsive design ensures that the interface adapts seamlessly to different devices, maintaining a consistent and straightforward user experience across desktops, tablets, and smartphones. By prioritizing mobile-friendly designs, designers acknowledge the prevalence of mobile usage and tailor interfaces to the constraints and capabilities of smaller screens, promoting simplicity in interaction regardless of the device being used.

Effective use of whitespace is a subtle yet powerful strategy in preventing unnecessary complexity. Whitespace, or negative space, provides visual breathing room between elements, preventing visual clutter and improving overall readability. Well-applied whitespace guides users' attention, emphasizes important content, and contributes to a more harmonious visual composition. Designers must recognize that whitespace is not merely empty space but a strategic element that plays a pivotal role in creating a clean and uncluttered interface.

Another essential strategy for promoting a straightforward user experience is to employ clear and concise copywriting. Textual content should be crafted with the user's understanding in mind, avoiding jargon and unnecessary complexity. Instructions, labels, and error messages should be phrased in plain language, ensuring that users can easily comprehend the information presented to them. A collaborative effort between designers and content creators is crucial in achieving a balance between informative and easily understandable text, contributing to an interface that guides users without overwhelming them with unnecessary details.

Reducing the number of steps required to complete tasks is a fundamental approach to simplifying user interactions. Streamlining user flows and minimizing the number of clicks or actions needed to achieve a goal contribute to a more efficient and straightforward experience. By conducting usability testing and analyzing user journeys, designers can identify and eliminate unnecessary steps or barriers that may impede users' progress. A focus on task efficiency ensures that users can accomplish their objectives with minimal friction, fostering a positive and straightforward user experience.

Providing users with clear feedback is a strategy that not only enhances user understanding but also helps avoid unnecessary complexity. Immediate and informative feedback, whether visual, auditory, or haptic, communicates the outcome of user actions, guiding users through the interface. This feedback mechanism reduces uncertainty, preventing users from feeling lost or confused. Well-designed feedback systems contribute to a transparent and responsive user experience, where users can confidently interact with the interface without the fear of unintended consequences.

Usability testing and user feedback play a pivotal role in refining and optimizing interfaces for simplicity. By observing how users interact with the interface, designers gain valuable insights into potential pain points, areas of confusion, or unnecessary complexities. Regular usability testing sessions allow designers to validate design decisions, identify areas for improvement, and iteratively enhance the interface based on user feedback. This iterative approach ensures that the interface evolves in alignment with user needs and preferences, ultimately contributing to a more straightforward and user-friendly experience.

Personalization, when implemented thoughtfully, can contribute to simplicity by tailoring the interface to individual user preferences and behaviors. By understanding users' habits, preferences, and history, designers can provide customized content, recommendations, or shortcuts that streamline the user experience. However, it's essential to strike a balance, ensuring that personalization remains transparent and controllable by users. Overly aggressive personalization efforts that make assumptions about user preferences without clear user consent can lead to confusion and unintended complexities.

A comprehensive understanding of user personas and user journeys informs the design process and helps prevent unnecessary complexity. Designers must empathize with the diverse needs, goals, and challenges of the target audience. By creating detailed user personas and mapping out user journeys, designers gain insights into the contexts in which users will interact with the interface. This understanding enables designers to prioritize features, content, and interactions based on user priorities, reducing the likelihood of introducing unnecessary complexities that do not align with users' goals.

Documentation and tooltips can serve as effective aids in promoting a straightforward user experience, especially for complex or novel features. Providing users with contextual information, explanatory tooltips, or guided tours helps them understand the purpose and functionality of different elements within the interface. This proactive approach to user guidance can prevent confusion and mitigate the potential for users to get stuck or frustrated. However, designers must ensure that documentation is concise, accessible, and presented in a manner that complements the user's natural flow within the interface.

Accessibility considerations are integral to avoiding unnecessary complexity, as interfaces should be designed to cater to users with diverse needs and abilities. Implementing accessible design practices, such as providing alternative text for images, ensuring keyboard navigation, and considering color contrast, enhances the inclusivity of the interface. Designing with accessibility in mind not only aligns with ethical design principles but also contributes to a simplified and universally usable interface that accommodates users with varying levels of digital literacy and abilities.

Collaboration among cross-functional teams is a strategy that can significantly impact the simplicity of UI design. Involving stakeholders, developers, content creators, and user experience professionals in collaborative discussions ensures a holistic approach to design decisions. The diverse perspectives within a cross-functional team contribute to a more comprehensive understanding of user needs and potential complexities. Regular communication and collaboration foster a shared vision, preventing siloed decision-making that may inadvertently introduce unnecessary complexities.

In conclusion, strategies for avoiding unnecessary complexity and promoting a straightforward user experience are rooted in a holistic and user-centric approach to UI design. From information architecture and visual design to navigation, user feedback, and accessibility considerations, every aspect of the design process should be geared towards simplifying the user's journey. By prioritizing clarity, consistency, and user understanding, designers create interfaces that empower users to navigate, interact, and accomplish their goals with ease. As the digital landscape continues to evolve, the ongoing commitment to simplicity remains essential in creating interfaces that resonate with users and stand the test of time.

Chapter 4: Navigating the UI: A Deep Dive into User Experience

Define User Experience and its connection to UI design. User Experience (UX) is a multifaceted concept that encompasses the overall interaction and satisfaction a user derives from a product, system, or service. It goes beyond the traditional focus on usability and functionality, extending to emotions, perceptions, and the holistic journey of users as they engage with a product. UX design aims to create a positive, meaningful, and seamless experience that aligns with user needs and expectations. It involves understanding user behavior, preferences, and motivations to enhance every touchpoint of the user's journey, ultimately fostering a deep connection between the user and the product.

One crucial element intertwined with UX is User Interface (UI) design. UI is the visual and interactive aspect of a product, encompassing the graphical elements, buttons, icons, and other components that users interact with. The relationship between UX and UI design is symbiotic, as UI serves as the medium through which the broader UX goals are achieved. While UX focuses on the overall experience, UI design is concerned with the look and feel, ensuring that the visual elements are not only aesthetically pleasing but also functional and intuitive.

In the realm of UX, the journey begins with user research, where designers delve into the psyche of the target audience, identifying their needs, behaviors, and pain points. This insight becomes the foundation for creating user personas, which represent archetypal users and guide design decisions. The next phase involves creating wireframes and prototypes to outline the product's structure and functionality, allowing designers to iterate and refine based on feedback before committing to the final design.

As the user interacts with the product, the UI becomes the mediator of this interaction. UI elements, such as buttons, menus, and navigation bars, are strategically placed to guide users through the interface intuitively. Consistency in design elements fosters familiarity and ease of use, reducing cognitive load and enhancing the overall user experience. Typography, color schemes, and visual hierarchy play pivotal roles in UI design, influencing the user's perception and emotional response to the product.

Navigation design within the UI is a critical component of the overall UX, determining how easily users can move through the product. Intuitive navigation ensures that users can seamlessly access information and features, reducing frustration and enhancing satisfaction. The use of visual cues, such as clear calls-to-action and feedback mechanisms, contributes to a more transparent and user-friendly interface, aligning with the broader goals of positive user experience.

Beyond aesthetics, UI design is closely tied to the functionality of the product. Interactive elements, such as buttons and forms, should respond promptly and predictably to user inputs. The visual design should complement the functional aspects, creating a cohesive and harmonious user experience. Accessibility considerations, such as legible text and support for assistive technologies, further contribute to inclusivity and a positive user experience for individuals with diverse needs.

As technology evolves, responsive design has become integral to both UX and UI. Ensuring that the interface adapts seamlessly to different devices and screen sizes enhances accessibility and user satisfaction. Mobile responsiveness, in particular, has gained prominence as an increasing number of users access products through smartphones and tablets, necessitating designs that prioritize a consistent and enjoyable experience across various platforms.

User feedback is a crucial aspect of the UX/UI design process. Through usability testing, designers can gather insights into how users interact with the product, identifying pain points and areas for improvement. Iterative design based on user feedback allows for continuous refinement, aligning the product with evolving user expectations. This user-centric approach not only enhances the overall experience but also fosters user loyalty and positive word-of-mouth.

The psychology of user behavior is another facet that both UX and UI designers must consider. Understanding how users perceive and process information, make decisions, and respond to visual stimuli informs design choices. Cognitive psychology principles, such as Hick's Law and the Zeigarnik Effect, guide the creation of interfaces that optimize user engagement and task completion. By leveraging these insights, designers can create interfaces that resonate with users on a subconscious level, contributing to a more satisfying and engaging experience.

In conclusion, User Experience and User Interface design are integral components of creating products that resonate with users on both a functional and emotional level. UX encompasses the broader journey and satisfaction of users, while UI design serves as the visual and interactive conduit for delivering that experience. The synergy between UX and UI is evident throughout the design process, from user research to prototyping, and from navigation to responsive design. A successful product not only meets functional requirements but also engages users through an aesthetically pleasing, intuitive, and emotionally resonant interface, ultimately resulting in a positive and memorable user experience.

Discuss how positive UX is crucial for user satisfaction and overall system usability.

Positive User Experience (UX) is paramount in shaping user satisfaction and influencing the overall usability of a system. At its core, UX extends beyond mere functionality, delving into the realm of emotions, perceptions, and the overall journey of users as they interact with a product or service. A well-designed UX not only meets the functional needs of users but also addresses their psychological and emotional aspects, contributing to a sense of satisfaction that goes beyond mere task completion.

One key aspect of positive UX is the seamless and intuitive nature of interactions within the system. When users can effortlessly navigate through the interface, locate information, and perform tasks without unnecessary friction, it fosters a sense of ease and efficiency. This intuitive navigation is crucial for overall system usability, as it reduces the cognitive load on users, allowing them to focus on their goals rather than grappling with complex or confusing interfaces. A positive UX ensures that users can accomplish their tasks without unnecessary hurdles, leading to heightened satisfaction and a more positive perception of the system.

Furthermore, positive UX is closely tied to the concept of user delight. When a system not only meets but exceeds user expectations, it creates a sense of delight that elevates the overall user experience. This delight can manifest in various forms, such as unexpected but helpful features, aesthetically pleasing design elements, or interactive elements that engage and entertain users. User delight contributes significantly to user satisfaction, creating a positive emotional connection with the system that transcends utilitarian functionality.

Consistency in design is another critical factor in positive UX that directly impacts user satisfaction and system usability. When users encounter a consistent visual language, layout, and interaction patterns throughout the system, it fosters a sense of familiarity. This consistency allows users to build mental models of how the system works, reducing the learning curve and making the overall experience more predictable. A cohesive and consistent design language enhances usability by providing users with a sense of control and confidence in their interactions with the system.

In the context of positive UX, the concept of accessibility plays a pivotal role in ensuring that the system is inclusive and usable for a diverse user base. Accessibility considerations, such as providing alternative text for images, ensuring keyboard navigation, and designing for users with various abilities, contribute to a positive UX for all users. When a system is accessible to individuals with different needs, it not only reflects ethical design practices but also enhances overall user satisfaction by accommodating a broader range of users.

The emotional resonance of a system is an often overlooked but crucial aspect of positive UX. Design choices, such as color schemes, typography, and visual elements, can evoke specific emotions and shape the overall perception of the system. A well-crafted emotional experience contributes to user satisfaction by creating a positive and memorable interaction. Whether through calming visuals, vibrant colors, or engaging animations, the emotional impact of design choices influences how users feel about the system, ultimately affecting their satisfaction and continued engagement.

Positive feedback mechanisms within the system also play a significant role in enhancing user satisfaction and overall usability. When users receive clear and timely feedback for their actions, whether through visual cues, notifications, or success messages, it provides a sense of confirmation and assurance. Positive feedback not only validates user interactions but also contributes to a more transparent and responsive system. On the other hand, thoughtful error messages and guidance in case of mistakes or missteps contribute to a positive UX by helping users recover from errors seamlessly, minimizing frustration and ensuring a more forgiving user experience.

The concept of user empowerment is intrinsic to positive UX and contributes directly to user satisfaction. When users feel in control of their interactions and can customize settings or preferences to align with their needs, it enhances their sense of agency. Empowering users to tailor their experience fosters a feeling of ownership and personalization, contributing to a positive and satisfying interaction. Customization options, whether in terms of interface preferences, notifications, or user settings, empower users to shape the system according to their preferences, fostering a sense of individuality and control.

Usability testing and continuous iteration based on user feedback are integral components of ensuring positive UX and overall system usability. Through usability testing, designers can gain insights into how users interact with the system, identifying pain points, areas for improvement, and opportunities for enhancement. Iterative design based on user feedback allows designers to refine the system, addressing user needs and expectations. This user-centric approach not only enhances the overall user experience but also ensures that the system evolves to meet changing user requirements, fostering long-term satisfaction and usability.

Positive UX is a key driver of user satisfaction, influencing user perceptions, attitudes, and behaviors towards a system. When users have a positive experience, they are more likely to engage with the system consistently, recommend it to others, and remain loyal over time. This loyalty is particularly crucial in today's competitive landscape, where users have a myriad of choices for digital products and services. A positive UX contributes to user retention and loyalty, as users are more inclined to stick with a system that consistently delivers a satisfying and enjoyable experience.

In conclusion, positive User Experience is intricately linked to user satisfaction and overall system usability. It goes beyond functional efficiency, encompassing intuitive navigation, user delight, consistency in design, accessibility, emotional resonance, feedback mechanisms, user empowerment, and iterative design based on user feedback. A positive UX not only meets user needs but also address-es their emotional and psychological aspects, fostering a sense of sat-isfaction that transcends utilitarian functionality. In today's digital landscape, where user expectations are high, prioritizing positive UX is not just a design choice but a strategic imperative for creating sys-tems that resonate with users and stand the test of time.

Explore common navigation patterns in UI design.

UI design relies heavily on effective navigation patterns to guide users seamlessly through digital interfaces. These patterns play a cru-cial role in enhancing user experience by providing clear pathways and intuitive interactions. One prevalent navigation pattern is the "Top Navigation Bar," positioned at the top of the interface. It often houses primary navigation links, offering users a quick overview of key sections or pages within the application or website. This pattern is widely adopted due to its familiarity and ease of use, making it an effective choice for organizing essential information.

Another common navigation pattern is the "Sidebar Menu," which typically resides on the left or right side of the interface. The sidebar can include primary navigation links, sub-menus, or even icons representing different sections. This pattern is advantageous for applications or websites with a substantial amount of content, as it allows for hierarchical organization and easy access to various sec-tions without cluttering the main view.

Tabs, positioned horizontally or vertically, represent a versatile navigation pattern. They are often used to organize content into dif-ferent categories or views, allowing users to switch between them seamlessly. Tab navigation is prevalent in both desktop and mobile applications, providing a visual and interactive way for users to ex-plore diverse content within the same interface.

The "Hamburger Menu" has become synonymous with mobile navigation. Characterized by three horizontal lines, the icon conceals a menu that reveals additional navigation options when clicked. While initially popularized for mobile interfaces to save screen space, the hamburger menu has found its way into desktop designs as well. However, its use on desktop interfaces has been a topic of debate due to concerns about discoverability and accessibility.

Dropdown menus are another widely used navigation pattern, often employed to present a list of choices or options related to a specific category. Dropdowns conserve screen real estate by only displaying options when activated, offering a clean and organized layout. However, designers need to ensure that dropdowns are implemented with attention to accessibility and user-friendliness, avoiding issues like hover-dependent interactions on touch devices.

Breadcrumb navigation provides users with a hierarchical trail indicating their current location within the application or website. It typically appears horizontally at the top of the page and allows users to backtrack easily through the path they've taken. Breadcrumbs enhance user orientation, especially in platforms with intricate structures or deep content hierarchies, by offering a clear visual representation of the user's navigation history.

The "Floating Action Button" (FAB) is a distinctive navigation pattern commonly found in mobile applications. Positioned at a prominent location, often in the lower-right corner, the FAB serves as a shortcut to a primary action or frequently used feature. While it enhances user efficiency, designers must exercise caution to ensure that the FAB does not obstruct essential content or become intrusive.

Infinite scrolling is a navigation pattern prevalent in web interfaces that continuously load content as users scroll down the page. This pattern eliminates the need for pagination, providing a seamless and uninterrupted browsing experience. While effective for content-heavy platforms, designers must consider potential challenges, such as maintaining a sense of context and ensuring accessibility for users with limited scrolling capabilities.

Card-based navigation has gained popularity, particularly in content-driven applications. Each card represents a distinct piece of content or functionality, making it easy for users to scan and select items of interest. Card layouts are commonly associated with responsive design, adapting fluidly to various screen sizes and orientations.

An emerging navigation pattern is the "Bottom Navigation Bar," frequently employed in mobile applications. Placed at the bottom of the screen, it usually accommodates primary navigation options, enabling users to access key features with their thumbs. This pattern aligns with the ergonomic considerations of mobile interfaces, prioritizing user convenience.

The use of "Sticky Navigation" involves keeping certain elements, such as the navigation bar or menu, fixed at the top or side of the screen as users scroll. This persistent navigation ensures that essential options remain accessible, enhancing user convenience. However, designers must strike a balance to prevent excessive clutter and obstruction of content.

In conclusion, the world of UI design encompasses a variety of navigation patterns, each tailored to meet specific needs and enhance user experience. From the conventional top navigation bar to innovative patterns like card-based layouts and bottom navigation bars, designers continually explore and adapt these patterns to create interfaces that are not only aesthetically pleasing but also intuitive and user-friendly. The selection of a navigation pattern depends on factors such as the type of content, user preferences, and the overall design goals, with the ultimate aim of providing users with a seamless and efficient journey through digital interfaces.

Discuss how understanding user flow contributes to creating intuitive and efficient interfaces.

Understanding user flow is paramount in the creation of intuitive and efficient interfaces, as it allows designers to map out the journey users take through a digital product or service. User flow encompasses the series of steps a user follows to accomplish a specific task, from the initial interaction to the final outcome. By gaining insights into user behavior, preferences, and expectations, designers can align the interface with the natural progression of user actions, ultimately enhancing the overall user experience.

A comprehensive understanding of user flow begins with thorough user research. Designers delve into the intricacies of user needs, motivations, and pain points, allowing them to create user personas that represent archetypal users. This foundational step sets the stage for anticipating user actions and tailoring the interface to cater to their specific requirements. By empathizing with users and placing them at the center of the design process, designers can develop interfaces that resonate with the target audience, resulting in a more intuitive and user-friendly experience.

Mapping out user journeys through the product or service is a crucial aspect of understanding user flow. This involves identifying entry points, decision-making moments, and exit points within the interface. Through techniques like user flow diagrams and wireframes, designers visualize the sequential steps users will take, enabling them to identify potential bottlenecks or points of confusion. This visual representation aids in streamlining the user's path, ensuring a coherent and logical flow that aligns with their expectations.

The role of information architecture is pivotal in shaping user flow. Designers must organize content in a hierarchy that makes sense to users, facilitating easy navigation and comprehension. A well-structured information architecture contributes to an intuitive interface by grouping related content, establishing clear categories, and providing logical pathways. Users should be able to effortlessly locate information, features, or functions, reinforcing a sense of control and mastery over the interface.

Consistent and recognizable patterns contribute significantly to an intuitive user flow. Users rely on visual cues and familiar elements to navigate through interfaces seamlessly. Design conventions, such as placing the navigation menu at the top or using recognizable icons, help users establish mental models that guide their interactions. Consistency in design elements fosters a sense of predictability, reducing cognitive load and enabling users to focus on their tasks rather than deciphering unfamiliar interface elements.

Effective use of calls-to-action (CTAs) is a key component in guiding user flow. CTAs serve as signposts, prompting users to take specific actions within the interface. Well-designed CTAs are clear, concise, and strategically placed, ensuring users can progress through the intended flow without ambiguity. Designers must consider the language, placement, and visual design of CTAs to optimize their effectiveness in guiding users through the desired pathways.

The concept of progressive disclosure is a valuable strategy in creating intuitive interfaces. Instead of overwhelming users with a plethora of information or options upfront, designers strategically reveal information progressively as users navigate deeper into the interface. This approach minimizes cognitive overload, allowing users to absorb information gradually and make informed decisions at each step of the user flow. Progressive disclosure aligns with the natural way users explore and learn, contributing to a more efficient and user-friendly experience.

Responsive design is integral to understanding user flow in the context of various devices and screen sizes. Interfaces must adapt seamlessly to different resolutions, ensuring a consistent and optimized experience across desktops, tablets, and smartphones. Designers need to consider how the user flow may vary on smaller screens and prioritize content based on device-specific considerations. Responsive design contributes to the overall efficiency of interfaces by accommodating users across diverse contexts and devices.

User feedback mechanisms play a crucial role in refining and optimizing user flow. Through usability testing and iterative design, designers gather insights into how users interact with the interface, identifying pain points or areas of confusion. Continuous refinement based on user feedback ensures that the user flow evolves to align with changing user expectations and preferences. This user-centric approach contributes to the creation of interfaces that not only meet but exceed user needs, fostering a positive and efficient user experience.

Effective onboarding processes are a key component of understanding user flow, particularly for first-time users. By guiding users through a series of introductory steps and explaining key features, designers can facilitate a smooth entry into the interface. Onboarding experiences set the tone for subsequent interactions, influencing how users navigate the interface and encouraging them to explore its full potential. Understanding the user flow during onboarding helps designers create experiences that are not only welcoming but also set users up for success from the outset.

Accessibility considerations are paramount in shaping an inclusive user flow. Designers must account for users with diverse needs and abilities, ensuring that the interface is usable for everyone. This involves providing alternative text for images, implementing keyboard navigation, and considering color contrast for users with visual impairments. A user flow that prioritizes accessibility contributes to the overall efficiency of the interface by making it available and usable to a broader audience.

In conclusion, understanding user flow is a cornerstone in the creation of intuitive and efficient interfaces. It involves empathizing with users, mapping out their journeys, optimizing information architecture, leveraging consistent design patterns, and incorporating user feedback. A well-crafted user flow aligns with the natural progression of user actions, guiding them seamlessly through the interface and minimizing friction. By prioritizing user needs and expectations, designers can create interfaces that not only meet functional requirements but also deliver a positive, efficient, and memorable user experience.

Highlight the significance of usability testing in refining UI designs.

Usability testing stands as a cornerstone in the iterative design process, playing a pivotal role in refining User Interface (UI) designs. This essential methodology involves systematically evaluating a product or system with real users to identify potential usability issues, gather insights, and make informed design decisions. The significance of usability testing extends beyond mere validation of design choices; it serves as a powerful tool for enhancing user experience, streamlining interfaces, and ultimately creating products that resonate with users on a profound level.

At the core of usability testing is the recognition that users bring a unique perspective and set of expectations to the interaction with a UI. By actively involving real users in the evaluation process, designers gain valuable insights into how the interface aligns with user needs, behaviors, and preferences. This user-centric approach ensures that the design is not solely driven by assumptions or internal perspectives but is grounded in the reality of user experiences, fostering empathy and understanding between designers and end-users.

Usability testing is particularly effective in uncovering usability issues that might not be apparent during the design phase. As users engage with the interface, their interactions reveal aspects of the design that may impede task completion, cause confusion, or lead to frustration. Observing users navigate through the product in a controlled testing environment provides designers with a firsthand understanding of pain points, stumbling blocks, and areas for improvement. This direct feedback loop empowers designers to address issues that may have otherwise gone unnoticed, resulting in a more refined and user-friendly UI.

One of the key advantages of usability testing lies in its ability to assess the learnability of an interface. Through observation and feedback, designers can gauge how easily users grasp the functionalities and navigation within the UI, especially for first-time users. This insight is invaluable for refining onboarding processes, optimizing the placement of key features, and ensuring that the interface aligns with users' cognitive processes. Usability testing, therefore, contributes significantly to the creation of interfaces that are not only functional but also accessible and intuitive for a diverse user base.

The iterative nature of usability testing aligns seamlessly with the agile design methodology, allowing designers to make incremental improvements based on real-world feedback. As users interact with the UI, their input serves as a catalyst for continuous refinement. Designers can implement changes, tweak design elements, and iterate on the UI in response to observed user behaviors and preferences. This iterative loop ensures that the design evolves in tandem with user expectations, leading to a more polished and user-centric final product.

Usability testing is instrumental in identifying and addressing navigation challenges within an interface. Whether it involves clarifying the placement of navigation elements, optimizing the flow of information, or improving the structure of menus, usability testing sheds light on how users navigate through the UI. Clear and efficient navigation is fundamental to a positive user experience, and usability testing serves as a compass for designers, guiding them to make informed decisions that enhance the overall flow and usability of the interface.

The significance of usability testing extends beyond identifying issues to uncovering positive aspects of the UI that contribute to user satisfaction. By observing users successfully complete tasks, designers gain insights into what elements of the design are working well and resonating positively with users. This recognition of strengths, combined with user feedback, allows designers to amplify successful design elements, ensuring that the interface retains its strengths while addressing areas for improvement. Usability testing, therefore, serves as a catalyst for reinforcing and optimizing the positive aspects of the UI.

Usability testing is integral to validating design decisions and mitigating risks associated with assumptions. Designers may have a vision for how users will interact with the interface, but it is through testing that these assumptions are put to the test. Usability testing provides a reality check, offering designers a tangible understanding of how users perceive and engage with the UI. This validation not only instills confidence in design choices but also allows designers to course-correct early in the process, preventing the propagation of potentially flawed assumptions throughout the development lifecycle.

Accessibility considerations are paramount in today's design landscape, and usability testing is a crucial tool in ensuring that interfaces are inclusive and usable for all. By including participants with diverse abilities and needs in usability tests, designers can identify barriers that may hinder accessibility. Usability testing sheds light on issues related to screen readers, keyboard navigation, color contrast, and other accessibility features. This awareness enables designers to make informed decisions that prioritize accessibility, ensuring that the UI is not only usable but also respectful of diverse user needs.

Usability testing fosters collaboration and communication within design teams and across stakeholders. By sharing user testing results, designers can effectively communicate the impact of design decisions on the user experience. Usability testing findings serve as a common language that aligns designers, developers, and product managers, facilitating a shared understanding of user needs and priorities. This collaborative approach enhances team cohesion, promotes a user-centered mindset, and encourages a collective commitment to delivering a UI that meets and exceeds user expectations.

The role of usability testing extends beyond the early stages of design, encompassing post-launch evaluations to ensure ongoing optimization. Regular usability testing after the product's release allows designers to gather insights into user behaviors in real-world scenarios. This longitudinal perspective helps designers identify evolving user needs, respond to changing technology landscapes, and address any emerging issues. Continuous usability testing contributes to the longevity and relevance of the UI, supporting a commitment to user satisfaction and maintaining a competitive edge in the ever-evolving digital landscape.

In conclusion, the significance of usability testing in refining UI designs cannot be overstated. This methodology stands as a cornerstone in the user-centered design process, offering designers a direct window into user experiences, preferences, and pain points. Usability testing empowers designers to iterate on designs, validate assumptions, address accessibility considerations, optimize navigation, and foster collaboration within design teams. By placing users at the forefront of the design process, usability testing ensures that UI designs are not only functional but also resonate with users, ultimately contributing to the creation of interfaces that are intuitive, efficient, and capable of delivering a superior user experience.

Discuss the iterative design process and how user feedback informs improvements.

The iterative design process is a dynamic and cyclical approach that revolves around continuous refinement based on feedback, testing, and insights gained from real-world usage. At its core, this methodology acknowledges that the creation of effective and user-centric designs is an evolving journey rather than a one-time event. Each iteration involves a cycle of design, testing, and refinement, with the ultimate goal of aligning the product more closely with user needs, preferences, and expectations.

One of the fundamental principles of the iterative design process is its emphasis on empathy for the end-users. By understanding the perspectives, behaviors, and pain points of users, designers can craft solutions that genuinely address their needs. This empathetic approach becomes particularly apparent in the initial stages of iteration, where designers immerse themselves in user research. This phase involves interviews, observations, and usability testing, laying the foundation for informed design decisions and the subsequent iterative cycle.

User feedback serves as the backbone of the iterative design process, providing valuable insights into the strengths and weaknesses of a design. Feedback is gathered through various channels, including usability testing sessions, surveys, analytics, and direct user engagement. This multifaceted approach ensures a comprehensive understanding of user experiences, enabling designers to identify patterns, uncover pain points, and recognize areas for improvement. The richness of user feedback becomes a guiding light in the iterative process, steering designers toward informed and user-centric design decisions.

The initial design iteration is often characterized by the creation of prototypes or wireframes. These low-fidelity representations allow designers to quickly test and gather feedback on the basic structure and functionality of the interface. Usability testing during this phase serves as a reality check, revealing how users interact with the prototype and what elements may need adjustment. The iterative loop begins as designers incorporate user feedback, refining the design and addressing any identified issues to create an improved iteration.

Prototyping and user feedback are not limited to the early stages of design; they continue to play a crucial role throughout the entire iterative process. As designs evolve and become more detailed, higher-fidelity prototypes are created to simulate the final product. Usability testing sessions are conducted at each stage, ranging from early wireframes to more polished designs, ensuring that user feedback informs decisions at every level of granularity. This iterative loop ensures that the design remains aligned with user expectations as it progresses towards completion.

The iterative design process is particularly effective in addressing usability concerns. Usability testing helps identify obstacles users may encounter in completing tasks, navigating through the interface, or understanding the system. Designers leverage this feedback to make adjustments that enhance the overall user experience. Whether it's refining the placement of key features, improving navigation pathways, or clarifying the language used in the interface, the iterative process allows designers to systematically address usability issues and create interfaces that are intuitive and user-friendly.

A crucial aspect of the iterative design process is the incorporation of divergent and convergent thinking. In the early stages of iteration, designers explore a range of design possibilities, allowing for creativity and innovation. This divergent phase involves generating multiple design concepts and exploring various solutions. Subsequently, through user feedback and testing, the process converges towards the most effective and user-friendly design solutions. This interplay between exploration and refinement ensures that the final design is not only creative but also grounded in real-world usability.

The iterative design process is closely aligned with the principles of agile development methodologies. The iterative cycle of design, test, and refine dovetails seamlessly with agile sprints, allowing for frequent and incremental updates to the product. This iterative-agile synergy accelerates the development timeline while maintaining a user-centric focus. Each iteration builds upon the successes and lessons of the previous ones, fostering a nimble and adaptive approach that is well-suited to the rapidly changing landscape of technology and user expectations.

User feedback goes beyond the identification of issues; it also illuminates positive aspects of the design that resonate with users. Understanding what elements are working well allows designers to amplify those strengths and ensure they are retained or enhanced in subsequent iterations. Positive user feedback becomes a source of inspiration and validation, reinforcing design decisions that contribute to a positive and memorable user experience. This acknowledgment of strengths, combined with constructive criticism, shapes the trajectory of the iterative process, balancing refinement with the preservation of successful design elements.

A crucial facet of the iterative design process is the ability to pivot and adapt based on user feedback and changing requirements. As the product evolves, user needs may shift, technological landscapes may change, and new insights may emerge. Iterative design embraces this flexibility, allowing designers to pivot in response to feedback and evolving contexts. This adaptability ensures that the final product is not only aligned with current user expectations but is also resilient to future shifts in the digital landscape.

Usability testing in the iterative design process is not a one-time event but a continuous and cyclical practice. Regular testing sessions, even after the product's release, provide designers with ongoing insights into real-world user interactions. This longitudinal perspective helps identify emerging issues, evolving user preferences, and areas for optimization. Continuous usability testing ensures that the product remains responsive to changing user needs, maintaining relevance and effectiveness over time.

The iterative design process fosters a culture of continuous improvement within design teams. Each iteration serves as a learning opportunity, allowing designers to reflect on the effectiveness of their decisions and the impact on user experience. This reflective practice contributes to a collective growth mindset, encouraging designers to embrace challenges, learn from failures, and celebrate successes. The iterative loop becomes not only a mechanism for refining designs but also a catalyst for professional and team development.

In conclusion, the iterative design process is a dynamic and user-centric approach that places feedback at its core. By embracing a cycle of design, test, and refine, designers ensure that their creations evolve in response to user needs and preferences. User feedback becomes a guiding force, informing decisions, uncovering usability issues, and validating successful design elements. The iterative process is not confined to the early stages of design but extends throughout the entire product lifecycle, fostering adaptability, continuous improvement, and a commitment to delivering interfaces that resonate with users and stand the test of time.

Explore the role of interactive elements in enhancing user engagement.

The role of interactive elements in enhancing user engagement is pivotal, shaping the way users interact with digital interfaces and fostering a more dynamic and immersive user experience. Interactive elements, ranging from buttons and sliders to complex animations and dynamic content, serve as the conduits through which users engage with and manipulate the interface. These elements not only facilitate functionality but also play a crucial role in capturing user attention, guiding their interactions, and creating a sense of responsiveness that is fundamental to user engagement.

One of the primary functions of interactive elements is to provide clear and intuitive navigation pathways within the interface. Navigation menus, buttons, and links serve as entry points for users to explore different sections of a website or application. The responsiveness of these elements, coupled with smooth transitions and visual feedback, contributes to a seamless and enjoyable navigation experience. Clear and well-designed interactive navigation elements not only enhance user engagement but also influence the overall perception of the interface's usability and accessibility.

Interactive elements contribute significantly to the overall aesthetics of a digital interface, elevating the visual appeal and creating a more engaging and visually stimulating experience. Thoughtful use of animations, transitions, and interactive design elements enhances the aesthetic appeal of the interface, making it more dynamic and lively. Whether it's a subtle hover effect on a button or a captivating animation that responds to user interactions, these visual enhancements contribute to a more memorable and delightful user experience, reinforcing positive engagement.

The role of interactive elements extends beyond mere aesthetics to the creation of immersive and interactive storytelling experiences. In digital media, particularly on websites and applications, storytelling is not limited to static text and images; it involves interactive elements that invite users to actively participate in the narrative. Elements like sliders, carousels, and interactive timelines enable users to engage with content in a nonlinear and exploratory manner, enhancing their involvement and deepening their connection with the presented information. Interactive storytelling elements create a sense of agency for users, allowing them to shape their journey and experience the content in a more personalized and engaging way.

Interactive elements play a crucial role in user feedback mechanisms, providing users with immediate responses to their actions. From button clicks to form submissions, interactive elements offer visual cues and feedback, confirming to users that their inputs have been recognized and processed. This real-time feedback fosters a sense of control and transparency, reducing uncertainty and enhancing user confidence. Well-designed interactive feedback mechanisms contribute to a more responsive and user-friendly interface, ultimately influencing user engagement by creating an environment of trust and reliability.

The gamification of digital interfaces relies heavily on interactive elements to enhance user engagement. Gamification involves incorporating game-like elements, such as points, badges, and rewards, into non-game contexts to motivate user behavior. Interactive elements, such as progress bars, achievement pop-ups, and interactive challenges, serve as the building blocks of gamified experiences. By introducing elements of play and competition, gamification leverages interactive design to captivate users' attention, stimulate their curiosity, and encourage repeated interactions. This approach transforms routine tasks into engaging and rewarding experiences, ultimately boosting user engagement.

Forms and input fields are integral interactive elements that play a critical role in user engagement, particularly in web applications. Well-designed forms contribute to a seamless and efficient user experience by guiding users through the input process with clarity and simplicity. Interactive form validation, auto-suggestions, and conditional logic enhance the responsiveness of forms, reducing errors and improving the overall efficiency of data entry. The thoughtful integration of interactive elements in forms ensures that users are actively engaged throughout the information submission process, leading to higher completion rates and a more positive overall experience.

Interactive elements are key facilitators of user interactions with multimedia content, such as images, videos, and 3D models. Elements like image carousels, video players, and interactive galleries enable users to manipulate and explore multimedia content on their terms. This hands-on approach to content consumption enhances user engagement by providing a more immersive and personalized experience. Users can zoom in on images, control video playback, or interact with 3D models, creating a sense of exploration and interactivity that goes beyond passive viewing.

The role of microinteractions, subtle and often overlooked interactive elements, cannot be overstated in user engagement. Microinteractions include small animations, transitions, or feedback responses that occur in response to specific user actions. Examples include a button changing color upon hover or a notification icon animating when new content is available. While seemingly minor, these microinteractions contribute to a more delightful and engaging user experience by adding a layer of sophistication and responsiveness to the interface. The cumulative effect of well-designed microinteractions enhances the overall sense of polish and attention to detail, influencing user perceptions and engagement positively.

Social media platforms heavily leverage interactive elements to enhance user engagement through features like likes, comments, and shares. These elements not only provide users with tools to express themselves but also create a social ecosystem where interactions and reactions contribute to a sense of community. The gamification of social interactions, such as streaks or badges for active engagement, further encourages users to participate regularly. The seamless integration of interactive elements in social media platforms transforms them into dynamic and vibrant spaces where users actively contribute to the content ecosystem, fostering sustained engagement.

E-commerce platforms harness the power of interactive elements to create immersive and persuasive shopping experiences. Features like product zoom, 360-degree views, and interactive product configurators allow users to explore products in detail before making purchase decisions. Interactive elements, such as add-to-cart animations and real-time price updates, contribute to a more dynamic and responsive shopping journey. The seamless integration of interactive design elements in e-commerce interfaces not only enhances user engagement but also influences purchasing behavior by providing users with a rich and interactive exploration of products and services.

The responsive design of interfaces for various devices relies on interactive elements to adapt seamlessly to different screen sizes and orientations. Interactive elements, such as collapsible menus, responsive navigation bars, and touch-friendly buttons, ensure that users can interact with the interface efficiently across a range of devices. This adaptability contributes to a consistent and user-friendly experience, regardless of whether users are accessing the interface on a desktop, tablet, or smartphone. The role of interactive elements in responsive design is paramount in maintaining engagement by catering to the diverse ways users interact with digital content.

Voice interfaces and chatbots represent a frontier where interactive elements take on new dimensions. Conversational interfaces rely on interactive elements to guide users through spoken interactions, providing cues and responses that mimic human conversation. In the realm of chatbots, interactive buttons and quick-reply options streamline user interactions, making the conversational experience more intuitive and engaging. The effective integration of interactive elements in voice interfaces and chatbots contributes to a natural and conversational interaction flow, enhancing user engagement in environments where traditional graphical interfaces may not be applicable.

The accessibility of interactive elements plays a crucial role in ensuring inclusivity and engagement for users with diverse needs. Accessibility considerations, such as keyboard navigation, screen reader compatibility, and adherence to color contrast standards, ensure that interactive elements can be effectively utilized by users with varying abilities. By prioritizing accessibility, designers create interfaces that are usable by a broad audience, fostering inclusivity and engagement among users with disabilities.

In conclusion, the role of interactive elements in enhancing user engagement is multifaceted and integral to the success of digital interfaces. From providing clear navigation pathways to creating immersive storytelling experiences, interactive elements shape the way users interact with and experience digital content. Whether through the gamification of interactions, the incorporation of microinteractions, or the responsive design for various devices, these elements contribute to a more dynamic, visually appealing, and user-centric experience. The effective integration of interactive elements not only captures user attention but also fosters a sense of agency, creating interfaces that users actively engage with, enjoy, and find memorable.

Discuss the impact of animations, transitions, and interactive feedback on the overall user experience.

The impact of animations, transitions, and interactive feedback on the overall user experience is profound, as these elements contribute to a more dynamic, engaging, and user-centric interaction with digital interfaces. Animations, when thoughtfully designed and implemented, serve as powerful tools for conveying information, guiding user attention, and creating a sense of fluidity within the interface. Whether it's a subtle hover effect on a button, a smooth transition between pages, or a captivating loading animation, these dynamic elements elevate the user experience by providing a visually rich and seamless interaction.

Animations play a crucial role in capturing user attention and directing it towards important elements within the interface. By leveraging motion, designers can draw focus to specific areas, guiding users through a logical flow and highlighting key information. For instance, the use of entrance animations can make elements appear gradually, creating a sense of anticipation and drawing attention to newly presented content. Conversely, exit animations can gracefully remove elements, signaling changes and maintaining a visually coherent transition between different states of the interface. This intentional use of animations ensures that users are not overwhelmed with static information, enhancing the overall visual hierarchy and aiding in the absorption of content.

Transitions contribute to the continuity and smoothness of the user experience, bridging the gap between different states or views within an interface. When transitioning between pages or sections, a well-crafted animation or transition provides users with a sense of spatial awareness and context. Instead of abrupt changes, users are guided through a visual journey that helps them maintain a mental map of their interactions. This contributes to a more intuitive navigation experience, reducing disorientation and improving overall usability. Seamless transitions create a sense of cohesion, making the interface feel like a unified and interconnected environment rather than a collection of disparate elements.

Interactive feedback, manifested through animations and visual cues, plays a pivotal role in enhancing the responsiveness of the interface. When users interact with elements, whether it's clicking a button, submitting a form, or hovering over an item, providing instant and meaningful feedback reinforces their actions. For example, a button changing color or displaying a subtle animation upon hover communicates to the user that the element is interactive and responsive. Similarly, when a form is successfully submitted, a well-designed animation or notification assures users that their action was acknowledged, reducing uncertainty and enhancing the overall sense of control. Interactive feedback creates a more tangible and responsive connection between the user and the interface, fostering a positive and engaging experience.

The impact of animations, transitions, and interactive feedback extends to the realm of user engagement and emotional resonance. When implemented thoughtfully, these elements contribute to the creation of a more enjoyable and memorable user experience. For instance, delightfully designed microinteractions, such as a heart icon pulsating when clicked or a subtle bounce effect on a confirmation message, add a layer of personality to the interface. These microinteractions go beyond mere functionality, creating moments of surprise and joy that leave a lasting impression on users. The emotional resonance fostered by well-crafted animations and interactive feedback contributes to a positive perception of the brand or product, enhancing user satisfaction and loyalty.

In the context of storytelling and content presentation, animations play a vital role in creating engaging narratives and conveying information in a compelling manner. Infographics, data visualizations, and storytelling elements can be enhanced through animations that reveal information gradually, guiding users through a narrative journey. For instance, a data chart that animates to showcase trends over time or a timeline that unfolds with each scroll adds a layer of interactivity, making the content more digestible and engaging. These animated storytelling elements not only communicate information effectively but also capture and maintain user interest, fostering a more immersive and enjoyable content consumption experience.

The impact of animations, transitions, and interactive feedback on user experience is particularly pronounced in the context of mobile applications. The limited screen real estate on mobile devices necessitates careful consideration of how information is presented and how users navigate through the interface. Fluid animations and intuitive transitions contribute to the creation of mobile interfaces that feel natural and responsive. Gesture-based interactions, such as swiping between screens or tapping on interactive elements, can be complemented by animations that provide visual cues, enhancing the overall touch-driven experience. In the mobile environment, the judicious use of animations and transitions becomes even more critical in ensuring a user-friendly and enjoyable interaction.

Accessibility considerations play a significant role in determining the impact of animations on the overall user experience. While animations can enhance engagement for many users, they may pose challenges for individuals with certain visual or cognitive impairments. Designers need to ensure that animations are not overly distracting or disorienting, and they should provide options for users to adjust or disable animations based on their preferences and needs.

This inclusivity in design ensures that the impact of animations remains positive for all users, regardless of their abilities or preferences.

The impact of animations on the loading experience is a noteworthy consideration, especially in the context of web interfaces. Loading animations, often accompanied by progress indicators, serve to manage user expectations and provide reassurance that the system is actively responding to their request. A well-designed loading animation not only prevents users from perceiving wait times as tedious but also contributes to a perception of efficiency and responsiveness. The loading experience, when coupled with engaging animations, transitions, and interactive feedback, can transform what might be perceived as a passive wait into an opportunity for user engagement and brand reinforcement.

In conclusion, animations, transitions, and interactive feedback are integral components of the overall user experience, contributing to a more dynamic, engaging, and emotionally resonant interaction with digital interfaces. These elements go beyond mere embellishments, playing crucial roles in guiding user attention, creating seamless transitions between states, and providing responsive feedback. When implemented thoughtfully, animations enhance the visual appeal of interfaces, contribute to storytelling, and foster a sense of delight. Their impact on mobile experiences, accessibility, and loading interactions underscores their importance in shaping a user-centric and enjoyable digital journey. The strategic use of animations and interactive elements not only elevates the functionality of interfaces but also leaves a lasting impression, enhancing user satisfaction and contributing to the success of digital products and platforms.

Discuss the importance of designing interfaces that adapt to various screen sizes and devices.

The importance of designing interfaces that adapt to various screen sizes and devices cannot be overstated in the contemporary digital landscape. With the proliferation of diverse devices, ranging from desktop computers and laptops to tablets and smartphones, users access digital content through a multitude of screens. Responsive design, which involves creating interfaces that dynamically adjust to different screen sizes and orientations, has become a fundamental principle in ensuring a seamless and consistent user experience across the ever-expanding spectrum of devices.

User expectations regarding accessibility and usability have evolved, making responsive design a prerequisite for success in the digital realm. A responsive interface ensures that users can access content and interact with features regardless of the device they are using. This adaptability is especially critical as users increasingly transition between devices throughout their daily routines. A website or application that seamlessly transforms from a desktop view to a mobile-friendly layout as users switch from their computers to smartphones reflects a commitment to meeting users where they are and providing a cohesive experience regardless of the chosen device.

The mobile-first approach, a cornerstone of responsive design, recognizes the prevalence of mobile devices in today's digital landscape. Designing interfaces with a mobile-first mindset means prioritizing the user experience on smaller screens before scaling up to larger displays. This approach acknowledges the constraints of mobile devices, such as limited screen real estate and touch-based interactions, and ensures that the interface remains functional and user-friendly in these scenarios. By starting with the smallest screens in mind, designers can create interfaces that are inherently adaptable and optimized for a wide range of devices.

The diversity of screen sizes and resolutions across devices necessitates a flexible and grid-based layout system. A responsive design relies on a fluid grid that scales proportionally to the screen size, ensuring that content is appropriately arranged and readable regardless of the device's dimensions. This adaptability is achieved through the strategic use of breakpoints, where the layout adjusts to accommodate different screen widths. The importance of a flexible grid lies in its ability to maintain the integrity of the interface's structure while accommodating variations in screen size, contributing to a harmonious and visually pleasing user experience.

The impact of responsive design on search engine optimization (SEO) cannot be overlooked. Search engines, such as Google, prioritize mobile-friendly websites in their rankings, considering the growing number of users accessing the internet through mobile devices. Responsive design ensures that the same content is served across all devices, eliminating the need for separate URLs or duplicate content. This unified approach not only simplifies maintenance for website administrators but also positively influences SEO rankings, leading to improved visibility and discoverability in search engine results.

Responsive design aligns with the principles of inclusivity, addressing the needs of users with diverse abilities and preferences. An interface that adapts to various screen sizes and devices enhances accessibility, allowing individuals with disabilities to access digital content in a way that suits their needs. Considerations such as font size, contrast ratios, and touch-friendly interactions become integral in creating an inclusive user experience. By embracing responsive design, designers contribute to making digital content more accessible to a broader audience, fostering inclusivity and equal access for users with varying abilities.

The financial implications of responsive design also underscore its importance for businesses and organizations. Maintaining separate designs for desktop and mobile versions can be resource-intensive, requiring additional development, testing, and maintenance efforts. Responsive design streamlines these processes by creating a single codebase that adapts to different devices. This efficiency not only reduces development costs but also ensures consistency in branding and user experience across devices, contributing to a cohesive and cost-effective digital presence for businesses.

The rise of e-commerce further accentuates the importance of responsive design, as users increasingly make online purchases through a variety of devices. An e-commerce platform that provides a seamless and intuitive shopping experience on both desktop and mobile devices enhances user satisfaction and encourages conversions. Responsive design ensures that product catalogs, checkout processes, and payment gateways are optimized for various screen sizes, reducing friction in the user journey and fostering a positive relationship between users and e-commerce platforms.

The advent of wearable devices, smart TVs, and other emerging technologies underscores the ongoing evolution of the digital landscape. Responsive design anticipates these changes and positions interfaces to adapt seamlessly to new and diverse devices entering the market. Designing interfaces with future scalability in mind ensures that digital products remain relevant and functional as technology continues to advance. The forward-looking approach of responsive design positions businesses and organizations to navigate the ever-changing digital landscape with agility and adaptability.

Social media platforms exemplify the impact of responsive design on user engagement. Users access social media through a myriad of devices, from laptops and tablets to smartphones and smartwatches. Responsive design ensures that social media interfaces are optimized for each device, providing a consistent and enjoyable experience for users regardless of the screen size. This adaptability contributes to sustained user engagement, as individuals seamlessly transition between devices to interact with content, share updates, and connect with others.

The importance of responsive design is evident in the context of content consumption, where users expect a consistent and enjoyable reading experience across devices. Responsive typography, which adjusts font size and line spacing based on the screen size, plays a crucial role in ensuring readability on various devices. By tailoring the presentation of text to accommodate different screens, responsive design enhances the accessibility and legibility of content, fostering a positive reading experience for users on desktops, tablets, and smartphones alike.

The global reach of digital content emphasizes the cultural and regional diversity of users accessing interfaces. Responsive design allows for localization and adaptation to different languages and writing systems, accommodating variations in content length and structure. The flexibility of responsive layouts ensures that interfaces can seamlessly integrate translations without compromising the overall design integrity. This consideration contributes to a user-centric approach that respects linguistic diversity and cultural nuances, fostering a more inclusive and globally accessible digital experience.

Educational platforms, whether for formal learning institutions or online courses, benefit significantly from responsive design. Students and learners engage with educational content through a variety of devices, each with its own screen size and interaction capabilities. Responsive design ensures that learning materials, quizzes, and interactive elements are optimized for different devices, facilitating a consistent and effective learning experience. The adaptability of responsive design in educational contexts supports accessibility and encourages a more flexible and personalized approach to learning.

The importance of responsive design in government and public service websites is underscored by the need to provide accessible and user-friendly information to citizens. Government websites serve as crucial channels for delivering public services, information, and resources. Responsive design ensures that citizens can access government services and information seamlessly, irrespective of the device they use. This inclusivity fosters transparency, efficiency, and citizen engagement, contributing to a positive perception of government services.

In conclusion, the importance of designing interfaces that adapt to various screen sizes and devices lies at the core of creating a user-centric, accessible, and future-ready digital experience. Responsive design addresses the diverse ways users access digital content, ensuring a seamless transition between devices and providing a consistent user experience. From enhancing SEO rankings to supporting inclusivity and accommodating emerging technologies, the impact of responsive design resonates across industries and user scenarios. Embracing responsive design not only meets the expectations of modern users but also positions digital interfaces to navigate the dynamic landscape of technology with flexibility and agility.

Explore responsive design principles for creating a seamless experience across platforms.

Responsive design principles are instrumental in crafting digital interfaces that seamlessly adapt to various screen sizes and devices, ensuring a consistent and user-friendly experience across platforms. At the heart of responsive design lies a commitment to flexibility, adaptability, and user-centricity, guiding designers to create interfaces that transcend the limitations of traditional fixed layouts. Fluid grids, flexible images, and media queries are foundational elements that define the landscape of responsive design, facilitating the creation of interfaces that harmoniously evolve with the diversity of devices in the modern digital ecosystem.

The cornerstone of responsive design is the implementation of a fluid grid system, wherein the layout proportions are defined not in fixed pixels but in relative units such as percentages. A fluid grid enables the content to dynamically adjust its size and arrangement based on the screen width, ensuring that the interface remains visually cohesive across a spectrum of devices. This principle empowers designers to create layouts that are proportionate and scalable, allowing the same content to be presented in a user-friendly manner on both desktop monitors and smaller screens like smartphones or tablets.

In conjunction with a fluid grid, flexible images play a pivotal role in responsive design. Images are a substantial component of digital content, and their adaptability is crucial in providing a seamless experience across platforms. Responsive images are defined using relative units, ensuring that they can scale proportionately within the fluid grid. This adaptability not only caters to different screen sizes but also considers the varying resolutions of devices, optimizing the loading speed and visual quality of images. By implementing flexible images, designers enhance the overall aesthetics of the interface and contribute to a responsive and visually appealing user experience.

Media queries constitute a key responsive design principle, allowing designers to apply specific styles based on the characteristics of the device or screen. These queries enable the adaptation of stylesheets to different conditions such as screen width, device orientation, or even specific features of the device, like whether it is a touchscreen. Media queries facilitate a tailored presentation of content, ensuring optimal readability and usability across devices. This dynamic adjustment of styles based on device characteristics is crucial for creating interfaces that are not only visually consistent but also optimized for the diverse ways users interact with digital content.

Viewport meta tag is another responsive design principle that addresses the nuances of mobile devices. By setting the viewport meta tag in the HTML head, designers can control the initial scale and dimensions of the viewport, ensuring that the content is rendered appropriately on mobile screens. This tag plays a crucial role in eliminating the need for users to zoom in or out to view content, creating a more user-friendly and accessible experience on smaller screens. The viewport meta tag exemplifies the attention to detail required in responsive design to cater to the specific characteristics of different devices.

Progressive enhancement is a guiding principle in responsive design that emphasizes the importance of starting with a solid foundation and progressively enhancing the user experience based on the capabilities of the device. This approach ensures that all users, regardless of their device's capabilities, can access the core content and functionality. As the capabilities of the device increase, additional features and enhancements are progressively introduced, providing an optimized experience for users with more advanced devices. Progressive enhancement aligns with the inclusive nature of responsive design, accommodating a diverse user base and acknowledging the varied technological landscapes users navigate.

Mobile-first design is an extension of the progressive enhancement principle that places a particular emphasis on designing for the smallest screens first and then scaling up to larger screens. In a mobile-first approach, designers prioritize the core functionality and content essential for smaller screens, ensuring that the interface is optimized for mobile devices. This approach not only aligns with the prevalence of mobile usage but also encourages a more focused and streamlined design process. By starting with the constraints of mobile screens, designers create interfaces that are inherently adaptable, setting a strong foundation for responsive design across a range of devices.

Content prioritization is a responsive design principle that recognizes the importance of delivering relevant and impactful content to users, regardless of the device they are using. Designers must prioritize content based on its significance, ensuring that users receive the most relevant information prominently displayed on their screens. This prioritization becomes especially crucial on smaller screens, where space constraints demand a more strategic approach to content presentation. By aligning content priorities with the principles of responsive design, designers create interfaces that deliver a consistent and meaningful user experience across platforms.

Flexible navigation is a responsive design principle that addresses the challenges of adapting navigation menus to various screen sizes.

Traditional navigation menus designed for desktop screens may become unwieldy on smaller screens, leading to a compromised user experience. Flexible navigation involves rethinking menu structures, using techniques such as collapsible menus, off-canvas navigation, or prioritizing key menu items based on screen width. By optimizing navigation for different devices, designers ensure that users can seamlessly access and navigate through the interface, regardless of the screen size they are using.

Touch-friendly design is a responsive design principle that recognizes the prevalence of touchscreens on many devices, particularly mobile devices and tablets. Designing interfaces with touch-friendly elements involves considerations such as appropriately sized touch targets, spacing between interactive elements to prevent accidental taps, and minimizing reliance on hover interactions. By prioritizing touch-friendly design, interfaces become more accessible and enjoyable for users interacting with touchscreens, contributing to a responsive and user-centric experience.

Performance optimization is an integral aspect of responsive design, acknowledging the varying network conditions and device capabilities users encounter. Optimizing performance involves considerations such as minimizing the use of large images, leveraging browser caching, and prioritizing the loading of critical resources. A performance-optimized responsive design ensures that users, irrespective of their network speed or device specifications, can access content efficiently. This principle aligns with the goal of creating interfaces that are not only visually consistent but also deliver a fast and responsive user experience.

User testing across devices is a responsive design principle that emphasizes the importance of validating the user experience on various devices through thorough testing. Conducting user testing across devices allows designers to identify and address any usability or functionality issues that may arise on specific platforms. This iterative testing process ensures that the interface performs seamlessly and provides a consistent user experience across the diverse array of devices that users may use to access the content. By prioritizing user testing across devices, designers validate the effectiveness of responsive design principles and refine the interface based on real-world user interactions.

Cross-browser compatibility is a responsive design principle that recognizes the need for consistent performance across different web browsers. Users access digital content through a variety of browsers, each with its own rendering engine and specifications. Ensuring cross-browser compatibility involves testing and optimizing the interface to function consistently across popular browsers, avoiding discrepancies in rendering or functionality. This principle reinforces the commitment to delivering a seamless experience, irrespective of the browser preferences of the users.

The strategic use of breakpoints is a responsive design principle that allows designers to define specific points at which the layout of the interface should adapt to different screen sizes. Breakpoints act as triggers for changes in the layout, enabling designers to optimize the presentation of content based on the width of the screen. By strategically defining breakpoints, designers ensure that the interface remains visually cohesive and user-friendly across a range of devices, contributing to a seamless and responsive experience.

In conclusion, responsive design principles form the foundation for creating interfaces that seamlessly adapt to various screen sizes and devices, fostering a consistent and user-centric experience. From fluid grids and flexible images to media queries and progressive enhancement, these principles guide designers in crafting interfaces that transcend the constraints of fixed layouts. The holistic approach of responsive design considers the diverse characteristics of devices, prioritizes user experience, and embraces adaptability, ensuring that digital interfaces evolve seamlessly with the dynamic landscape of technology. As users continue to navigate an array of devices, responsive design principles stand as essential guidelines for designers striving to deliver accessible, inclusive, and cohesive experiences across platforms.

Chapter 5: Accessibility and Inclusivity in OS Interfaces

Define accessibility and its significance in creating interfaces that cater to diverse user needs.

Accessibility, in the context of digital design, refers to the inclusive practice of creating interfaces and content that can be accessed, understood, and interacted with by a diverse range of users, including those with disabilities. The overarching goal of accessibility is to ensure that digital experiences are barrier-free, allowing individuals with varying abilities and needs to navigate, perceive, and interact with digital content effectively. This encompasses a wide spectrum of disabilities, including visual, auditory, motor, cognitive, and neurological impairments, as well as situational limitations that users may encounter, such as temporary disabilities or environmental constraints. The significance of accessibility lies not only in legal and ethical considerations but also in the broader pursuit of fostering inclusivity, equal access, and a user-centric approach in the digital landscape.

One of the fundamental aspects of accessibility is creating interfaces that are perceivable by users with diverse sensory abilities. For users with visual impairments, this involves providing alternatives to visual content through methods such as descriptive text for images, captions for videos, and transcripts for audio content. The use of clear and legible fonts, appropriate color contrasts, and scalable text ensures that content is easily readable for individuals with varying levels of visual acuity. By prioritizing perceivability, designers lay the groundwork for interfaces that cater to users with different sensory capabilities, fostering an inclusive and equitable digital experience.

Operable interfaces are a key tenet of accessibility, ensuring that users can interact with and navigate digital content using various input methods. This includes providing keyboard navigation options for users who may rely on assistive technologies or have motor impairments that limit their use of a traditional mouse. Additionally, operability entails avoiding time-based interactions that may pose challenges for users with motor or cognitive disabilities. Designing interfaces with clear and consistent navigation structures, logical tab orders, and focus indicators contributes to an operable experience, enabling users to engage with digital content seamlessly, regardless of their physical abilities.

Understanding the importance of clarity and simplicity in digital interfaces is paramount for ensuring accessibility. Users with cognitive disabilities or learning difficulties may benefit from straightforward and intuitive designs that minimize cognitive load. This involves organizing content logically, avoiding unnecessary complexity, and providing clear instructions and cues. By embracing simplicity, designers create interfaces that are more user-friendly for individuals with cognitive challenges, fostering a digital environment that accommodates a diverse range of cognitive abilities and learning styles.

The principle of robustness in accessibility emphasizes the creation of digital content that remains functional and consistent across various assistive technologies, browsers, and devices. By adhering to web standards, semantic HTML, and best coding practices, designers ensure that their interfaces are compatible with screen readers, voice recognition software, and other assistive technologies commonly used by individuals with disabilities. A robust approach to accessibility enhances the resilience of digital content, providing a more reliable and consistent user experience for individuals relying on diverse assistive technologies.

Perceivable, operable, understandable, and robust design principles collectively contribute to the overarching goal of inclusivity in digital interfaces. Understanding the significance of accessibility extends beyond compliance with legal standards, such as the Web Content Accessibility Guidelines (WCAG), to encompass a commitment to social responsibility and ethical design practices. Inclusive design benefits not only users with disabilities but also a broader audience, including older adults, individuals with temporary impairments, and those navigating challenging environmental conditions. The adoption of accessibility principles aligns with the ethos of universal design, emphasizing that products and services should be usable by as many people as possible, regardless of their abilities or circumstances.

The legal landscape surrounding accessibility reinforces its significance in the digital domain. Many countries, including the United States with the Americans with Disabilities Act (ADA) and the European Union with the Web Accessibility Directive, have enacted regulations that mandate accessible digital experiences. Non-compliance with these regulations may result in legal consequences and financial penalties. Beyond legal obligations, adherence to accessibility standards reflects a commitment to social justice, equity, and the recognition of the rights of individuals with disabilities to participate fully in the digital realm.

The business case for accessibility further underscores its significance, as creating inclusive digital experiences can lead to a broader user base, increased customer loyalty, and improved brand reputation. Catering to users with disabilities represents a significant market segment, with billions of individuals worldwide who may benefit from accessible design. Moreover, accessible interfaces often provide a superior user experience for all users, regardless of their abilities, leading to increased user satisfaction, positive word-of-mouth recommendations, and a competitive advantage in the marketplace. The positive impact on brand perception and customer loyalty, coupled with the potential for expanded market reach, highlights the strategic importance of integrating accessibility into the overall design and development process.

Accessibility considerations play a crucial role in the context of emerging technologies and the evolving digital landscape. As new technologies, platforms, and devices continue to shape the way users interact with digital content, designers must ensure that accessibility remains a core consideration. The advent of voice interfaces, augmented reality, virtual reality, and other immersive technologies introduces new challenges and opportunities for inclusive design. Ensuring that individuals with disabilities can fully participate in these evolving digital experiences requires proactive consideration of accessibility principles, contributing to a future where technology is inherently inclusive and accessible to all.

Social media platforms exemplify both the challenges and opportunities associated with accessibility in the digital age. These platforms serve as vital communication channels, and their accessibility has significant implications for users with disabilities. Features such as alternative text for images, closed captions for videos, and customizable text sizes contribute to a more accessible social media experience. However, challenges persist, particularly in areas like real-time communication and the accessibility of emerging features. Social media companies play a pivotal role in advancing accessibility by addressing these challenges and proactively incorporating inclusive design practices.

The role of assistive technologies in accessibility cannot be overstated. These technologies, ranging from screen readers and magnifiers to speech recognition software and alternative input devices, empower individuals with disabilities to interact with digital content effectively. Designing interfaces with compatibility for assistive technologies is essential for ensuring that users with disabilities can independently access information, engage with applications, and participate in online activities. The collaboration between designers and assistive technology developers contributes to a more cohesive and supportive digital ecosystem for individuals with diverse abilities.

In the context of education, accessibility is a critical consideration to ensure that digital learning materials are inclusive and usable by all students. Designing accessible educational interfaces involves providing alternatives for multimedia content, ensuring compatibility with screen readers, and offering navigational structures that accommodate diverse learning styles. Accessible educational technology not only benefits students with disabilities but also promotes a more inclusive and equitable learning environment for all learners, fostering a culture of diversity and accessibility in educational settings.

Accessibility in healthcare technology is of paramount importance, as digital interfaces play a crucial role in facilitating communication, information access, and healthcare management for individuals with diverse health conditions. Patient portals, telehealth platforms, and health information systems must prioritize accessibility to ensure that individuals with disabilities can effectively engage with healthcare services. From clear and concise information presentation to compatibility with assistive technologies, healthcare interfaces that embrace accessibility principles contribute to patient empowerment, improved healthcare outcomes, and an inclusive healthcare ecosystem.

The gaming industry, traditionally associated with visual and auditory experiences, has witnessed a paradigm shift towards greater inclusivity through accessible design. Accessibility features in video games, such as customizable controls, subtitles, and options for colorblind players, enhance the gaming experience for individuals with disabilities. The recognition of gaming as a form of entertainment and social interaction for individuals with disabilities has led to a growing emphasis on accessible game design, fostering a more inclusive gaming culture.

In conclusion, accessibility in digital design is a multifaceted and essential practice that goes beyond compliance with standards and regulations. It embodies a commitment to inclusivity, equality, and social responsibility, recognizing the diverse needs and abilities of users in the digital landscape. The significance of accessibility is evident in legal frameworks, business advantages, and the ethical imperative to ensure that technology is accessible to all. As technology continues to evolve, the integration of accessibility principles remains pivotal in shaping a digital future that prioritizes inclusivity, empowers individuals with disabilities, and fosters a more equitable and user-centric digital experience for everyone.

Discuss the impact of inclusive design on user experience.

Inclusive design, a philosophy rooted in the principle that digital interfaces and products should be accessible and usable by as many people as possible, regardless of their abilities or disabilities, has a profound impact on user experience. At its core, inclusive design fosters an environment where diversity is not only acknowledged but celebrated, recognizing that users have a wide range of needs, preferences, and capabilities. By prioritizing inclusivity, designers create interfaces that go beyond catering to a specific user group and instead accommodate the diverse and unique characteristics of a broad audience, contributing to a more empathetic, equitable, and user-centric user experience.

One of the key impacts of inclusive design on user experience is evident in improved accessibility for individuals with disabilities. By considering the needs of users with visual, auditory, motor, cognitive, or neurological impairments, inclusive design ensures that digital interfaces are navigable and comprehensible for everyone. Features such as alternative text for images, closed captions for videos, and keyboard navigation options empower users with disabilities to access information and interact with digital content independently. This enhanced accessibility not only aligns with ethical considerations but also opens up new possibilities for individuals who might have faced barriers in the past, fostering a sense of empowerment and inclusion.

Inclusive design extends its positive impact to a broader audience beyond those with disabilities. Users with varying levels of technological proficiency, language skills, or cultural backgrounds benefit from interfaces designed with inclusivity in mind. Clear and intuitive navigation, straightforward language, and culturally sensitive design choices contribute to a more user-friendly experience for diverse user groups. Inclusive design recognizes the richness of human diversity and strives to create interfaces that resonate with users from different backgrounds and contexts, fostering a sense of belonging and cultural sensitivity in the digital space.

Another significant impact of inclusive design lies in creating interfaces that are adaptable to diverse contexts and environments. Users access digital content in varied circumstances, including different devices, network conditions, and environmental constraints. Inclusive design anticipates these challenges and ensures that interfaces remain functional and usable across a spectrum of situations. This adaptability contributes to a seamless user experience, irrespective of the device being used or the environmental factors at play. By embracing inclusivity, designers empower users to engage with digital content in ways that suit their preferences and circumstances, reinforcing the notion that technology should adapt to users, not the other way around.

Inclusive design also plays a pivotal role in enhancing usability and user satisfaction. Interfaces that prioritize clarity, simplicity, and ease of use benefit all users, not just those with specific needs. By streamlining complex navigation structures, avoiding unnecessary visual clutter, and providing straightforward interactions, inclusive design creates interfaces that are intuitive and user-friendly. This simplicity not only reduces the learning curve for new users but also enhances the overall user experience, leading to increased satisfaction and positive perceptions of the brand or product.

The emotional impact of inclusive design on user experience should not be understated. When users feel seen, heard, and valued through interfaces that consider their diverse needs, it fosters a positive emotional connection. Inclusive design goes beyond functional considerations to address the emotional resonance of users interacting with digital content. Features such as customizable preferences, personalization options, and representations that reflect diversity contribute to a sense of empathy and inclusivity. This emotional connection translates into increased user loyalty, positive word-of-mouth recommendations, and a brand image that resonates with users on a deeper, more meaningful level.

Inclusive design also contributes to enhanced creativity and innovation in the design process. When designers intentionally seek to accommodate diverse perspectives, they tap into a wealth of insights and ideas that may not have been considered otherwise. Inclusive design involves collaboration with users, stakeholders, and experts from various domains, fostering a multidisciplinary approach to problem-solving. This collaborative and diverse mindset sparks creativity, leading to innovative solutions that benefit all users. The iterative nature of inclusive design encourages ongoing feedback, allowing designers to refine and improve their creations based on real-world user experiences, ensuring continuous innovation and adaptation.

The economic impact of inclusive design is increasingly recognized as a strategic advantage in the business world. Companies that prioritize inclusivity in their digital products and services often find themselves better positioned in the market. Inclusivity enhances market reach by appealing to a broader audience, including individuals with disabilities who represent a significant consumer base. Moreover, inclusive design contributes to positive brand perception, customer loyalty, and differentiation in a competitive landscape. Businesses that embrace inclusivity not only comply with legal standards but also demonstrate a commitment to social responsibility, contributing to a positive corporate image and fostering long-term relationships with diverse customer demographics.

Education is an arena where the impact of inclusive design on user experience is particularly pronounced. Inclusive educational interfaces ensure that learning materials are accessible to students with diverse abilities and learning styles. Features such as captions for videos, text-to-speech functionality, and adaptable reading interfaces accommodate a wide range of learning preferences. Inclusive design in education contributes to a learning environment where all students, regardless of their abilities, can participate fully, fostering a culture of diversity and equality in educational settings. The positive impact extends beyond the classroom, preparing students for a future where inclusivity is valued and celebrated.

Social media platforms exemplify the transformative impact of inclusive design on user engagement and community building. By embracing inclusivity, social media companies create environments where users from diverse backgrounds, abilities, and cultures can connect, share experiences, and engage in meaningful conversations. Features such as customizable privacy settings, content warnings, and accessible multimedia contribute to a more inclusive and supportive social media experience. Inclusive design in social media not only reflects the diversity of users but also plays a role in shaping online communities that celebrate individuality and promote positive interactions.

In the realm of healthcare, inclusive design has far-reaching implications for patient engagement and healthcare accessibility. Digital healthcare interfaces that prioritize inclusivity ensure that individuals with diverse health conditions can access and manage their health information effectively. Features such as customizable font sizes, voice interfaces, and clear navigation contribute to an inclusive healthcare experience. Inclusive design in healthcare extends to telehealth platforms, patient portals, and health apps, creating a more accessible and patient-centric healthcare ecosystem.

The impact of inclusive design on user experience extends to the gaming industry, challenging traditional notions of gaming as a niche activity. Inclusive design in gaming involves features such as customizable controls, subtitles, and representation of diverse characters, creating gaming experiences that are accessible to players with disabilities. This inclusivity not only broadens the gaming audience but also fosters a gaming culture that celebrates diversity and embraces players with varying abilities. Inclusive design in gaming reflects a shift towards recognizing the universal appeal of interactive and immersive experiences for individuals of all backgrounds.

In conclusion, the impact of inclusive design on user experience is profound and multi-faceted. Beyond the functional considerations of accessibility, inclusive design contributes to emotional connections, usability improvements, creative innovation, economic advantages, and the cultivation of inclusive communities. By embracing diversity in the design process and prioritizing the needs of users with varying abilities and backgrounds, designers create interfaces that resonate with a broad audience, fostering a digital landscape that is welcoming, equitable, and responsive to the unique characteristics of individuals. The enduring impact of inclusive design extends beyond the digital realm, influencing societal perceptions, cultural attitudes, and the way individuals interact with technology, ultimately contributing to a more inclusive and empathetic world.

Explore design considerations for making UI elements accessible to users with disabilities.

Designing accessible user interface (UI) elements is a fundamental aspect of creating digital experiences that cater to users with disabilities, fostering inclusivity and ensuring equal access to information and functionality. In this exploration, we will delve into various design considerations that play a pivotal role in making UI elements accessible for users with diverse abilities, encompassing visual, auditory, motor, cognitive, and neurological impairments. These considerations go beyond mere compliance with accessibility standards, embodying a commitment to creating interfaces that prioritize user experience for all.

Visual accessibility is a critical consideration in UI design, and designers must address the needs of users with visual impairments. One key element is ensuring sufficient contrast between text and background colors, making content readable for individuals with low vision or color blindness. Additionally, designers should choose fonts that are clear, legible, and resizable, accommodating users who may need to adjust text size for readability. Icons and images should be accompanied by descriptive alternative text, providing context and information for users relying on screen readers. The use of meaningful and consistent color coding, combined with clear labels, aids users with color blindness in comprehending and navigating the interface effectively.

For users with auditory impairments, UI design should consider alternatives to audio-based information and alerts. Closed captions for videos and transcripts for audio content are essential, ensuring that users who are deaf or hard of hearing can access information presented through multimedia. Visual indicators for alerts or notifications, such as flashing lights or icon changes, provide alternatives to sound-based feedback. Ensuring that critical information is not solely conveyed through audio cues guarantees that users with auditory impairments can fully participate in and comprehend the interactive aspects of the interface.

Motor accessibility involves accommodating users with limited dexterity or mobility challenges. Designers should consider providing larger clickable areas for interactive elements, minimizing the risk of accidental clicks and facilitating ease of interaction for users with motor impairments. Touch-friendly design, with well-spaced and appropriately sized interactive elements, benefits users who interact with the interface through touchscreens or alternative input devices. Implementing keyboard shortcuts and ensuring that all interactive elements are reachable using keyboard navigation is crucial for users who may not be able to use a mouse effectively.

Cognitive accessibility focuses on creating interfaces that are easily understandable and navigable for users with cognitive disabilities or learning difficulties. Clarity and simplicity in design are paramount, involving straightforward language, clear instructions, and a logical flow of information. Consistency in layout and navigation aids users in understanding the structure of the interface, reducing cognitive load. Providing tooltips, help text, and contextual guidance ensures that users receive additional information when needed, supporting comprehension and task completion for individuals with cognitive challenges.

Neurological accessibility addresses the needs of users with conditions such as epilepsy, migraines, or attention disorders. Design considerations include avoiding rapid or flashing animations that may trigger seizures and providing options to disable or customize motion effects. Ensuring a predictable and stable interface experience reduces the risk of discomfort or sensory overload for users with neurological conditions. Thoughtful design that minimizes distractions, supports focus, and allows users to control the pace of interaction contributes to a more neurologically inclusive user experience.

Semantic HTML, a cornerstone of accessible UI design, ensures that the structure and content of the interface are conveyed in a meaningful way to assistive technologies. Using appropriate HTML elements for headers, lists, and navigation contributes to a well-organized and navigable interface for users relying on screen readers. Descriptive and concise link text enhances the comprehensibility of navigation for screen reader users, allowing them to understand the purpose of each link without relying on surrounding context. Ensuring that form elements are associated with labels and providing helpful error messages contributes to a seamless experience for users with disabilities interacting with forms.

Focus management is a crucial consideration for ensuring keyboard accessibility, benefiting users who navigate the interface without a mouse. Designers should ensure that all interactive elements, including links, buttons, and form fields, can be navigated and activated using keyboard controls. Clear visual indicators of focus, such as highlighting or an outline, help users understand their current position within the interface. Managing focus order logically and consistently contributes to an intuitive navigation experience for users relying on keyboard input, promoting equal access and usability.

A well-designed and accessible navigation structure is essential for users with disabilities to efficiently move through the interface. Providing skip navigation links allows users to bypass repetitive content and jump directly to the main content area, benefiting screen reader users who may otherwise need to navigate through extensive menus. Logical and consistent navigation menus enhance predictability and ease of use for all users, contributing to a more intuitive experience. Descriptive and informative labels for navigation links assist users in understanding the purpose and destination of each link, supporting users with cognitive or visual impairments.

Image accessibility involves providing alternative text for all images, ensuring that users with visual impairments can comprehend the content and context conveyed by visuals. Descriptive alternative text should convey the purpose or information of the image, avoiding generic or non-informative descriptions. Decorative images should have empty or null alternative text, indicating to assistive technologies that the image is purely aesthetic and does not convey meaningful content. This consideration ensures that users with visual impairments receive equivalent information and context when navigating and interacting with the interface.

Responsive design principles play a significant role in ensuring that UI elements adapt seamlessly to different screen sizes and devices, benefitting users with varied abilities and preferences. A responsive layout, which dynamically adjusts based on screen width, allows users to access content across devices without sacrificing usability. Ensuring that interactive elements remain functional and well-spaced on smaller screens benefits users with motor impairments or those who rely on touchscreens. By prioritizing a mobile-first approach, designers create interfaces that are inherently adaptable and optimized for diverse devices, contributing to a more inclusive user experience.

Form design considerations are vital for creating accessible and usable interfaces for users with disabilities. Labeling form fields with clear and descriptive text ensures that users understand the information required and provides context for screen reader users. Additionally, using the appropriate input types and attributes, such as email, phone, or date, supports users in entering information accurately. Error messages should be concise, clearly associated with the relevant form field, and provide guidance on resolving issues, aiding users with cognitive or attention-related challenges. Designing forms with a logical and linear flow supports users in completing tasks efficiently, benefiting users with cognitive disabilities.

Consistent and predictable navigation enhances the user experience for individuals with cognitive or neurological impairments.

Providing clear indicators of the user's location within the interface, such as breadcrumbs or highlighted navigation items, supports orientation. Consistency in the placement of navigation menus, buttons, and interactive elements reduces cognitive load and aids users in forming a mental model of the interface. Predictable navigation contributes to a sense of control for users with cognitive or neurological conditions, fostering a more comfortable and comprehensible user experience.

Audio and video media considerations involve providing alternatives and controls for users with visual or auditory impairments. Closed captions for videos, transcripts for audio content, and audio descriptions for visual elements ensure that users with disabilities receive equivalent information and context. Providing controls for users to pause, play, or adjust the volume of media content supports users with auditory impairments or those who may need to review information at their own pace. Implementing accessible media elements ensures that users with disabilities can fully engage with multimedia content, contributing to a more inclusive user experience.

Customization options are essential for allowing users to adapt the interface to their individual needs and preferences. Designers should provide options for users to adjust text size, contrast settings, and background colors, benefiting users with visual or cognitive impairments. Color customization options contribute to a more inclusive experience for users with color blindness or sensitivity to certain color combinations. By offering customization features, designers empower users to tailor the interface to their specific needs, promoting a more personalized and user-centric experience.

Usability testing with users with disabilities is a critical step in ensuring that UI elements are truly accessible and meet the diverse needs of the user base. Involving individuals with disabilities in usability testing provides valuable insights into the effectiveness and usability of the interface for users with varied abilities. Real-world testing scenarios allow designers to identify and address potential barriers, refine interactions, and validate the accessibility of the UI elements. This iterative testing process ensures that the final interface reflects the diverse perspectives and needs of users with disabilities, contributing to a more inclusive and user-friendly design.

In conclusion, the design considerations for making UI elements accessible to users with disabilities encompass a wide range of factors, from visual and auditory accessibility to motor, cognitive, and neurological considerations. By integrating these considerations into the design process, designers contribute to the creation of digital interfaces that prioritize inclusivity, equal access, and a user-centric approach. Accessibility goes beyond compliance with standards; it embodies a commitment to recognizing and addressing the diverse needs of users, ensuring that digital experiences are accessible and usable for everyone, regardless of their abilities or disabilities. Through thoughtful and intentional design, UI elements become a gateway to a more inclusive and equitable digital landscape.

Discuss features such as alternative text, keyboard navigation, and screen reader compatibility.

Features such as alternative text, keyboard navigation, and screen reader compatibility are integral components of accessible design, playing a crucial role in ensuring that digital interfaces are inclusive and usable for individuals with disabilities. Alternative text, commonly known as alt text, is a vital feature that provides descriptive information for images, enabling users with visual impairments to comprehend the content and context conveyed by visuals. Alt text is especially significant for screen reader users, as it allows assistive technologies to convey the meaning of images through synthesized speech or braille displays. By incorporating meaningful and descriptive alt text, designers enhance the accessibility of visual content, fostering a more inclusive experience for users who rely on screen readers to navigate and understand the interface.

Keyboard navigation is a cornerstone of accessible design, catering to users who may have difficulty using a traditional mouse or pointing device. This feature allows users to navigate through the interface, interact with interactive elements, and access content using keyboard controls alone. Designers must ensure that all interactive elements, including links, buttons, and form fields, are reachable and operable through keyboard navigation. Clear visual indicators, such as focus outlines, highlight the currently focused element, aiding users in understanding their position within the interface. Keyboard navigation not only benefits users with motor impairments but also provides an alternative and efficient means of interaction for a broader range of users.

Screen reader compatibility is a pivotal aspect of creating accessible interfaces, addressing the needs of users with visual impairments who rely on screen reader software to interpret and convey digital content audibly. Screen readers convert on-screen text and information into synthesized speech or braille output, allowing users to navigate, interact, and consume digital content effectively. Designers must ensure that the interface is structured using semantic HTML to convey content hierarchy, relationships, and meaningful information to assistive technologies. This includes using proper heading elements, labeling form fields, and providing alternative text for images. By prioritizing screen reader compatibility, designers empower users with visual impairments to access and engage with digital content, fostering an inclusive and equitable user experience.

The role of alternative text in fostering accessibility cannot be overstated. When images are used in digital content, alternative text serves as a textual description that conveys the content and function of the images. For users with visual impairments who rely on screen readers, this feature is essential as it provides information about the visual elements they cannot see. Meaningful and descriptive alternative text ensures that users receive equivalent information and context, contributing to a comprehensive understanding of the content. Additionally, alternative text is crucial in situations where images fail to load or are not displayed properly, ensuring that users, regardless of their abilities, have access to the intended information.

Keyboard navigation is a fundamental feature that enhances accessibility by providing an alternative means of interacting with digital interfaces. While traditional navigation involves using a mouse or other pointing device, keyboard navigation allows users to navigate, select, and activate interactive elements using keyboard controls. This feature is particularly valuable for individuals with motor impairments or those who may have difficulty using a mouse. Designing interfaces with robust keyboard navigation ensures that all users, regardless of their physical abilities or preferences, can access and interact with content efficiently. Clear visual indicators of focus, such as outlined or highlighted elements, help users understand their position within the interface and contribute to a more intuitive and user-friendly experience.

Screen reader compatibility is a cornerstone of accessibility for users with visual impairments. Screen readers are assistive technologies that interpret and vocalize digital content, allowing users to navigate and interact with websites, applications, and documents. To ensure screen reader compatibility, designers must prioritize semantic HTML and provide information that can be accurately conveyed through synthesized speech or braille output. Properly structured headings, labeled form fields, and alternative text for images contribute to a meaningful and coherent experience for users relying on screen readers. By embracing screen reader compatibility, designers empower individuals with visual impairments to access information, engage with digital content, and participate fully in the online environment.

Alternative text, keyboard navigation, and screen reader compatibility collectively contribute to creating a more inclusive and accessible digital landscape. When these features are thoughtfully implemented, they ensure that individuals with disabilities, particularly those with visual, motor, or cognitive impairments, can navigate, understand, and interact with digital content effectively. The synergy of these features addresses diverse user needs, fostering an environment where digital interfaces become a gateway to information and interaction for all users, regardless of their abilities or disabilities.

The effectiveness of alternative text is most evident in the context of images. Images play a crucial role in conveying information, enhancing aesthetics, and providing context within digital content. For users with visual impairments, alternative text serves as a textual representation of images, allowing them to grasp the content and meaning conveyed by visuals. The provision of meaningful alternative text is not only an accessibility requirement but also a design consideration that enriches the user experience. By crafting descriptive alternative text, designers contribute to a more inclusive and informative digital environment, ensuring that users with visual impairments receive a comparable and meaningful experience while navigating through image-rich content.

Keyboard navigation, as a feature, embodies the principle of flexibility and inclusivity. While mouse-based navigation is the conventional method, not all users can rely on this input method due to physical limitations or personal preferences. Keyboard navigation allows users to navigate through interactive elements, menus, and content using a keyboard. This is particularly beneficial for individuals with motor impairments who may have challenges using a mouse or other pointing devices. In addition, keyboard navigation caters to a broader audience by offering an alternative means of interaction. By designing interfaces that support keyboard navigation, designers acknowledge the diversity of user needs and create digital experiences that are accessible to a wider range of individuals.

Screen reader compatibility is a cornerstone of digital inclusivity for individuals with visual impairments. Screen readers are assistive technologies that convert digital text into synthesized speech or braille output. To ensure screen reader compatibility, designers must structure content using semantic HTML, providing clear and meaningful information to assistive technologies. Properly labeled form fields, headings, and alternative text for images enable screen readers to convey the content and context accurately. The integration of screen reader compatibility is not just a technical requirement but a commitment to making digital content accessible and navigable for users who rely on auditory or tactile feedback. By prioritizing screen reader compatibility, designers contribute to a digital landscape where users with visual impairments can independently access and interact with online information.

The collaborative impact of these features is exemplified when considering a user with visual and motor impairments. For such users, the combination of alternative text, keyboard navigation, and screen reader compatibility ensures a comprehensive and accessible experience. Alternative text provides textual descriptions of images, allowing the user to understand visual content, while keyboard navigation enables efficient navigation and interaction without relying on a mouse. Simultaneously, screen reader compatibility ensures that the user receives audible information about the interface elements, enhancing their understanding and engagement. In this way, the synergy of these features addresses multiple dimensions of accessibility, creating a user experience that is not only functional but also empowering for individuals with diverse abilities.

The inclusive design philosophy recognizes that accessibility features are not isolated elements but interconnected components that work together to create a holistic and user-centric experience. Alternative text, keyboard navigation, and screen reader compatibility, when implemented cohesively, contribute to a digital environment where individuals with disabilities can participate fully, independently, and meaningfully. By embracing these features, designers champion a user-centric approach that goes beyond compliance, fostering an inclusive digital landscape that celebrates diversity and ensures equal access for all users. In this way, alternative text, keyboard navigation, and screen reader compatibility become catalysts for change, shaping digital experiences that prioritize accessibility and empower users of varying abilities to navigate and interact with the online world.

Discuss strategies for creating visually inclusive interfaces.

Creating visually inclusive interfaces involves adopting design strategies that prioritize accessibility, accommodate diverse user needs, and ensure that the visual elements of a digital interface are inclusive and equitable for users of all abilities. One crucial strategy is to prioritize high contrast and legibility in the color scheme and typography. High contrast between text and background colors improves readability, benefiting users with low vision or color blindness. Ensuring legible font sizes and styles contributes to a more accessible reading experience, catering to users with varying visual acuity. By embracing a visually inclusive color and typography palette, designers create interfaces that are not only aesthetically pleasing but also considerate of users with different visual abilities.

The use of meaningful and descriptive imagery is another essential strategy for creating visually inclusive interfaces. Visual content should convey information clearly and be complemented by alternative text that provides a textual description. This practice ensures that users with visual impairments, who may rely on screen readers, receive equivalent information about the visual elements. Additionally, avoiding the overuse of complex or ambiguous visuals enhances clarity and comprehension, benefiting users with cognitive or visual challenges. By integrating thoughtful and purposeful imagery, designers contribute to an inclusive visual experience that transcends aesthetic appeal to deliver meaningful content and context for all users.

Responsive design principles play a pivotal role in ensuring that interfaces adapt seamlessly to various screen sizes and devices, contributing to a visually inclusive experience. A responsive layout accommodates users who access digital content on a diverse range of devices, from large desktop monitors to smaller mobile screens. This adaptability is particularly beneficial for users with motor impairments or those who may rely on touchscreens, ensuring that interactive elements remain accessible and well-spaced across different devices. By prioritizing a responsive design approach, designers create interfaces that are inherently inclusive and optimized for diverse user experiences, fostering a visually cohesive and adaptable digital environment.

Consideration for font choice and readability is a key component of visually inclusive design. Fonts should be selected with attention to legibility, ensuring that users of all ages and visual abilities can comfortably read the content. Sans-serif fonts are often preferred for digital interfaces due to their clean and straightforward appearance. Additionally, providing options for users to adjust text size enhances customization for individuals with varying visual needs. By offering a range of accessible fonts and size options, designers acknowledge the diversity of user preferences and visual requirements, promoting a visually inclusive design that caters to the individual needs of all users.

Incorporating clear and consistent navigation structures is fundamental to creating visually inclusive interfaces. Navigation menus, buttons, and interactive elements should be designed with clarity and predictability, ensuring that users can easily understand and navigate through the interface. Consistent placement of navigation elements across pages and sections reduces cognitive load and aids users in forming a mental model of the interface. Clear labels and visual cues for interactive elements contribute to a more intuitive experience, benefiting users with cognitive or visual impairments. A well-designed navigation system is a cornerstone of visual inclusivity, providing a user-friendly experience that transcends potential barriers.

Color choices and combinations play a crucial role in creating visually inclusive interfaces. Designers must consider color contrast to ensure that text and interactive elements are easily distinguishable from the background. High contrast is particularly beneficial for users with low vision or color blindness. Additionally, avoiding reliance on color alone to convey information is essential, as some users may have difficulty differentiating certain color combinations. Providing alternative visual cues, such as icons or patterns, enhances the comprehensibility of content for users with visual challenges. A thoughtful and inclusive approach to color selection contributes to a more accessible and visually harmonious interface.

Embracing universal design principles is a fundamental strategy for creating visually inclusive interfaces. Universal design aims to make products and environments usable by people of all abilities and disabilities. Applying this approach involves anticipating diverse user needs from the outset of the design process. Designers should consider factors such as legibility, contrast, navigation, and overall user experience with inclusivity in mind. By proactively addressing potential barriers and incorporating inclusive features, designers ensure that the interface is accessible to a broad spectrum of users. Universal design fosters a mindset where inclusivity is not an afterthought but an integral part of the design philosophy, resulting in visually inclusive interfaces that prioritize equal access for everyone.

Ensuring compatibility with assistive technologies is a central strategy for visual inclusivity. Assistive technologies, such as screen readers and magnifiers, are crucial tools for users with visual impairments. Designers must prioritize semantic HTML, providing clear information about the structure and content of the interface to assistive technologies. This includes proper labeling of form fields, meaningful headers, and alternative text for images. Compatibility with assistive technologies ensures that users with visual impairments can navigate, comprehend, and interact with digital content effectively. By embracing this strategy, designers contribute to a visually inclusive experience that extends beyond the visual layer to encompass the diverse ways users access and engage with digital interfaces.

Customization options are powerful tools for enhancing visual inclusivity. Providing users with the ability to customize aspects such as text size, color contrast, and interface layout allows individuals to tailor the visual experience to their specific needs and preferences. This strategy is particularly valuable for users with varying degrees of visual acuity or those who may benefit from personalized adjustments. By offering customization options, designers empower users to create a visual environment that suits their unique requirements, fostering a sense of control and inclusivity in the digital experience.

Consideration for animation and motion effects is pivotal in creating visually inclusive interfaces. While animations can enhance the user experience, they may pose challenges for users with certain visual or neurological conditions, such as motion sensitivity or vestibular disorders. Providing options to disable or adjust the speed of animations accommodates users who may find them distracting or discomforting. Additionally, ensuring that important information is not solely conveyed through motion or visual effects guarantees that users with visual impairments or those who prefer reduced motion can access content effectively. By incorporating thoughtful and adjustable animation features, designers contribute to a visually inclusive experience that respects diverse user preferences and needs.

Usability testing with a diverse user base is a fundamental strategy for creating visually inclusive interfaces. Engaging users with varying abilities, including those with visual impairments, allows designers to gather valuable insights into the effectiveness and usability of the interface. Real-world testing scenarios reveal potential barriers, highlight areas for improvement, and validate the overall visual inclusivity of the design. Usability testing is an iterative process that ensures the interface meets the diverse needs of users, guiding designers in refining and optimizing the visual elements based on user feedback. By embracing usability testing, designers foster a user-centric approach that prioritizes inclusivity, resulting in visually inclusive interfaces that resonate with a broad audience.

In conclusion, the strategies for creating visually inclusive interfaces encompass a holistic and user-centric approach that considers diverse user needs, embraces accessibility principles, and prioritizes equal access for individuals of all abilities. From color choices and typography to navigation structures and customization options, each strategy plays a vital role in fostering visual inclusivity. By integrating these strategies into the design process, designers contribute to a digital landscape that is welcoming, equitable, and considerate of the diverse ways users perceive and interact with visual content. Visual inclusivity transcends aesthetics to become a fundamental aspect of creating interfaces that prioritize accessibility, usability, and a positive user experience for everyone.

Explore color contrast, font choices, and other design elements that accommodate users with visual impairments.

Creating digital interfaces that accommodate users with visual impairments involves thoughtful consideration of various design elements, encompassing color contrast, font choices, and additional components that contribute to an inclusive and accessible user experience. Color contrast, a fundamental aspect of visual design, plays a crucial role in ensuring readability and visibility for users with low vision or color blindness. Designers must prioritize sufficient contrast between text and background colors, making content easily discernible. Adhering to accessibility standards, such as those outlined in the Web Content Accessibility Guidelines (WCAG), guides designers in selecting color combinations that meet the criteria for readability. This not only benefits users with visual impairments but also enhances the overall legibility and clarity of content for a diverse audience.

Font choices are integral to creating accessible interfaces, particularly for users with varying degrees of visual acuity. Selecting legible fonts that prioritize clarity and simplicity is essential. Sans-serif fonts are often preferred for digital interfaces due to their clean and straightforward appearance. Additionally, designers must consider font size to accommodate users with low vision. Offering options for users to adjust text size ensures a customizable experience, allowing individuals to set font sizes that align with their specific visual needs. By providing a range of accessible fonts and size options, designers acknowledge the diversity of user preferences and visual requirements, contributing to a more inclusive design.

Typography considerations extend beyond font choices to include aspects such as line spacing and letter spacing. Adequate spacing between lines of text, known as line height, enhances readability and reduces visual clutter. Users with visual impairments, such as those with dyslexia or low vision, benefit from well-spaced text that is easier to follow. Similarly, letter spacing, or kerning, influences the legibility of text. Designers should avoid cramped letter spacing, as it can impede readability for users with visual challenges. Striking a balance between line spacing and letter spacing contributes to an accessible typographic design that ensures content is clear and comprehensible.

The use of alternative text for images is a vital component of accessible design, addressing the needs of users with visual impairments who rely on screen readers. Alternative text provides a textual description of images, conveying their content and context to users who cannot perceive visual elements. Designers must craft meaningful and descriptive alternative text that goes beyond mere functional descriptions, providing users with a rich understanding of the visual content. Ensuring that all images, including decorative ones, have appropriate alternative text is crucial for creating a comprehensible and inclusive experience for users relying on assistive technologies.

Contrast considerations extend beyond text and background colors to include other interface elements, such as buttons, icons, and interactive components. Designers should ensure that these elements exhibit sufficient contrast to be easily distinguishable. This is especially important for users with low vision or color blindness, who may struggle to differentiate between elements with insufficient contrast. Embracing a design approach that prioritizes clear visual distinctions between interactive and non-interactive elements contributes to a more navigable and user-friendly interface for individuals with visual impairments.

Implementing clear and consistent navigation structures is paramount for users with visual impairments, as well as for those with cognitive challenges. Designers should prioritize straightforward and predictable navigation menus, buttons, and interactive elements. Consistent placement of navigation elements across pages and sections reduces cognitive load and aids users in forming a mental model of the interface. Clear labels and visual cues for interactive elements contribute to a more intuitive experience, benefiting users with visual or cognitive impairments. Well-designed navigation enhances accessibility by ensuring that users can navigate the interface with ease and confidence, fostering inclusivity.

Consideration for animations and motion effects is crucial for users with visual impairments, as well as those with neurological conditions that may be sensitive to motion stimuli. Designers should provide options for users to disable or adjust the speed of animations to accommodate individuals who find them distracting or discomforting. Additionally, ensuring that critical information is not solely conveyed through motion or visual effects guarantees that users with visual impairments can access content effectively. By incorporating thoughtful and adjustable animation features, designers contribute to an accessible and visually inclusive experience that respects diverse user preferences and needs.

Ensuring compatibility with assistive technologies, such as screen readers and magnifiers, is fundamental in creating interfaces that cater to users with visual impairments. Designers must prioritize semantic HTML, providing clear information about the structure and content of the interface to assistive technologies. Properly labeled form fields, meaningful headers, and alternative text for images enable screen readers to convey the content and context accurately. Compatibility with assistive technologies ensures that users with visual impairments can navigate, comprehend, and interact with digital content effectively. By embracing this strategy, designers contribute to a visually inclusive experience that extends beyond the visual layer to encompass the diverse ways users access and engage with digital interfaces.

The use of customizable color schemes is a powerful strategy for accommodating users with visual impairments, allowing individuals to adjust the interface colors based on their specific needs and preferences. Designers can implement features that enable users to choose high-contrast color schemes or invert colors, catering to users with low vision or color blindness. Customizable color options empower users to create a visual environment that suits their unique requirements, fostering a sense of control and inclusivity in the digital experience. By providing flexibility in color choices, designers contribute to a visually inclusive design that acknowledges and respects the diverse ways users perceive and interact with content.

Designing accessible forms is essential for users with visual impairments, as well as those with cognitive or motor challenges. Clear and concise labels for form fields ensure that users understand the information required and provide context for screen reader users. Additionally, designers should use appropriate input types and attributes, such as email, phone, or date, to support users in entering information accurately. Error messages should be well-crafted, clearly associated with the relevant form field, and provide guidance on resolving issues, aiding users with cognitive or attention-related challenges. By prioritizing accessible form design, designers contribute to a visually inclusive experience that facilitates efficient and error-free interaction for users with diverse abilities.

Engaging in usability testing with a diverse user base, including individuals with visual impairments, is a fundamental strategy for ensuring the effectiveness and inclusivity of design choices. Real-world testing scenarios allow designers to observe how users with diverse visual needs interact with the interface, identify potential barriers, and gather valuable insights into areas for improvement. Usability testing is an iterative process that ensures the interface meets the diverse needs of users, guiding designers in refining and optimizing the visual elements based on user feedback. By embracing usability testing, designers foster a user-centric approach that prioritizes inclusivity, resulting in visually inclusive interfaces that resonate with a broad audience.

In conclusion, the design elements that accommodate users with visual impairments form a multifaceted approach that integrates considerations for color contrast, font choices, alternative text, navigation structures, animation effects, compatibility with assistive technologies, customizable color schemes, and accessible forms. By thoughtfully addressing these elements, designers contribute to the creation of visually inclusive interfaces that prioritize accessibility, usability, and a positive user experience for individuals of all abilities. The synergy of these design strategies ensures that digital content is not only visually appealing but also welcoming and accessible to a diverse user base. In embracing these considerations, designers play a pivotal role in shaping a digital landscape that values inclusivity and equal access for users with varying visual needs.

Highlight the importance of user testing specifically focused on accessibility.

User testing specifically focused on accessibility is a pivotal and indispensable phase in the design and development process, ensuring that digital products and interfaces are inclusive, equitable, and usable for individuals with diverse abilities. Accessibility in this context refers to the design and implementation of digital content and interfaces that consider the needs of users with disabilities, such as visual, auditory, motor, cognitive, and neurological impairments. The importance of user testing for accessibility lies in its ability to uncover potential barriers, validate design choices, and provide invaluable insights into the real-world experiences of users with disabilities. Traditional usability testing often falls short in addressing the unique challenges faced by individuals with disabilities, making dedicated accessibility testing an imperative step towards creating a digital landscape that is accessible to all.

One of the fundamental reasons why user testing focused on accessibility is crucial is its role in uncovering barriers that may impede users with disabilities from fully engaging with and benefiting from digital interfaces. Individuals with disabilities often encounter obstacles that are not immediately apparent during the design and development stages. By conducting dedicated accessibility testing with users who have diverse abilities, designers gain a deeper understanding of how different disabilities may impact the user experience. This process sheds light on potential challenges such as unclear navigation, lack of keyboard accessibility, or issues with screen reader compatibility. Identifying these barriers early in the development process allows designers to proactively address and rectify issues, ultimately creating a more inclusive and accessible digital product.

Moreover, user testing focused on accessibility serves as a crucial validation mechanism for design choices related to accessibility features. While adhering to established accessibility guidelines and standards is essential, user testing provides a reality check by assessing how well these features function in practice. For instance, the effectiveness of alternative text for images, proper labeling of form fields, and keyboard navigation can be confirmed through user testing. This validation process ensures that the implemented accessibility features not only meet technical specifications but also align with the practical needs and preferences of users with disabilities. The feedback obtained from users during these tests contributes to refining accessibility features and enhancing their usability, ultimately leading to a more effective and user-friendly accessible design.

An essential aspect of user testing focused on accessibility is its ability to capture the authentic experiences of individuals with disabilities in real-world scenarios. While designers may possess a theoretical understanding of accessibility requirements, user testing provides valuable insights into the day-to-day challenges faced by users with disabilities. Users with visual impairments may encounter difficulties navigating complex interfaces, individuals with motor impairments may struggle with interactive elements that are not optimized for keyboard navigation, and those with cognitive impairments may face challenges in understanding complex instructions. Observing and understanding these challenges through user testing empowers designers to make informed decisions that go beyond meeting compliance standards, contributing to a more empathetic and user-centric approach to accessibility.

Furthermore, user testing focused on accessibility is integral to the iterative design process, allowing designers to refine and improve digital interfaces based on continuous feedback from users with disabilities. The iterative nature of user testing aligns with the principles of user-centered design, emphasizing an ongoing dialogue between designers and users to ensure that the final product meets the evolving needs of its diverse user base. As users with disabilities provide feedback and insights during testing, designers can implement iterative changes, addressing identified issues and optimizing the accessibility of the interface. This iterative cycle fosters a dynamic design process where accessibility is not a one-time consideration but an ongoing commitment to refinement and improvement, resulting in digital products that continuously evolve to better serve users with diverse abilities.

The significance of user testing focused on accessibility is heightened by the fact that individuals with disabilities often face unique and diverse challenges that cannot be fully anticipated through theoretical assessments alone. This testing process serves as a bridge between design intentions and actual user experiences, offering a reality check on the effectiveness of accessibility features in accommodating the specific needs of users with disabilities. For example, individuals with color blindness may struggle with certain color combinations that designers may not have anticipated. By engaging users with diverse abilities in the testing process, designers gain firsthand insights into the nuanced challenges faced by different user groups, enabling them to make informed adjustments that cater to a broader range of accessibility needs.

Moreover, the legal and ethical implications of accessibility underscore the importance of dedicated user testing in this domain. Many countries and regions have established legal frameworks and regulations that mandate digital accessibility, emphasizing the need for organizations to ensure that their digital products are inclusive and accessible to individuals with disabilities. User testing focused on accessibility becomes a crucial component of compliance, allowing organizations to demonstrate their commitment to creating digital experiences that adhere to legal standards. Beyond legal considerations, there is an ethical imperative to prioritize accessibility in design, recognizing the rights of individuals with disabilities to access information and participate fully in the digital world. User testing becomes a tangible and measurable way for organizations to uphold these ethical principles and ensure their digital offerings are accessible to all.

Additionally, the insights gained from user testing focused on accessibility have broader implications for the overall user experience. Accessibility features that benefit users with disabilities often lead to improved usability and satisfaction for the entire user base. For example, designing for keyboard accessibility not only aids users with motor impairments but also benefits users who prefer using keyboard shortcuts or have situational limitations, such as when a mouse is not available. Captioned videos, initially designed for users with hearing impairments, enhance the experience for users in noisy environments or those who prefer muted content. Thus, the positive outcomes of accessibility-focused user testing extend beyond compliance and inclusion, positively impacting the usability and satisfaction of the entire user community.

In conclusion, user testing specifically focused on accessibility is an indispensable and multifaceted process that addresses the unique needs of individuals with disabilities, ensures compliance with legal standards, and contributes to a more inclusive and user-friendly digital landscape. Through the identification of barriers, validation of accessibility features, capturing authentic user experiences, and supporting the iterative design process, user testing plays a pivotal role in the development of digital interfaces that prioritize accessibility. The insights gained from testing not only contribute to compliance with legal standards but also align with ethical considerations, recognizing the rights of individuals with disabilities to access and engage with digital content on an equal footing. As technology continues to evolve, user testing focused on accessibility remains a cornerstone in the pursuit of digital inclusivity, equal access, and the creation of a more accessible and empathetic digital world.

Discuss how involving users with diverse abilities contributes to a more inclusive interface.

Involving users with diverse abilities in the design and development of interfaces is essential for creating a truly inclusive digital environment. This approach recognizes the vast spectrum of user capabilities and ensures that technological solutions cater to the needs of a broad and varied user base. By actively engaging individuals with diverse abilities, ranging from physical and cognitive disabilities to different cultural and linguistic backgrounds, designers gain invaluable insights into the challenges faced by users across the accessibility spectrum. This collaborative process fosters empathy and understanding, driving the creation of interfaces that go beyond mere compliance with accessibility standards to embrace a philosophy of universal design.

A key benefit of involving users with diverse abilities is the identification and elimination of barriers that may unintentionally exist in digital interfaces. Users with different needs and preferences provide nuanced feedback that enables designers to uncover potential pitfalls and make informed decisions about interface elements. For instance, individuals with visual impairments may offer insights into the effectiveness of alternative text for images, while those with motor impairments can highlight challenges related to navigation and interaction. This iterative feedback loop empowers designers to refine their creations, resulting in interfaces that are not only accessible but also intuitive and user-friendly for everyone.

Moreover, involving users with diverse abilities promotes the development of assistive technologies and features that can enhance the overall user experience. By understanding the specific requirements of different user groups, designers can implement functionalities such as screen readers, voice commands, or customizable interfaces that adapt to individual preferences. This proactive approach not only accommodates users with disabilities but also creates a more adaptable and customizable interface for all users, acknowledging the inherent diversity in how individuals interact with technology.

The inclusivity achieved through user involvement extends beyond the realm of physical or cognitive disabilities. By engaging individuals from various cultural and linguistic backgrounds, designers can create interfaces that resonate with a global audience. Language choices, culturally sensitive design elements, and considerations for diverse communication styles all contribute to a more inclusive interface that transcends geographical and cultural boundaries. This cultural inclusivity not only enhances the user experience for people from different backgrounds but also reflects a commitment to breaking down digital divides and fostering a sense of belonging for all users.

Furthermore, involving users with diverse abilities promotes a shift from a one-size-fits-all mentality to an approach centered on individual user needs. This user-centric paradigm recognizes that accessibility is not a checkbox but an ongoing process that evolves with technology and user expectations. By incorporating feedback from users with diverse abilities, designers gain a deeper understanding of the varied ways in which individuals engage with digital interfaces. This understanding informs the development of interfaces that are adaptable, scalable, and future-proof, ensuring that technological advancements do not inadvertently create new barriers but instead continue to enhance inclusivity.

The collaborative nature of involving users with diverse abilities also extends to the testing phase, where real-world scenarios and usage patterns are considered. By including individuals with different abilities in usability testing, designers can observe firsthand how their creations perform in diverse contexts. This dynamic testing process not only identifies potential issues but also validates the effectiveness of accessibility features and ensures that they enhance rather than hinder the user experience. This iterative testing and refinement cycle results in interfaces that are robust, reliable, and capable of withstanding the complexities of real-world usage.

In conclusion, involving users with diverse abilities in the design and development of interfaces is instrumental in creating a more inclusive digital landscape. This approach not only addresses the specific needs of users with disabilities but also fosters a culture of empathy, understanding, and adaptability. By actively engaging with individuals across the accessibility spectrum, designers gain invaluable insights that lead to the creation of interfaces that are not only accessible but also intuitive, adaptable, and culturally sensitive. The ultimate goal is to transcend the limitations of traditional design paradigms and embrace a universal design philosophy that ensures digital interfaces are welcoming and usable for everyone, regardless of their abilities or backgrounds.

Discuss legal requirements and ethical considerations related to accessibility.

Legal requirements and ethical considerations surrounding accessibility are pivotal components of the digital landscape, emphasizing the importance of inclusivity and equal access for individuals with diverse abilities. From a legal standpoint, various international and national legislations mandate accessibility standards to ensure that digital interfaces are barrier-free. The Americans with Disabilities Act (ADA) in the United States, for example, requires that public accommodations, including digital platforms, are accessible to individuals with disabilities. Similarly, the Web Content Accessibility Guidelines (WCAG) provide a global framework developed by the World Wide Web Consortium (W3C) to guide organizations in creating accessible web content. Compliance with such legal frameworks is not just a matter of meeting regulatory requirements; it is an ethical imperative that underscores the principles of equality, dignity, and respect for all individuals.

Ethical considerations in the realm of accessibility extend beyond mere legal compliance, emphasizing the moral responsibility of technology creators to foster inclusivity. Designers and developers must recognize that accessibility is not merely a checkbox to be ticked off but an ongoing commitment to creating technology that serves everyone, regardless of their abilities. The ethical obligation to prioritize accessibility is rooted in the principles of justice and fairness, acknowledging that exclusionary digital experiences perpetuate systemic inequalities. Upholding these ethical considerations involves embracing a user-centric approach that actively involves individuals with diverse abilities in the design and testing processes, ensuring their voices are heard and their needs are addressed.

Moreover, ethical considerations extend to the broader societal impact of digital exclusion. In an interconnected world where digital platforms play a central role in various aspects of life, from education and employment to social interaction, excluding certain individuals from these spaces amplifies existing inequalities. The ethical imperative, therefore, demands a commitment to dismantling barriers and actively working towards a more inclusive digital society. This includes a recognition that accessibility is not solely the responsibility of individuals with disabilities but a collective societal effort to create an environment where everyone can participate fully and contribute meaningfully.

A critical ethical dimension of accessibility involves designing with empathy, considering the diverse ways individuals interact with technology. This requires going beyond the minimum standards set by regulations and striving for user experiences that are not just accessible but also enjoyable, empowering, and respectful of individual autonomy. Ethical designers recognize the unique challenges faced by different user groups and actively seek to address these challenges in their creations, fostering a sense of belonging and dignity for all users.

Additionally, ethical considerations underscore the importance of staying abreast of technological advancements and proactively addressing emerging accessibility challenges. As technology evolves, so do the potential barriers that may arise for individuals with diverse abilities. Ethical designers and developers remain vigilant in anticipating and mitigating these challenges, ensuring that technological progress does not inadvertently exclude certain segments of the population. This proactive approach aligns with the ethical principle of continuous improvement, recognizing that the pursuit of accessibility is an ongoing journey rather than a static destination.

Ethical considerations also emphasize the significance of transparency and accountability in the development process. Designers and developers should communicate openly about their commitment to accessibility, the steps taken to ensure inclusivity, and any challenges encountered along the way. Transparency builds trust and encourages collaboration with stakeholders, including individuals with disabilities, advocacy groups, and the wider community. Moreover, transparency fosters a culture of learning and improvement, allowing the industry as a whole to benefit from shared insights and best practices.

In conclusion, legal requirements and ethical considerations play integral roles in shaping the landscape of digital accessibility. Legal frameworks provide a foundation for ensuring compliance and accountability, establishing a baseline for creating digital interfaces that are accessible to all. However, ethical considerations elevate the discourse beyond legal obligations, emphasizing the moral imperative to create inclusive, respectful, and empowering digital experiences. The synergy between legal requirements and ethical principles creates a robust foundation for fostering a digital ecosystem where accessibility is not just a regulatory checkbox but a fundamental aspect of designing technology that serves the diverse needs of all individuals. Upholding both legal and ethical standards ensures that the digital landscape becomes a more inclusive and equitable space for everyone, regardless of their abilities or backgrounds.

Explore the impact of accessibility regulations on UI design practices.

Accessibility regulations wield a profound influence on UI (User Interface) design practices, reshaping the landscape and instigating a paradigm shift towards inclusivity. As digital platforms become increasingly integral to daily life, regulations such as the Web Content Accessibility Guidelines (WCAG) emerge as beacons, directing UI designers to create interfaces that accommodate users with diverse abilities. These regulations act as catalysts, compelling designers to transcend traditional approaches and adopt more holistic methodologies. The impact is most evident in the meticulous consideration given to various elements, ranging from color contrast and font sizes to navigation structures and interactive components. The imperative to adhere to accessibility regulations drives designers to scrutinize every aspect of the UI, ensuring that it is not only aesthetically pleasing but also functional and accessible to a broad spectrum of users.

The influence of accessibility regulations on UI design practices extends beyond mere compliance; it fosters a cultural shift towards user-centricity and empathy. Designers are prompted to view accessibility not as a checkbox to be marked off but as an integral aspect of their creative process. By incorporating accessibility considerations from the outset, designers actively engage with the principles of universal design, striving to create interfaces that are inherently inclusive. This shift in mindset results in the integration of features that cater to users with various needs, such as alternative text for images, keyboard navigation options, and resizable text. Accessibility ceases to be a retrofitting exercise and becomes an integral part of the design ethos, enhancing the user experience for everyone.

Furthermore, accessibility regulations propel UI designers to collaborate more closely with individuals who have diverse abilities. This collaborative approach ensures that the lived experiences of users with disabilities are taken into account during the design process. User testing involving individuals with various abilities becomes a cornerstone of UI design practices, providing invaluable insights into the effectiveness of different interface elements. This collaborative effort not only enhances the accessibility of the UI but also contributes to a more robust and user-friendly design. Designers, through such collaboration, gain a deeper understanding of the challenges faced by users with diverse abilities, allowing for the creation of interfaces that go beyond the minimum requirements of regulations and cater to the nuanced needs of the user community.

The impact of accessibility regulations on UI design practices is especially evident in the meticulous attention given to visual and interactive elements. Color contrast, for instance, becomes a critical consideration to ensure legibility for users with visual impairments. Designers must navigate the nuances of color choices to guarantee readability and comprehension for all users, aligning their creations with the specific guidelines outlined in accessibility regulations. Similarly, interactive components such as buttons and links are scrutinized to ensure they are operable via various input methods, including keyboard navigation and screen readers. These considerations, driven by accessibility regulations, lead to UI designs that are not only visually appealing but also functional and accessible to a diverse audience.

Moreover, accessibility regulations serve as a catalyst for innovation in UI design. Designers are compelled to think creatively and problem-solve to meet accessibility standards while maintaining a high level of user engagement. This drive for innovation often results in the development of novel design patterns and solutions that benefit all users, not just those with disabilities. For instance, efforts to enhance keyboard navigation may lead to streamlined and efficient interactions for all users. The pursuit of accessible and inclusive design fosters a culture of continuous improvement and innovation, pushing UI designers to explore new possibilities and challenge conventional norms.

The influence of accessibility regulations extends to the development of design tools and frameworks, which, in turn, shape UI design practices. Design software and platforms increasingly incorporate features that facilitate the creation of accessible interfaces. Templates and components are designed with accessibility in mind, simplifying the process for designers to adhere to regulations without compromising on creativity. The integration of accessibility features into design tools not only streamlines the design process but also serves as an educational tool, raising awareness among designers about the importance of inclusive design practices.

Furthermore, accessibility regulations have a ripple effect on the overall design ecosystem, influencing not only individual designers but also educational institutions and industry standards. Design education now emphasizes the significance of accessibility, ensuring that the next generation of designers is well-versed in creating interfaces that prioritize inclusivity. Industry standards evolve to reflect the growing importance of accessibility, with organizations recognizing the benefits of creating products and services that cater to a diverse audience. This holistic impact extends the influence of accessibility regulations beyond individual design practices to shape the broader design landscape.

In conclusion, accessibility regulations wield a transformative influence on UI design practices, ushering in an era where inclusivity is not just encouraged but mandated. These regulations drive designers to adopt a more user-centric and empathetic approach, prompting a shift in mindset towards universal design principles. The impact is evident in the meticulous consideration given to visual and interactive elements, the collaboration with users of diverse abilities, and the drive for innovation in UI design. As accessibility regulations continue to evolve, their influence will likely shape not only individual design practices but also the collective ethos of the design community, fostering a commitment to creating digital interfaces that are accessible, functional, and enriching for users with diverse abilities.

Chapter 6: Innovations in UI Technology: Past, Present, and Future

Establish the dynamic nature of UI technology and its continuous evolution.

The field of User Interface (UI) technology is inherently dynamic, characterized by a continuous and rapid evolution that reflects the relentless progress of the digital landscape. This dynamism stems from a confluence of technological advancements, changing user expectations, and the perpetual quest for improved user experiences. One of the driving forces behind the dynamic nature of UI technology is the ever-advancing hardware and software capabilities. As processors become more powerful, graphics rendering technologies advance, and storage capacities expand, UI designers are presented with new possibilities for creating interfaces that are not only visually stunning but also functionally sophisticated. The constant march of technology enables the incorporation of innovative features, such as augmented reality, virtual reality, and gesture-based interactions, transforming the way users engage with digital interfaces.

The evolution of UI technology is also intricately tied to the shifting landscape of user behaviors and expectations. Users, influenced by the prevalence of technology in their daily lives, develop a more sophisticated understanding of what constitutes a seamless and intuitive user experience. This evolving user consciousness prompts UI designers to adapt and refine their approaches continually. User feedback, gathered through analytics and direct engagement, becomes a compass guiding the evolution of UI elements and interactions. The rise of mobile devices, for example, has necessitated responsive design practices, as users increasingly expect interfaces that seamlessly transition across various screen sizes and orientations. The dynamic interplay between user expectations and UI technology evolution fuels a perpetual cycle of innovation and refinement.

Furthermore, the dynamic nature of UI technology is evident in the iterative design processes employed by UI designers. The development of user interfaces is seldom a linear journey; instead, it involves a constant cycle of prototyping, testing, and refinement. Designers harness the power of iterative design to gather user feedback, identify pain points, and make informed adjustments. This iterative approach allows for the incorporation of user insights into the design process, ensuring that UIs evolve in response to real-world usage patterns and user preferences. Whether through A/B testing, usability studies, or user interviews, designers engage in an ongoing dialogue with users, adapting and refining UI elements to align with changing needs and expectations.

The dynamic nature of UI technology is further accentuated by the iterative releases of software and applications. Continuous updates and feature releases are common in the digital realm, driven by the need to address bugs, improve performance, and introduce new functionalities. Each update represents an opportunity for UI designers to refine and enhance the user interface based on real-world usage data and evolving design principles. This perpetual cycle of updates ensures that UIs remain relevant, secure, and aligned with the ever-changing technological landscape.

Another dimension of the dynamic nature of UI technology is the influence of design trends and aesthetics. Design trends, influenced by cultural shifts, emerging technologies, and societal changes, shape the visual language of UIs. UI designers are not only tasked with creating interfaces that are functional and user-friendly but also with staying attuned to the latest design trends. The shift from skeuomorphic design to flat design, for example, reflects a broader cultural shift towards minimalism and simplicity. Designers navigate this dynamic landscape, striking a balance between adhering to established design principles and incorporating innovative visual elements that resonate with contemporary sensibilities.

Moreover, the dynamic nature of UI technology is intertwined with the globalization of design practices. As digital interfaces transcend geographical boundaries, UI designers must consider cultural nuances and diverse user expectations. The evolution of UI technology involves a recognition that design solutions need to be adaptable and culturally sensitive to cater to a global audience. Localization efforts, considering language, cultural symbolism, and regional preferences, become integral aspects of UI design, reflecting the dynamic nature of technology as it reaches users from diverse backgrounds.

The advent of emerging technologies also contributes to the dynamic evolution of UI design. Technologies such as artificial intelligence, machine learning, and voice recognition introduce new dimensions to user interactions, requiring designers to explore innovative ways of integrating these capabilities into interfaces. Conversational interfaces, for instance, leverage natural language processing to create more intuitive interactions, reshaping the way users engage with digital platforms. The integration of such technologies into UI design represents not only a response to technological advancements but also a proactive exploration of possibilities, marking the dynamic nature of UI technology as it embraces cutting-edge innovations.

Additionally, the dynamic nature of UI technology is closely tied to the ever-evolving regulatory landscape. As concerns about privacy, security, and accessibility gain prominence, UI designers must navigate a complex web of compliance requirements. Regulatory frameworks, such as the General Data Protection Regulation (GDPR) and accessibility standards like the Web Content Accessibility Guidelines (WCAG), introduce new considerations that shape the evolution of UI design practices. The need to ensure ethical design, prioritize user privacy, and adhere to accessibility principles adds layers of complexity to the dynamic landscape of UI technology, necessitating constant vigilance and adaptation.

In conclusion, the dynamic nature of UI technology is an inherent and defining characteristic of the digital era. It is fueled by the relentless march of technological progress, changing user expectations, iterative design processes, software updates, design trends, globalization, and the integration of emerging technologies. UI designers navigate this dynamic landscape by embracing iterative design methodologies, staying attuned to user feedback, and incorporating the latest technological advancements. The constant evolution of UI technology reflects not only the adaptability of designers but also the industry's commitment to creating interfaces that resonate with users, push the boundaries of innovation, and remain responsive to the ever-changing digital landscape.

Discuss the symbiotic relationship between technological advancements and interface innovations.

The symbiotic relationship between technological advancements and interface innovations is at the core of the dynamic evolution observed in the digital landscape. Technological progress, marked by continuous breakthroughs in hardware, software, and connectivity, serves as the catalyst for pushing the boundaries of interface design. As hardware capabilities advance, offering more processing power, enhanced graphics rendering, and improved sensors, designers are empowered to create interfaces that were previously unthinkable. High-resolution displays, seamless animations, and immersive experiences become not only possible but expected as technology continues to march forward. The synergy between technological advancements and interface innovations propels the design community into uncharted territories, unlocking new possibilities and reshaping the way users interact with digital platforms.

Conversely, the demand for innovative interfaces drives technological advancements as designers explore ways to deliver richer and more engaging user experiences. The pursuit of enhanced usability, aesthetics, and functionality prompts a continuous cycle of innovation in response to user expectations. For instance, the proliferation of touchscreens in smartphones and tablets was not just a technological breakthrough but a deliberate response to the evolving needs of users who sought more intuitive and direct ways of interaction. The interplay between user demands and technological capabilities fuels a reciprocal relationship where each side spurs the other towards greater heights.

One significant area where technological advancements and interface innovations intertwine is in the realm of user interaction modalities. The evolution from traditional mouse and keyboard inputs to touchscreens, voice commands, gesture recognition, and even brain-computer interfaces is a testament to the symbiotic relationship at play. Technological advancements in sensors, machine learning, and natural language processing enable the development of interfaces that understand and respond to a diverse array of inputs. Conversely, as new interaction modalities emerge, designers are challenged to create interfaces that leverage these capabilities effectively, ushering in an era where user interactions become more fluid, natural, and context-aware.

Moreover, the symbiotic relationship between technological advancements and interface innovations is evident in the realm of augmented reality (AR) and virtual reality (VR). The advancement of display technologies, along with improvements in graphics processing units (GPUs) and motion tracking, has fueled the rise of immersive interfaces. AR overlays digital information onto the real world, enhancing users' perception and interaction with their environment. VR, on the other hand, transports users to entirely virtual spaces, creating experiences that go beyond the constraints of the physical world. The marriage of technological prowess and interface design in AR and VR exemplifies how each propels the other forward, creating novel and transformative user experiences.

Furthermore, the symbiotic relationship extends to the democratization of technology through accessibility and inclusivity. As technological advancements make devices more powerful and affordable, designers are presented with opportunities to create interfaces that cater to a broader audience. The push for inclusivity drives innovations such as screen readers, voice commands, and customizable interfaces, ensuring that individuals with diverse abilities can engage with digital platforms. In turn, the demand for accessible interfaces stimulates advancements in assistive technologies, creating a positive feedback loop that aligns technological progress with the values of inclusivity and equal access.

The convergence of mobile technology and connectivity provides another lens through which to examine the symbiotic relationship between technological advancements and interface innovations. The evolution from feature phones to smartphones and, subsequently, to the era of ubiquitous connectivity with 5G, has fundamentally transformed how users interact with digital interfaces. The increased bandwidth and reduced latency afforded by advanced networks enable seamless streaming, real-time collaboration, and the integration of cloud-based services, shaping user expectations for responsive and always-connected interfaces. Designers, in turn, leverage these capabilities to create interfaces that leverage the power of the cloud, facilitate real-time interactions, and provide a consistent user experience across devices.

Additionally, the symbiotic relationship is evident in the evolution of design tools and frameworks. As technological advancements provide more powerful computing resources, designers gain access to sophisticated tools that streamline the design process. High-fidelity prototyping, real-time collaboration, and augmented reality design tools are manifestations of how technological progress enhances the capabilities of designers. Simultaneously, the demand for more efficient design workflows and the need to accommodate diverse design requirements drive the development of tools and frameworks that leverage the latest technological advancements. This reciprocal influence between technology and design tools shapes the landscape in which designers operate, enabling them to push the boundaries of creativity and efficiency.

The concept of the Internet of Things (IoT) serves as another testament to the symbiotic relationship between technological advancements and interface innovations. As an increasing number of devices become interconnected, from smart home appliances to wearable devices and industrial sensors, designers are tasked with creating interfaces that facilitate meaningful interactions within this complex ecosystem. The integration of IoT technologies not only demands advanced connectivity solutions but also challenges designers to develop interfaces that provide a cohesive and seamless experience across a diverse array of devices. The symbiosis between technological advancements and interface design in the IoT space reflects the intricate dance between hardware capabilities and the need for intuitive, user-friendly interfaces in an increasingly interconnected world.

Furthermore, artificial intelligence (AI) represents a domain where the symbiotic relationship is particularly pronounced. Technological advancements in machine learning, natural language processing, and computer vision empower AI to comprehend user behavior, preferences, and context. AI-driven interfaces, such as chatbots and virtual assistants, adapt to user interactions, providing personalized and context-aware experiences. Simultaneously, the demand for interfaces that leverage AI capabilities drives further research and development in AI technologies, resulting in a continuous cycle of improvement and innovation.

In conclusion, the symbiotic relationship between technological advancements and interface innovations defines the ever-evolving landscape of digital experiences. This intricate dance shapes how users interact with technology, pushing the boundaries of what is possible and redefining the expectations for seamless and engaging interfaces. As technological progress unlocks new capabilities, designers respond by envisioning and creating interfaces that leverage these advancements to provide richer, more intuitive, and more immersive user experiences. The reciprocal influence between technology and interface design not only propels innovation but also reflects a profound interconnectedness that defines the trajectory of the digital era.

Explore historical milestones in UI technology.

The historical journey of User Interface (UI) technology is a captivating narrative that unfolds through a series of transformative milestones, each contributing to the evolution of digital interactions. The earliest days of computing, characterized by massive mainframes and punch cards, set the stage for the rudimentary interfaces that marked the dawn of human-computer interaction. It was in the 1960s that the first graphical user interfaces (GUIs) emerged, notably with the work done at the Stanford Research Institute, where Douglas Engelbart presented the groundbreaking concept of a mouse as a pointing device. Engelbart's "Mother of All Demos" in 1968 showcased not only the mouse but also collaborative editing, hypermedia, and video conferencing, laying the foundation for the interactive computing experience.

The 1970s witnessed the advent of the Xerox Alto, a groundbreaking computer that featured the first GUI with icons, windows, and a mouse. Developed at Xerox PARC (Palo Alto Research Center), this revolutionary system marked a leap forward in UI design by introducing visual metaphors for interacting with digital content. Although the Xerox Alto did not reach commercial success, its influence was profound, serving as an inspiration for subsequent UI innovations. The Xerox Star, introduced in the early 1980s, can be considered the first commercial computer system with a GUI, featuring a desktop metaphor and the use of a mouse for navigation.

The year 1984 saw the launch of the Apple Macintosh, a milestone that catapulted GUIs into the mainstream. Apple's iconic "1984" Super Bowl commercial heralded a new era of computing, introducing the masses to the concept of a user-friendly interface. The Macintosh GUI, with its desktop metaphor, icons, and point-and-click interaction, became a hallmark of intuitive computing. This watershed moment not only defined Apple's trajectory but also set a standard for UI design that would influence the industry for years to come.

Microsoft Windows, first released in 1985, further popularized the GUI concept in the personal computing realm. Windows 3.0, launched in 1990, marked a significant upgrade with improved graphics and the introduction of scalable TrueType fonts. Windows gradually became the dominant operating system for personal computers, solidifying the GUI as the standard interface paradigm for mainstream users. The competition between Microsoft and Apple during this era fueled innovation, leading to the refinement of GUI elements and the introduction of features such as drag-and-drop functionality.

The 1990s witnessed the rise of the World Wide Web, ushering in a new era of UI design with the advent of web browsers. Tim Berners-Lee's creation of the first web browser, WorldWideWeb (later renamed Nexus), in 1990 marked the genesis of the internet as we know it. Subsequently, the introduction of Mosaic in 1993 and Netscape Navigator in 1994 popularized web browsing, making the internet accessible to a broader audience. The browser wars between Netscape and Microsoft's Internet Explorer in the late 1990s spurred innovations in UI design for web interfaces, laying the groundwork for the interactive and dynamic web experiences we have today.

As the internet continued to evolve, the early 2000s brought forth a shift towards a more dynamic and interactive web with the advent of Web 2.0. This era saw the rise of social media platforms, such as Facebook and Twitter, which introduced novel UI patterns like real-time updates and asynchronous content loading. The emergence of AJAX (Asynchronous JavaScript and XML) allowed web pages to update without requiring a full reload, enhancing the user experience and paving the way for more responsive and interactive web applications.

The mid-2000s witnessed the entry of mobile technology into the UI landscape, forever altering the way users interact with digital content. Apple's introduction of the iPhone in 2007, with its touch-based interface and the App Store, set a new standard for mobile UI design. The capacitive touchscreens and gesture-based interactions revolutionized the concept of a mobile interface, making it more intuitive and user-friendly. Google's Android operating system, launched in 2008, contributed to the diversification of mobile UIs, fostering competition and innovation in the smartphone market.

The concept of skeuomorphic design, where digital interfaces mimicked real-world objects, gained prominence during the early smartphone era. Apple, under the guidance of Steve Jobs, favored this approach, as seen in the design of apps like the Notes and Calendar, which resembled physical counterparts. However, as the industry matured, a shift towards flat design gained momentum. Microsoft's Windows 8, introduced in 2012, embraced flat design principles with its Metro UI, eschewing skeuomorphic elements for a cleaner and more modern aesthetic. This marked a significant departure from the visual styles of the past and influenced subsequent design trends.

The 2010s witnessed the rise of responsive design, a paradigm shift prompted by the proliferation of various devices with different screen sizes and resolutions. Ethan Marcotte coined the term "responsive web design" in a seminal article in 2010, advocating for designing websites that adapt to various screen sizes, creating a consistent user experience across devices. This approach became pivotal as the diversity of devices used for internet access expanded, encompassing smartphones, tablets, laptops, and desktops.

Voice user interfaces (VUIs) gained prominence in the latter half of the 2010s, driven by the widespread adoption of virtual assistants like Apple's Siri, Google Assistant, and Amazon's Alexa. The integration of voice commands into digital interfaces represented a shift towards more natural and conversational interactions. Users could now interact with their devices and applications using voice, contributing to the multimodal nature of contemporary UIs.

In recent years, the concept of "dark mode" has become a notable trend in UI design. Originating as a feature for reducing eye strain in low-light conditions, dark mode has become a popular aesthetic choice for applications and operating systems. It not only addresses usability concerns but also aligns with the visual preferences of many users.

Looking ahead, the future of UI technology is poised for further evolution, shaped by emerging technologies such as augmented reality (AR), virtual reality (VR), and the Internet of Things (IoT). AR interfaces, like those seen in applications like Pokémon GO, overlay digital information on the real world, blurring the lines between the physical and digital realms. VR interfaces, as seen in immersive gaming experiences, offer entirely virtual environments for user interaction. The interconnected nature of IoT introduces interfaces that facilitate interactions between a myriad of connected devices, from smart homes to industrial sensors.

In conclusion, the historical milestones in UI technology narrate a compelling story of continuous innovation and adaptation. From the humble beginnings of punch cards and command-line interfaces to the touchscreens, gestures, and voice commands of the present day, the journey of UI technology reflects the relentless pursuit of creating interfaces that are not only functional but also intuitive, engaging, and responsive to the needs of users. The milestones mentioned here represent pivotal moments in this ongoing narrative, each contributing to the rich tapestry of UI evolution that has defined the digital era.

Discuss innovations such as the mouse, touchscreens, and gesture controls that shaped the UI landscape.

The evolution of User Interface (UI) technology has been punctuated by transformative innovations that have fundamentally shaped the way users interact with digital systems. One such groundbreaking invention was the mouse, introduced in the late 1960s by Douglas Engelbart and his team at the Stanford Research Institute. The mouse was a paradigm shift from the conventional punch cards and command-line interfaces of the time, offering a tangible and intuitive means of interacting with computers. This handheld pointing device, coupled with a graphical user interface (GUI), introduced a novel way of navigating and manipulating digital content. The introduction of the mouse marked the beginning of a more user-centric approach to computing, providing users with an unprecedented level of control over their interactions with computers.

In the realm of touchscreens, another pivotal innovation unfolded, reshaping the UI landscape in profound ways. The concept of touch-based interaction gained prominence with the advent of the Apple iPhone in 2007. Apple's incorporation of a capacitive touchscreen, sensitive to the electrical impulses of human touch, revolutionized the smartphone industry. Touchscreens eliminated the need for physical keyboards and buttons, offering users an immersive and tactile way to engage with their devices. The swipe, pinch-to-zoom, and tap gestures became ubiquitous, fundamentally altering user expectations and paving the way for a new era of mobile computing. Touchscreens not only transformed the design of smartphones but also influenced the development of tablets, interactive kiosks, and other digital interfaces, fostering a more direct and intimate connection between users and technology.

Building on the success of touchscreens, gesture controls emerged as a novel and futuristic way to interact with digital systems. Gesture controls enable users to manipulate digital content through hand movements, without the need for physical contact with a device. Microsoft's Kinect, released in 2010, represented a milestone in gesture-based UI technology, allowing users to control gaming consoles and other applications through body movements. Similarly, hand-tracking technology, as seen in devices like the Leap Motion controller, enables users to interact with computers using natural hand gestures. These innovations transcend the traditional input methods of mice and keyboards, offering a more immersive and intuitive means of interaction. Gesture controls have found applications not only in gaming but also in areas such as virtual reality (VR), where users can navigate and manipulate virtual environments using hand gestures, further expanding the possibilities of UI design.

Furthermore, voice recognition technology has played a pivotal role in shaping the UI landscape, providing users with a hands-free and natural means of interaction. Early voice recognition systems, characterized by limited accuracy, paved the way for advancements in natural language processing and machine learning. The integration of voice assistants like Apple's Siri, Google Assistant, and Amazon's Alexa into smartphones and smart speakers marked a transformative shift. Users could now perform a myriad of tasks, from setting reminders to controlling smart home devices, using voice commands. Voice recognition has extended beyond personal assistants, finding applications in dictation software, accessibility features, and automotive interfaces. This innovation has not only enhanced convenience but has also contributed to the development of more inclusive and accessible UI designs.

The advent of multitouch technology represents another milestone that has significantly impacted the UI landscape. Multitouch screens, capable of detecting multiple points of contact simultaneously, introduced a new level of interactivity and responsiveness. This innovation was popularized by devices like the Apple iPhone, where users could perform complex gestures using multiple fingers, such as pinch-to-zoom or two-finger scrolling. Multitouch technology has become integral to the design of smartphones, tablets, and touch-enabled laptops, enabling users to manipulate digital content with greater precision and fluidity. This innovation has transcended personal devices, influencing the design of interactive displays, kiosks, and collaborative workspaces, fostering more dynamic and engaging user experiences.

The concept of haptic feedback, or the sense of touch in UI interactions, has emerged as an innovative approach to enhance the user experience. Haptic feedback technologies, such as vibration motors or actuators embedded in devices, provide tactile sensations in response to user interactions. This tactile feedback adds a layer of realism to touch-based interfaces, mimicking the feel of physical buttons or textures. Haptic feedback is utilized in various applications, from smartphones that provide subtle vibrations during typing to virtual reality controllers that simulate the sensation of touching virtual objects. This innovation adds a sensory dimension to UI interactions, creating a more immersive and engaging user experience.

In the realm of augmented reality (AR), innovations such as spatial computing have redefined how users interact with digital content in physical spaces. Spatial computing involves the understanding and integration of digital information into the user's physical environment. Devices like Microsoft's HoloLens and Magic Leap utilize spatial computing to overlay holographic images onto the real world. Users can interact with digital content as if it coexists with their physical surroundings, introducing a new paradigm for UI design. Spatial computing has applications beyond entertainment, extending to fields such as education, healthcare, and industrial design, where users can manipulate and visualize digital information in three-dimensional space.

Moreover, the advent of biometric authentication has reshaped security measures and user access in UI design. Biometric technologies, including fingerprint recognition, facial recognition, and iris scanning, offer a secure and convenient means of user identification. Mobile devices, in particular, have embraced biometric authentication as a method to unlock devices, authorize payments, and access sensitive information. This innovation not only enhances security but also streamlines the user experience by eliminating the need for traditional password-based authentication. Biometric authentication has found applications in various contexts, from unlocking smartphones to securing access to buildings and financial transactions, contributing to a more seamless and secure UI landscape.

As technology continues to advance, the integration of artificial intelligence (AI) into UI design has become a transformative force. AI-driven interfaces leverage machine learning algorithms to understand user behavior, preferences, and context, enabling personalized and adaptive interactions. Recommendations, predictive typing, and smart assistants are examples of AI-driven features that enhance user experiences by anticipating user needs. Chatbots and virtual assistants, powered by natural language processing, engage users in conversational interactions, providing information and performing tasks. The intersection of AI and UI design introduces a level of sophistication that goes beyond traditional rule-based systems, opening avenues for more dynamic and context-aware user interfaces.

In conclusion, the innovations of the mouse, touchscreens, gesture controls, and other advancements have played instrumental roles in shaping the UI landscape throughout history. These innovations have not only revolutionized how users interact with digital devices but have also influenced the design principles and expectations that underpin modern UIs. The journey from the mouse to touchscreens, gestures, and beyond illustrates the ongoing quest for more intuitive, engaging, and inclusive user interfaces. As technology continues to evolve, the symbiotic relationship between innovation and UI design remains at the forefront, ushering in an era of ever-expanding possibilities for human-computer interaction.

Discuss the contemporary technological landscape in UI design.

The contemporary technological landscape in UI (User Interface) design is characterized by a dynamic interplay of diverse elements, reflecting the relentless pace of technological evolution and its profound impact on how users interact with digital interfaces. One of the defining features of the contemporary UI design landscape is the prevalence of responsive and adaptive design principles. With users accessing digital content across a myriad of devices, including smartphones, tablets, laptops, and desktops, designers embrace responsive design to ensure a consistent and optimized user experience across various screen sizes and resolutions. The flexibility inherent in responsive design caters to the diverse ways users engage with digital interfaces, fostering accessibility and usability in the modern multi-device ecosystem.

The rise of mobile technology has been a transformative force in shaping the contemporary UI landscape. Mobile devices, particularly smartphones, have become ubiquitous tools for accessing information, communication, and entertainment. As a result, UI designers prioritize mobile-first or mobile-friendly approaches, acknowledging the significance of creating interfaces that seamlessly adapt to the constraints and possibilities of smaller screens. Mobile UI design extends beyond mere responsiveness, encompassing considerations such as touch-friendly interactions, gesture controls, and optimizing performance for varied network conditions. The ubiquity of mobile devices has not only influenced UI design principles but has also catalyzed the development of mobile applications that redefine how users interact with digital content on the go.

In tandem with the mobile revolution, the concept of mobile apps has become a cornerstone of contemporary UI design. Mobile applications offer users a focused and tailored experience, often leveraging platform-specific design guidelines to ensure consistency with the native environment. App design extends beyond aesthetics, encompassing considerations of user engagement, intuitive navigation, and seamless functionality. The contemporary app landscape is diverse, ranging from social media platforms and productivity tools to gaming and e-commerce applications. As users increasingly rely on apps for various tasks, UI designers grapple with the challenge of creating interfaces that balance simplicity, functionality, and a visually appealing user experience.

The emergence of touchscreens as a dominant input method has profoundly influenced contemporary UI design. Touch gestures, such as swiping, tapping, and pinching, have become ingrained in user interactions across devices. The tactile nature of touchscreens not only necessitates considerations for touch-friendly interface elements but also opens avenues for more immersive and intuitive user experiences. Gesture controls, in particular, have evolved beyond touchscreens to include technologies like motion sensors and hand-tracking devices. These innovations redefine how users navigate and manipulate digital content, offering a more natural and fluid interaction paradigm that aligns with contemporary expectations.

The integration of voice user interfaces (VUIs) into the contemporary UI landscape represents a significant shift in how users interact with digital systems. Voice assistants, powered by natural language processing and machine learning, enable users to perform tasks, retrieve information, and control devices through spoken commands. VUIs add a layer of accessibility, particularly for users with mobility challenges, and contribute to the creation of hands-free and eyes-free interactions. As voice recognition technology advances, UI designers explore ways to incorporate VUIs seamlessly into various contexts, from smartphones and smart speakers to automotive interfaces and smart home devices.

Artificial intelligence (AI) stands as a transformative force in contemporary UI design, leveraging machine learning algorithms to enhance user experiences in sophisticated ways. AI-driven interfaces analyze user behavior, preferences, and contextual data to deliver personalized and adaptive interactions. Recommendations, predictive typing, and content curation are examples of AI features that elevate user engagement by anticipating user needs. Chatbots and virtual assistants, fueled by AI technologies, engage users in conversational interactions, providing information and performing tasks in a more natural and human-like manner. The fusion of AI with UI design introduces a level of intelligence that enables interfaces to evolve and adapt based on user input and evolving trends.

The contemporary UI design landscape is marked by the integration of augmented reality (AR) and virtual reality (VR) technologies. AR overlays digital information onto the real world, enhancing users' perception and interaction with their environment. AR applications, ranging from navigation tools to educational experiences, redefine how users engage with information in physical spaces. VR, on the other hand, transports users to entirely virtual environments, creating immersive and interactive experiences. VR interfaces, often seen in gaming and training applications, demand a reimagining of traditional UI elements to suit the three-dimensional and immersive nature of virtual environments. Both AR and VR contribute to a more spatial and experiential dimension in contemporary UI design, expanding the possibilities of human-computer interaction.

Dark mode, a contemporary design trend, has gained popularity in UI design across various platforms and applications. Dark mode offers an alternative color scheme that employs darker backgrounds and lighter text, reducing eye strain in low-light conditions and providing a visually pleasing aesthetic. Users appreciate the flexibility to choose between light and dark modes, and designers leverage this feature not only for its visual appeal but also for its practical benefits in enhancing readability and minimizing screen glare. Dark mode reflects the contemporary emphasis on user customization and the acknowledgment of diverse user preferences in the design of digital interfaces.

The contemporary UI design landscape is also characterized by an increased focus on inclusivity and accessibility. Designers recognize the importance of creating interfaces that cater to users with diverse abilities and needs. Accessibility features, such as screen readers, voice commands, and customizable text sizes, are integrated into UI designs to ensure that digital content is usable by a broad spectrum of users. This emphasis on inclusivity aligns with a broader societal awareness of the importance of accessibility in digital experiences and reflects a commitment to designing interfaces that prioritize usability for all.

Security considerations play a crucial role in the contemporary UI design landscape, given the increasing prevalence of digital transactions, personal data sharing, and online interactions. Designers incorporate secure authentication methods, encryption protocols, and user education strategies to enhance the security of digital interfaces. Two-factor authentication, biometric recognition, and secure user interfaces contribute to a safer digital environment, mitigating the risks associated with cyber threats and unauthorized access. The contemporary UI design landscape acknowledges the paramount importance of building trust and ensuring the protection of user information in the digital realm.

In conclusion, the contemporary technological landscape in UI design is characterized by a confluence of diverse influences, from the ubiquity of mobile devices and the prevalence of touchscreens to the integration of AI, AR, and VR technologies. UI designers navigate a multifaceted landscape where responsive and adaptive design principles, mobile applications, voice and gesture controls, AI-driven interfaces, and accessibility considerations converge to shape the digital experiences of users. As technology continues to advance, the contemporary UI design landscape is poised for further evolution, propelled by innovation, user-centric design philosophies, and an unwavering commitment to creating interfaces that are not only functional but also engaging, inclusive, and responsive to the needs of a diverse user base.

Explore current trends, such as augmented reality, voice interfaces, and AI-driven interactions.

In the ever-evolving landscape of technology and user interface (UI) design, current trends are shaping the way users interact with digital systems, ushering in a new era of immersive, intuitive, and intelligent experiences. Augmented reality (AR) stands out as a transformative trend that merges the digital and physical worlds. AR overlays digital content onto the real world, enhancing users' perception and interaction with their environment. This trend has gained momentum across various sectors, from gaming and education to retail and healthcare. Applications like Pokémon GO and IKEA Place showcase the potential of AR in creating engaging and context-aware user experiences. AR's ability to blend virtual elements with the real world adds a spatial and interactive dimension to UI design, paving the way for innovative applications that redefine how users engage with information and the environment.

Voice interfaces represent another significant trend reshaping the UI landscape, fueled by advancements in natural language processing and voice recognition technologies. Voice-driven interactions enable users to communicate with devices, applications, and services using spoken commands. Virtual assistants like Amazon's Alexa, Apple's Siri, and Google Assistant have become integral parts of daily life, providing information, controlling smart home devices, and performing tasks through conversational interactions. The rise of smart speakers and the integration of voice interfaces in smartphones and other devices underscore the growing importance of voice as a primary mode of interaction. This trend not only offers a hands-free and convenient user experience but also contributes to the development of more inclusive interfaces, catering to users with diverse abilities and preferences.

Artificial intelligence (AI) continues to be a driving force in shaping current trends in UI design. AI-driven interactions leverage machine learning algorithms to analyze user behavior, preferences, and context, enabling interfaces to deliver personalized and adaptive experiences. Recommendations, predictive typing, and content curation exemplify how AI enhances user engagement by anticipating and fulfilling user needs. Chatbots and virtual assistants, powered by natural language processing, engage users in conversational interactions, providing information and performing tasks in a more human-like manner. The integration of AI-driven features adds a layer of intelligence to UIs, enabling interfaces to evolve and adapt based on user input, thereby creating a more dynamic and context-aware user experience.

Conversational interfaces, a subset of voice interfaces, have emerged as a distinctive trend in UI design. These interfaces facilitate interactions through natural language conversations, enabling users to communicate with applications and services as if they were engaging in a dialogue. Chatbots, messaging apps, and virtual assistants exemplify the proliferation of conversational interfaces across various platforms. The appeal of this trend lies in its ability to mimic human communication patterns, creating a more user-friendly and approachable interaction model. Businesses leverage conversational interfaces for customer support, while messaging apps integrate AI-driven chatbots to enhance user engagement. The trend towards more conversational interactions reflects a shift towards user-centric design philosophies that prioritize intuitive and human-like communication.

Dark mode, characterized by a color scheme featuring darker backgrounds and lighter text, has become a prevailing trend in UI design across platforms and applications. Dark mode not only offers a visually appealing aesthetic but also provides practical benefits such as reducing eye strain in low-light conditions and minimizing screen glare. The popularity of this trend is evident in the widespread adoption by operating systems, social media platforms, and various applications, allowing users to choose between light and dark modes based on their preferences. Dark mode exemplifies the contemporary emphasis on user customization and the acknowledgment of diverse user needs, contributing to a more inclusive and user-centric UI design landscape.

The concept of microinteractions has gained prominence as a design trend that focuses on the subtle details and animations within an interface. Microinteractions are brief, often overlooked, interactions that occur in response to user actions or system events. These can include the subtle animation of a button when pressed or the notification sound when a message is received. Designers leverage microinteractions to enhance the overall user experience, providing feedback, guiding users through processes, and adding a sense of responsiveness to interfaces. This trend reflects a meticulous attention to detail and a recognition of the impact that small interactions can have on the overall user perception and engagement.

Progressive web apps (PWAs) represent a trend that bridges the gap between web and native mobile applications. PWAs combine the benefits of web technologies with the capabilities of native apps, offering a reliable, fast, and engaging user experience. These apps are designed to work seamlessly across various devices and screen sizes, providing users with a consistent experience. PWAs leverage technologies such as service workers to enable offline functionality, push notifications, and improved performance. This trend aligns with the growing demand for cross-platform experiences that offer the benefits of both web and native applications, contributing to a more versatile and accessible UI design landscape.

The trend of 3D elements and immersive design experiences has gained traction, particularly in gaming, entertainment, and e-commerce interfaces. Designers incorporate three-dimensional graphics, animations, and interactions to create more visually engaging and interactive experiences. This trend is closely tied to advancements in graphics rendering capabilities and the increased prevalence of devices with high-resolution displays. The integration of 3D elements adds a layer of realism to UIs, allowing users to interact with digital content in a more spatial and dynamic manner. From 3D product views in e-commerce to immersive storytelling in media applications, this trend exemplifies the contemporary push towards more visually stimulating and experiential UI designs.

User-centric design principles and a focus on inclusivity continue to drive trends in UI design. Designers increasingly prioritize creating interfaces that are not only visually appealing but also accessible to users with diverse abilities and needs. Accessibility features, such as screen readers, voice commands, and customizable text sizes, are integrated into UI designs to ensure usability for a broad spectrum of users. Inclusivity in design extends beyond accessibility to consider diverse cultural perspectives, ensuring that interfaces resonate with a global audience. This trend aligns with a broader societal awareness of the importance of inclusivity in digital experiences, emphasizing the responsibility of designers to create interfaces that prioritize usability for all.

The trend towards minimalism and simplicity in UI design remains a prevalent and enduring theme. Minimalist design principles prioritize clarity, simplicity, and the removal of unnecessary elements, creating interfaces that are clean, focused, and easy to navigate. This trend is exemplified by streamlined navigation menus, uncluttered layouts, and the use of ample white space. The minimalist approach not only enhances the visual aesthetics of interfaces but also contributes to improved user comprehension and ease of use. It reflects a commitment to distilling the essential elements of an interface, aligning with contemporary design philosophies that prioritize functionality and user-centered experiences.

In conclusion, the contemporary UI design landscape is characterized by a rich tapestry of trends that reflect the dynamic interplay of technological advancements, user expectations, and design philosophies. Augmented reality, voice interfaces, AI-driven interactions, conversational interfaces, dark mode, microinteractions, progressive web apps, 3D elements, inclusivity, and minimalism represent a diverse array of trends shaping the way users engage with digital interfaces. As technology continues to advance and user preferences evolve, these trends collectively contribute to a UI design landscape that is immersive, adaptive, and attuned to the needs and expectations of a diverse and global user base.

Explore emerging technologies expected to impact UI design in the future.

The future of User Interface (UI) design is intricately intertwined with the rapid advancement of emerging technologies, promising to reshape the way users interact with digital systems.

Augmented Reality (AR) stands out as a pioneering force set to redefine UI design by overlaying digital information onto the physical world. As AR continues to mature, designers are presented with the opportunity to create immersive and context-aware interfaces that seamlessly blend virtual elements with the real environment. Applications in fields such as navigation, education, and healthcare are anticipated to harness the potential of AR, offering users a more spatial and interactive dimension in their digital experiences. The convergence of AR with UI design opens new avenues for contextual information delivery, transforming the way users engage with their surroundings.

Voice interfaces, already a prominent trend, are poised to evolve significantly, driven by advancements in Natural Language Processing (NLP) and speech recognition. The future holds the promise of more sophisticated voice interactions, where AI-driven systems understand context, nuances, and user intent with greater precision. This evolution extends beyond virtual assistants to encompass a broader range of applications, from complex software interfaces to smart home systems. The integration of voice interfaces is expected to become more seamless and natural, contributing to the creation of hands-free and eyes-free interactions. As voice technology matures, designers will be challenged to explore innovative ways to leverage this medium, transforming the landscape of human-computer interaction.

Artificial Intelligence (AI) is poised to become an even more integral component of UI design, introducing a new era of adaptive and anticipatory interfaces. AI-driven interactions will leverage machine learning algorithms to analyze vast datasets of user behavior, preferences, and contextual information. This deeper understanding will enable interfaces to predict user needs, personalize experiences, and dynamically adjust to changing usage patterns. The fusion of AI with UI design is expected to elevate interfaces from static structures to intelligent systems capable of continuous learning and adaptation. The challenge for designers will be to strike a balance between the benefits of personalization and the importance of user privacy, ensuring that AI-driven interfaces enhance user experiences without compromising security and data ethics.

The emergence of Extended Reality (XR), which encompasses both Virtual Reality (VR) and AR, is set to revolutionize UI design by transcending the boundaries of physical and digital realms. VR interfaces, in particular, will transport users to entirely virtual environments, offering unparalleled levels of immersion and interaction. Designers will face the task of creating intuitive and user-friendly interfaces within these immersive spaces, where traditional UI elements need to be reconceptualized for a three-dimensional context. As XR technologies become more accessible and mainstream, industries ranging from gaming and entertainment to education and enterprise are expected to adopt these immersive interfaces, shaping the future of digital experiences.

The Internet of Things (IoT) is another transformative force that will profoundly impact UI design as more devices become interconnected. With a proliferation of smart homes, wearable devices, and industrial IoT applications, designers will need to navigate the challenge of creating interfaces that facilitate seamless communication between a myriad of connected devices. The emphasis will be on crafting cohesive and intuitive interfaces that empower users to interact with and manage the increasing complexity of their interconnected environments. UI designers will play a crucial role in simplifying the user experience within the expanding IoT ecosystem, ensuring that interactions are intuitive and that users can harness the full potential of connected technologies.

As touchscreens become more ubiquitous, haptic feedback technologies are expected to play a pivotal role in enhancing the tactile dimension of UI interactions. Haptic feedback, which provides users with tactile sensations in response to their actions, adds a layer of realism to touch-based interfaces. Future UI designs may incorporate more nuanced haptic feedback, simulating textures, resistance, and even temperature, creating a more immersive and engaging user experience. This technology is not limited to handheld devices but extends to wearables, VR controllers, and other interactive surfaces, presenting designers with the challenge of integrating haptic feedback in ways that enhance usability and user satisfaction.

Biometric technologies, such as facial recognition, fingerprint scanning, and iris recognition, are poised to become integral components of UI design, particularly in the realms of security and authentication. The future holds the promise of more seamless and secure user verification methods, where biometrics replace traditional passwords and PINs. Designers will need to consider the user experience implications of integrating biometric interfaces, ensuring that the balance between security and user convenience is maintained. Biometric authentication is expected to extend beyond smartphones to encompass various devices and applications, contributing to a more streamlined and secure digital experience.

The evolution of flexible and foldable display technologies is set to introduce novel possibilities for UI design, enabling devices with adaptable form factors. These technologies, which allow screens to bend and fold without compromising functionality, will challenge designers to envision interfaces that dynamically adjust to different screen configurations. Foldable smartphones and tablets are already entering the market, opening new avenues for multitasking and innovative UI layouts. Designers will need to explore how UI elements can intelligently adapt to changes in screen size and shape, providing users with a seamless and cohesive experience across various form factors.

Blockchain technology, primarily known for its applications in cryptocurrency, holds potential implications for UI design in terms of enhancing transparency, security, and user control. Decentralized applications (DApps) built on blockchain platforms introduce new paradigms where users have greater ownership and control over their data. UI designers will need to explore ways to convey complex blockchain concepts in user-friendly interfaces, ensuring that users can confidently engage with decentralized systems. The integration of blockchain principles in UI design may extend beyond financial applications to encompass areas such as identity verification, supply chain management, and secure communication.

The rise of quantum computing introduces a paradigm shift in computational power, potentially unlocking new possibilities for UI design. Quantum computers, with their ability to process vast amounts of data and solve complex problems exponentially faster than classical computers, may enable the creation of more sophisticated and dynamic UIs. The implications for UI design include the potential for real-time simulations, enhanced data visualization, and the optimization of complex algorithms within interfaces. As quantum computing progresses, UI designers will need to explore how to harness this computational power to create interfaces that push the boundaries of what is currently achievable.

In conclusion, the future of UI design is poised for radical transformation as emerging technologies continue to advance. From the immersive possibilities offered by augmented reality and extended reality to the intelligence infused by artificial intelligence, designers will navigate a landscape where the boundaries between physical and digital, real and virtual, become increasingly blurred. The challenges ahead include ensuring that these technologies are harnessed responsibly, ethically, and in a user-centric manner, with a commitment to creating interfaces that not only leverage technological advancements but also prioritize inclusivity, accessibility, and meaningful user experiences in the rapidly evolving digital era.

Discuss the potential influence of technologies like virtual reality, brain-computer interfaces, and immersive experiences.

The potential influence of transformative technologies such as Virtual Reality (VR), Brain-Computer Interfaces (BCIs), and immersive experiences on the landscape of human-computer interaction is profound and multifaceted. Virtual Reality, as a technology capable of creating immersive and synthetic environments, has the power to redefine how users perceive and interact with digital content. The immersive nature of VR allows users to be transported to entirely virtual worlds, providing a level of engagement and presence that transcends traditional interfaces. In the realm of user interface design, VR introduces a paradigm shift where conventional graphical elements are replaced by spatial and three-dimensional interactions. Designers grapple with creating intuitive interfaces within virtual environments, where gestures, gaze, and spatial awareness become primary means of interaction. The potential influence of VR extends beyond gaming and entertainment to fields such as education, training, and therapy, offering realistic simulations and experiential learning environments that are unprecedented in their depth and impact.

Brain-Computer Interfaces (BCIs) represent a revolutionary technological frontier that holds the promise of direct communication between the human brain and digital systems. These interfaces interpret neural signals to enable users to interact with computers, devices, and applications without traditional input methods. The potential influence of BCIs on UI design is transformative, as they challenge designers to reimagine interfaces that respond not only to explicit commands but also to the user's cognitive and emotional states. BCIs open up possibilities for creating interfaces that adapt in real-time based on the user's mental states, preferences, and intentions. Designing for BCIs involves understanding the intricacies of neural signals and translating them into meaningful and actionable interactions, offering a new dimension of accessibility and inclusivity for users with physical disabilities.

Immersive experiences, encompassing a spectrum of technologies such as augmented reality, virtual reality, and mixed reality, are poised to reshape the way users engage with digital content. The potential influence of immersive experiences lies in their ability to create environments where the boundaries between the physical and digital worlds blur. Augmented Reality (AR) overlays digital information onto the real world, enriching the user's perception of their surroundings. Mixed Reality (MR) combines elements of both physical and virtual worlds, allowing users to interact with digital content in real-world contexts. The immersive nature of these experiences challenges designers to create interfaces that seamlessly integrate with the user's environment, providing context-aware information and interactions. Immersive experiences have applications across diverse fields, from gaming and entertainment to education, healthcare, and industrial training, presenting designers with the task of crafting interfaces that enhance user experiences in both the physical and digital realms.

The potential influence of these transformative technologies extends beyond the immediate realm of interface design to impact broader aspects of human cognition, perception, and communication. In the context of Virtual Reality, the immersive nature of experiences can evoke powerful emotional responses and a sense of presence, influencing how users perceive information and engage with narratives. Designers need to consider the psychological and emotional implications of VR experiences, ensuring that interfaces are crafted with sensitivity to user well-being and ethical considerations. Moreover, the potential influence of Brain-Computer Interfaces on cognitive load and mental fatigue is a critical aspect to be addressed in design. As users engage in direct brain-machine communication, designers must prioritize user comfort, mitigate potential cognitive strain, and explore ways to enhance the overall cognitive experience.

The potential influence of these technologies also extends to the realm of accessibility and inclusivity. Virtual Reality, with its ability to create diverse and interactive environments, has the potential to enhance accessibility for users with disabilities. Designers are tasked with creating VR experiences that cater to individuals with varying needs, ensuring that interfaces are navigable and usable for everyone. Similarly, Brain-Computer Interfaces have the potential to empower individuals with severe physical disabilities, providing them with a means to interact with digital systems and the broader world. The inclusive design of BCIs involves understanding the diverse range of cognitive abilities and tailoring interfaces to accommodate individual differences, fostering a more equitable and accessible technological landscape.

The potential influence of these technologies also raises ethical considerations related to user privacy, data security, and the responsible use of neurotechnologies. Brain-Computer Interfaces, in particular, involve the direct interpretation of neural signals, raising concerns about the privacy and security of users' cognitive data. Designers must prioritize robust security measures, transparent data practices, and informed consent to address these ethical considerations. In the context of Virtual Reality, the collection of biometric data, tracking user movements, and creating detailed user profiles pose challenges to privacy and data protection. As designers navigate the potential influence of these technologies, ethical considerations become integral to the development of interfaces that respect user autonomy and safeguard sensitive information.

Furthermore, the potential influence of these technologies extends to the societal and cultural impact of digital experiences. Virtual Reality has the potential to revolutionize social interactions by creating shared virtual spaces where users can communicate, collaborate, and engage in social activities. Designers play a crucial role in shaping the social dynamics of virtual environments, ensuring that interfaces facilitate positive interactions, inclusivity, and cultural sensitivity. Brain-Computer Interfaces, by enabling direct communication between brains, have implications for telepathic communication and shared cognition. Designers must navigate the cultural and societal implications of these technologies, acknowledging diverse perspectives and fostering responsible use in a global context.

As designers grapple with the potential influence of these technologies, interdisciplinary collaboration becomes paramount. The convergence of expertise in neuroscience, psychology, human-computer interaction, and ethics is essential to navigate the complex challenges and opportunities presented by technologies like Virtual Reality and Brain-Computer Interfaces. Designers need to engage in ongoing dialogues with researchers, ethicists, and diverse user communities to ensure that interfaces are developed with a holistic understanding of their impact on users and society.

In conclusion, the potential influence of technologies like Virtual Reality, Brain-Computer Interfaces, and immersive experiences on UI design transcends the boundaries of traditional interaction paradigms. These technologies have the power to redefine how users perceive, interact, and communicate in digital environments. Designers are challenged to create interfaces that harness the transformative potential of these technologies while addressing ethical considerations, ensuring accessibility, and shaping positive societal impacts. The future of UI design lies at the intersection of technological innovation, user-centered principles, and a commitment to fostering experiences that enrich the human-computer relationship in ways previously unimagined.

Discuss ongoing research in the field of Human-Computer Interaction.

Ongoing research in the field of Human-Computer Interaction (HCI) reflects a dynamic and multidisciplinary landscape, where scholars and practitioners continually explore novel approaches, methodologies, and technologies to enhance the interaction between humans and digital systems. One prominent area of research focuses on the integration of artificial intelligence (AI) into HCI. As AI technologies advance, researchers are investigating ways to leverage machine learning algorithms to create more intelligent and adaptive interfaces. This involves exploring how AI can analyze user behavior, preferences, and context to personalize interactions, provide tailored recommendations, and enhance the overall user experience. The intersection of AI and HCI is a fertile ground for understanding how intelligent systems can augment human capabilities, leading to more intuitive and responsive digital interfaces.

Accessibility and inclusivity remain at the forefront of HCI research, reflecting a commitment to creating interfaces that cater to users with diverse abilities and needs. Ongoing efforts seek to enhance the usability of digital systems for individuals with disabilities through innovative design strategies, assistive technologies, and inclusive practices. Research in this domain explores advancements in screen readers, voice recognition, gesture controls, and other assistive technologies to empower users with varying abilities. Moreover, there is a growing emphasis on considering cultural and societal contexts in HCI research to ensure that interfaces resonate with a global audience and are sensitive to diverse perspectives.

The exploration of novel interaction modalities is a vibrant area of ongoing HCI research. This includes the investigation of touchless interfaces, where users can interact with digital systems without physical contact. Gesture-based controls, facial recognition, and motion sensing technologies are being studied to understand how they can be integrated into UI design to create more natural and immersive interactions. This research extends beyond traditional touchscreens to encompass a broader spectrum of devices, from smart homes and wearables to public interactive displays, pushing the boundaries of how users engage with digital content in various contexts.

The integration of Virtual Reality (VR) and Augmented Reality (AR) into HCI continues to be a focal point of exploration. Researchers are delving into the design principles, usability considerations, and user experiences within virtual and augmented environments. VR interfaces offer the potential for immersive and realistic simulations, impacting fields such as education, training, and healthcare. On the other hand, AR interfaces overlay digital information onto the real world, enriching users' perceptions of their surroundings. Ongoing research in this domain seeks to understand the optimal design practices, user comfort, and the cognitive implications of interacting within mixed reality environments.

As voice interfaces become increasingly prevalent, ongoing HCI research addresses the challenges and opportunities associated with natural language processing and voice recognition technologies. Researchers aim to enhance the accuracy and contextual understanding of voice commands, making voice interfaces more intuitive and versatile. The integration of conversational agents, chatbots, and virtual assistants into everyday interactions poses questions about user trust, privacy concerns, and ethical considerations. Ongoing research strives to navigate these complexities while optimizing voice interfaces for a wide range of applications, from smart homes and mobile devices to customer service and healthcare.

Another area of ongoing HCI research delves into the psychological and emotional aspects of user experiences. Researchers are exploring how design elements, interface aesthetics, and interactive features influence user emotions and perceptions. This includes investigations into the impact of color schemes, typography, and visual aesthetics on user mood and engagement. Emotion-aware interfaces, which adapt based on users' emotional states, represent a frontier in HCI research, aiming to create more empathetic and user-centered digital experiences. Understanding the emotional dimensions of human-computer interaction is crucial for designing interfaces that not only function optimally but also resonate on a deeper level with users.

In the context of HCI for health and well-being, ongoing research explores how digital interfaces can contribute to positive health outcomes. This includes the design of interfaces for health monitoring, telemedicine, mental health support, and behavior change interventions. Researchers investigate the usability and effectiveness of mobile health apps, wearable devices, and virtual health platforms, considering factors such as user engagement, adherence, and the impact on health-related behaviors. The integration of HCI principles into healthcare systems aims to enhance the patient experience, improve health outcomes, and foster a more collaborative and patient-centric approach to medical care.

Collaborative and social aspects of HCI are subjects of ongoing research, reflecting the increasing importance of digital collaboration in various domains. Researchers explore how interfaces can facilitate effective collaboration among distributed teams, leveraging technologies such as video conferencing, virtual collaboration tools, and shared digital spaces. The study of social computing examines the dynamics of online communities, social media platforms, and the impact of digital interfaces on social interactions. Ongoing research in this area delves into issues of online privacy, digital identity, and the role of interfaces in shaping social behaviors in the digital realm.

The ethical considerations surrounding HCI are gaining prominence in ongoing research efforts. As digital interfaces become integral to various aspects of daily life, researchers are grappling with questions related to user privacy, data security, algorithmic bias, and the responsible use of emerging technologies. Ethical HCI research involves exploring frameworks for ethical design, transparency in algorithmic decision-making, and strategies to mitigate potential harms associated with digital interfaces. The dialogue around ethical considerations in HCI extends to issues of inclusivity, cultural sensitivity, and the broader societal implications of technology-mediated interactions.

The ongoing exploration of HCI in the context of ubiquitous computing is a significant area of research. Ubiquitous computing envisions a seamlessly interconnected environment where digital technologies are woven into the fabric of daily life. Research in this domain investigates the challenges and opportunities associated with designing interfaces for a world where computing is pervasive, ranging from smart cities and connected homes to wearable devices and the Internet of Things (IoT). The aim is to create interfaces that seamlessly adapt to the user's context, providing a cohesive and integrated digital experience across diverse devices and environments.

In conclusion, ongoing research in the field of Human-Computer Interaction encompasses a diverse range of topics, reflecting the evolving nature of technology and its impact on how humans interact with digital systems. From the integration of artificial intelligence and novel interaction modalities to the exploration of immersive experiences, voice interfaces, and ethical considerations, HCI researchers contribute to a nuanced understanding of the complex dynamics between users and technology. The interdisciplinary nature of HCI research fosters collaborations between designers, psychologists, engineers, ethicists, and other stakeholders, driving the field forward in its quest to create more intuitive, inclusive, and ethically sound digital interfaces that enhance the human experience in the digital age.

Explore how HCI research contributes to shaping the future of UI technology.

Human-Computer Interaction (HCI) research plays a pivotal role in shaping the future of User Interface (UI) technology by delving into the intricacies of how users interact with digital systems and pushing the boundaries of design principles, technologies, and user experiences. One prominent contribution of HCI research lies in advancing the integration of artificial intelligence (AI) into UI technology. As researchers explore the capabilities of machine learning algorithms, they seek to create more intelligent and adaptive interfaces that can understand user behavior, preferences, and context. This research contributes to the development of UIs that can provide personalized experiences, anticipate user needs, and dynamically adjust to changing usage patterns. The fusion of AI and HCI represents a frontier where the interaction between humans and technology becomes more intuitive, intelligent, and responsive, thereby shaping the trajectory of UI technology towards a future where digital interfaces seamlessly align with the complexities of human cognition.

Accessibility and inclusivity are paramount considerations in HCI research, influencing the evolution of UI technology towards a more equitable and user-centric future. Researchers actively contribute to the development of UIs that cater to users with diverse abilities and needs. This involves exploring innovative design strategies, assistive technologies, and inclusive practices to enhance the usability of digital systems for individuals with disabilities. By addressing accessibility challenges, HCI research ensures that UI technology is not only functional but also accessible to a broad spectrum of users. This commitment to inclusivity contributes to shaping a future where digital interfaces prioritize diversity, equity, and accessibility, fostering a technological landscape that accommodates the needs of all users.

HCI research significantly contributes to the exploration of novel interaction modalities, redefining how users engage with digital content and envisioning the future of UI technology. Touchless interfaces, incorporating technologies like gesture-based controls, facial recognition, and motion sensing, emerge from HCI research endeavors. By investigating the design principles and usability of these modalities, researchers pave the way for UIs that transcend traditional touchscreens, offering more natural and immersive interactions. The future of UI technology is envisioned as one where users can interact seamlessly with devices, smart homes, and public displays through gestures and gaze, enriching the digital experience with a new dimension of user-friendly and intuitive interactions.

The integration of Virtual Reality (VR) and Augmented Reality (AR) into UI technology is a direct outcome of HCI research that explores the design principles, usability considerations, and user experiences within these immersive environments. As researchers delve into the complexities of designing for VR and AR, they contribute insights into creating interfaces that provide realistic simulations and overlay digital information onto the real world. The ongoing exploration of VR and AR within HCI research shapes the future of UI technology by envisioning interfaces that extend beyond the two-dimensional screen, offering users unprecedented levels of immersion and interaction. Whether applied to education, training, healthcare, or entertainment, the integration of VR and AR into UI technology reflects the ongoing quest to create interfaces that merge the physical and digital realms seamlessly.

Voice interfaces, a growing trend in UI technology, are a direct outcome of HCI research that explores natural language processing and voice recognition technologies. Researchers in HCI contribute to the development of voice interfaces that understand context, nuances, and user intent, making interactions more intuitive and user-friendly. This research not only enhances the accuracy and contextual understanding of voice commands but also delves into the integration of conversational agents, chatbots, and virtual assistants. The future of UI technology is envisioned as one where voice interfaces become ubiquitous, enabling users to interact with a wide range of devices, applications, and services through spoken commands. The ongoing dialogue in HCI research surrounding voice interfaces addresses challenges related to user trust, privacy, and ethical considerations, shaping a future where voice interactions are seamlessly integrated into the fabric of daily life.

HCI research is instrumental in understanding the psychological and emotional dimensions of user experiences, influencing the design of UI technology to elicit specific emotional responses and enhance user engagement. Researchers explore how design elements, interface aesthetics, and interactive features impact user emotions and perceptions. Emotion-aware interfaces, a frontier in HCI research, are designed to adapt based on users' emotional states, contributing to a more empathetic and user-centered digital experience. This research envisions a future where UI technology is not only functional but also emotionally intelligent, capable of recognizing and responding to users' emotional states to create more meaningful and engaging interactions.

In the context of HCI for health and well-being, research contributes to the development of UI technology that positively impacts users' health outcomes. Whether designing interfaces for health monitoring, telemedicine, mental health support, or behavior change interventions, HCI researchers actively shape the future of UI technology in the healthcare domain. The focus on usability, effectiveness, and user engagement in digital health interfaces reflects a commitment to creating technologies that enhance the patient experience, improve health outcomes, and foster a more collaborative and patient-centric approach to medical care.

Collaborative and social aspects of HCI research have a profound impact on shaping the future of UI technology in the context of digital collaboration and online communities. Researchers explore how interfaces can facilitate effective collaboration among distributed teams, leveraging technologies such as video conferencing, virtual collaboration tools, and shared digital spaces. The ongoing study of social computing delves into the dynamics of online communities and the impact of digital interfaces on social interactions. The future of UI technology is envisioned as one where collaborative and social elements are seamlessly integrated, enabling users to engage in effective digital collaboration and fostering positive social interactions in the online realm.

Ethical considerations surrounding HCI research contribute to shaping the future of UI technology by addressing issues related to user privacy, data security, algorithmic bias, and responsible use of emerging technologies. Researchers actively explore frameworks for ethical design, transparency in algorithmic decision-making, and strategies to mitigate potential harms associated with digital interfaces. As the ethical dialogue in HCI research evolves, it shapes a future where UI technology is not only innovative but also ethically sound, prioritizing user autonomy, transparency, and fairness in its design and implementation.

The exploration of HCI in the context of ubiquitous computing contributes to shaping the future of UI technology by envisioning interfaces that seamlessly adapt to the user's context. Researchers delve into the challenges and opportunities associated with designing interfaces for a world where computing is pervasive, ranging from smart cities and connected homes to wearable devices and the Internet of Things (IoT). The future of UI technology is imagined as one where interfaces provide a cohesive and integrated digital experience across diverse devices and environments, adapting to the user's needs and context seamlessly.

In conclusion, HCI research plays a transformative role in shaping the future of UI technology by influencing design principles, technologies, and user experiences. From the integration of AI to the exploration of novel interaction modalities, the evolution of VR and AR, the rise of voice interfaces, the consideration of psychological and emotional dimensions, and the ethical and inclusive dimensions of UI design, ongoing HCI research contributes to a future where digital interfaces are not only technologically advanced but also user-friendly, inclusive, and aligned with the ethical considerations of a rapidly evolving digital landscape. The interdisciplinary nature of HCI research ensures that the future of UI technology is shaped by a holistic understanding of the complex relationship between humans and technology, paving the way for more intuitive, adaptive, and human-centric interfaces in the years to come.

Chapter 7: Security Measures in Operating System Interfaces

Define the importance of security in operating system interfaces.

The importance of security in operating system interfaces is paramount, as these interfaces serve as the primary gateway through which users interact with and control the underlying system. Operating systems form the backbone of computing environments, managing hardware resources, running applications, and facilitating communication between different components. Security in this context is a multifaceted concept that encompasses various measures and practices designed to safeguard the integrity, confidentiality, and availability of both the operating system itself and the data processed by it.

One of the fundamental aspects of security in operating system interfaces is the protection of user data and system resources. Users interact with operating system interfaces to create, modify, and access files and applications. Ensuring the confidentiality of sensitive data is crucial, especially in multi-user environments where different individuals may share the same system. Security mechanisms, such as access control lists (ACLs) and file permissions, are implemented to restrict unauthorized access to files and directories. Encryption techniques are often employed to secure data both in transit and at rest, safeguarding it from unauthorized interception or access.

The integrity of the operating system itself is of utmost importance. Security mechanisms must prevent unauthorized modifications to the system files and configurations, as tampering with these elements could lead to system instability, data corruption, or the introduction of malicious software. Digital signatures, secure boot processes, and integrity checks are employed to verify the authenticity of system files and detect any alterations. Regular updates and patches, often distributed through secure channels, are essential to address vulnerabilities and ensure that the operating system remains resilient against evolving security threats.

Authentication mechanisms are integral to operating system security, as they control user access to the system. User authentication involves verifying the identity of individuals attempting to log in, preventing unauthorized access. Passwords, biometric authentication, and multi-factor authentication are common methods used to establish user identity. Strong authentication practices help mitigate the risk of unauthorized access, protecting not only user data but also the overall integrity of the operating system.

In the context of networked environments, the security of operating system interfaces extends to safeguarding communication channels and preventing unauthorized access to network resources. Firewalls, intrusion detection/prevention systems, and secure communication protocols are implemented to control and monitor network traffic. Operating systems often include features such as virtual private networks (VPNs) and secure sockets layer (SSL) support to encrypt communications, ensuring the confidentiality of data transmitted over networks.

The importance of security in operating system interfaces is particularly evident in the context of user privilege management. Operating systems implement role-based access control (RBAC) or discretionary access control (DAC) mechanisms to define and enforce user privileges. Users with administrative or superuser privileges have elevated access rights, enabling them to perform critical system tasks. The careful management of these privileges is crucial to prevent unauthorized modifications, installations, or deletions that could compromise system stability and security. Least privilege principles guide the assignment of minimal necessary permissions to users, minimizing potential security risks.

The significance of security in operating system interfaces becomes even more pronounced in the face of malware and other malicious activities. Operating systems are prime targets for various forms of malware, including viruses, worms, trojans, and ransomware. Security measures such as antivirus software, intrusion detection systems, and behavior monitoring are essential components of an operating system's defense against malicious code. Regular security updates and patches help address known vulnerabilities, reducing the risk of exploitation by malware.

The principle of isolation is a key element in operating system security. Modern operating systems often employ virtualization and containerization technologies to isolate processes and applications from each other. Virtual machines and containers create separate environments, preventing the compromise of one application or process from affecting others. This isolation extends to user accounts, ensuring that each user operates within their designated space without the ability to interfere with the system or other users' activities.

Security in operating system interfaces also encompasses the secure management of system logs and auditing. Logging mechanisms record various system events and user activities, providing a trail of information that can be crucial for identifying security incidents, investigating breaches, and ensuring accountability. Regular auditing helps detect anomalous behavior, unauthorized access attempts, and potential security threats. Secure handling of logs, including encryption and restricted access, is essential to maintain the integrity of this valuable security resource.

The concept of secure boot processes is fundamental to the security of operating system interfaces. During the boot-up sequence, the operating system is loaded into memory from non-volatile storage. Secure boot processes, often supported by hardware-based trusted platform modules (TPMs), verify the integrity and authenticity of the bootloader and subsequent components. This prevents the execution of malicious code during the boot process, establishing a secure foundation for the operating system to operate from.

The increasing prevalence of mobile and embedded systems further emphasizes the importance of security in operating system interfaces. Mobile operating systems, such as Android and iOS, are integral to smartphones and tablets, housing vast amounts of personal and sensitive data. Security measures in mobile operating systems include device encryption, secure boot, application sandboxing, and permissions systems to control app access to user data. Embedded operating systems, commonly found in IoT devices, rely on security features to protect against unauthorized access, data breaches, and potential exploitation for malicious purposes.

In conclusion, the importance of security in operating system interfaces cannot be overstated. Operating systems serve as the foundation for computing environments, managing resources, facilitating user interactions, and ensuring the overall integrity and functionality of digital systems. Security measures encompass a wide range of mechanisms, including access controls, authentication, encryption, integrity checks, and secure boot processes. The multifaceted approach to security in operating system interfaces is crucial for protecting user data, preventing unauthorized access, mitigating malware threats, and maintaining the stability and reliability of digital systems. As technology evolves, the continuous improvement and adaptation of security measures in operating system interfaces remain imperative to address emerging threats and ensure a resilient and secure computing environment.

Discuss the potential risks and consequences of insecure interfaces.

The potential risks and consequences of insecure interfaces are profound and wide-ranging, encompassing various aspects of information security, user privacy, and system integrity. Insecure interfaces, whether in software applications, web services, or networked devices, create vulnerabilities that malicious actors can exploit, leading to severe repercussions for individuals, organizations, and society at large. One of the primary risks associated with insecure interfaces is unauthorized access to sensitive information. When interfaces lack robust security measures, attackers may exploit vulnerabilities to gain unauthorized entry into systems, databases, or user accounts. This unauthorized access can lead to the exposure of confidential data, including personal information, financial records, and proprietary business data, resulting in identity theft, financial loss, and reputational damage.

Insecure interfaces also pose a significant threat to user privacy. When interfaces fail to implement adequate privacy safeguards, personal information may be exposed or misused. For instance, web applications that mishandle user data or transmit it over unsecured connections risk exposing sensitive information to eavesdroppers. This can have severe consequences, such as identity theft, unauthorized profiling, and the compromise of personal communications. The erosion of user privacy due to insecure interfaces not only violates individual rights but also erodes trust in digital systems, hindering the adoption of technology for fear of privacy breaches.

The potential for data breaches is a critical consequence of insecure interfaces, posing significant risks to both individuals and organizations. Insecure interfaces can be exploited by cybercriminals to execute attacks such as SQL injection, cross-site scripting (XSS), and other injection-based exploits, leading to unauthorized access to databases and the exfiltration of sensitive data. The fallout from data breaches includes financial losses, legal consequences, and reputational damage for the affected entities. Moreover, the compromise of personal and sensitive information can have long-lasting consequences for individuals, potentially leading to identity theft, fraud, and other forms of cybercrime.

In the context of networked systems, insecure interfaces amplify the risk of unauthorized system manipulation. Malicious actors may exploit vulnerabilities in network interfaces to gain control over devices, manipulate settings, or disrupt critical services. This can have severe consequences in sectors such as critical infrastructure, healthcare, and industrial control systems, where unauthorized access and manipulation could lead to physical harm, operational disruptions, and compromise of public safety. Insecure interfaces in networked devices, including Internet of Things (IoT) devices, can provide entry points for attackers to compromise entire ecosystems, leading to cascading security failures.

The potential for denial-of-service (DoS) and distributed denial-of-service (DDoS) attacks is heightened by insecure interfaces. Attackers can leverage vulnerabilities in interfaces to overload systems, leading to service disruptions and unavailability. In the case of DDoS attacks, insecure interfaces may be exploited to compromise a large number of devices, forming a botnet that collectively overwhelms targeted systems. The consequences of such attacks extend beyond inconvenience, affecting business continuity, disrupting critical services, and potentially causing financial losses. Insecure interfaces that lack sufficient safeguards against DoS and DDoS attacks contribute to a volatile online landscape where services can be rendered inaccessible at any moment.

The exploitation of insecure interfaces can lead to the injection of malicious code into systems, opening the door to a range of cyber threats. For instance, SQL injection attacks involve manipulating database queries through insecure interfaces, enabling attackers to execute arbitrary commands. Similarly, cross-site scripting attacks involve injecting malicious scripts into web applications through insecure interfaces, compromising user data and session information. The consequences of code injection attacks include the compromise of sensitive information, the unauthorized execution of commands, and the potential for complete system compromise. Insecure interfaces that allow for code injection undermine the integrity and security of software applications, putting users at risk of various cyber threats.

Insecure interfaces contribute to the proliferation of phishing attacks, which target users through deceptive means to extract sensitive information such as login credentials and financial details. Phishing often exploits insecure interfaces to create convincing replicas of legitimate websites or applications, tricking users into providing confidential information. The consequences of successful phishing attacks include unauthorized access to user accounts, identity theft, and financial fraud. Insecure interfaces that do not implement robust authentication mechanisms or fail to educate users about potential phishing threats exacerbate the risk of falling victim to such attacks.

The potential for malware propagation is heightened by insecure interfaces, enabling the distribution of malicious software through various channels. Insecure interfaces can be exploited to deliver malware payloads to users' devices, compromising system integrity and facilitating unauthorized access. Malware distributed through insecure interfaces may include ransomware, spyware, and other malicious software that can lead to data loss, financial extortion, and unauthorized surveillance. Insecure interfaces contribute to the ease with which malware can be disseminated, posing a significant threat to the security of digital ecosystems and individual users.

Insecure interfaces can lead to the compromise of authentication credentials, posing a direct threat to user accounts and sensitive information. Weak password policies, inadequate encryption, and insufficient protection against brute-force attacks are common vulnerabilities that malicious actors exploit to compromise user credentials. The consequences of unauthorized access to user accounts include identity theft, unauthorized financial transactions, and the compromise of personal data. Insecure interfaces that fail to implement strong authentication mechanisms and robust security practices put user accounts at risk, leading to severe consequences for individuals and organizations.

The potential for privilege escalation is a critical consequence of insecure interfaces, allowing attackers to gain unauthorized access to elevated privileges within systems. Exploiting vulnerabilities in interfaces, attackers may escalate their level of access from standard user privileges to administrative or superuser privileges. Privilege escalation can lead to the unauthorized modification of system settings, installation of malicious software, and compromise of critical system components. Insecure interfaces that do not implement effective privilege management mechanisms expose systems to the risk of unauthorized manipulation and control by malicious actors.

Insecure interfaces amplify the risks associated with software vulnerabilities, creating avenues for the exploitation of flaws that can lead to system compromise. Software vulnerabilities, including those in operating systems, applications, and plugins, are frequently targeted by attackers to gain unauthorized access, execute arbitrary code, or compromise user data. Insecure interfaces that do not facilitate timely software updates and patch management contribute to the persistence of vulnerabilities, leaving systems exposed to exploitation. The consequences of exploiting software vulnerabilities through insecure interfaces include data breaches, system compromise, and the propagation of malware.

The potential for legal and regulatory consequences is a significant outcome of insecure interfaces, especially in environments where data protection laws and regulations are in place. Organizations that fail to implement adequate security measures, leading to data breaches and unauthorized access, may face legal actions, regulatory fines, and reputational damage. Insecure interfaces contribute to non-compliance with data protection standards, such as the General Data Protection Regulation (GDPR), and expose entities to legal liabilities. The consequences of legal and regulatory actions extend beyond financial penalties, impacting the trust and credibility of organizations in the eyes of their customers, stakeholders, and regulatory authorities.

In conclusion, the potential risks and consequences of insecure interfaces are extensive, encompassing a spectrum of threats to information security, user privacy, and system integrity. From unauthorized access and data breaches to the compromise of user credentials and legal ramifications, insecure interfaces pose significant challenges to individuals, organizations, and the broader digital ecosystem. Mitigating these risks requires a holistic approach, involving robust security practices, regular vulnerability assessments, user education, and compliance with legal and regulatory standards. As technology continues to advance, the importance of securing interfaces becomes increasingly critical to ensuring the resilience, trustworthiness, and sustainability of digital systems in a dynamic and interconnected world.

Explore mechanisms for user authentication and authorization in UI design.

Mechanisms for user authentication and authorization in UI design play a pivotal role in ensuring the security and integrity of digital systems, applications, and services. User authentication, the process of verifying the identity of individuals accessing a system, is the first line of defense against unauthorized access. One of the traditional and widely-used authentication mechanisms in UI design is the username-password combination. Users input a unique username and a corresponding password to prove their identity. However, the security of this mechanism depends heavily on the strength of passwords chosen by users, making it vulnerable to brute-force attacks or password-related vulnerabilities. Multi-factor authentication (MFA) has emerged as a more robust approach, requiring users to provide additional proof of identity, such as a one-time code sent to their mobile device, a fingerprint scan, or facial recognition. MFA significantly enhances security by adding layers of verification beyond traditional passwords.

Biometric authentication represents another category of mechanisms within UI design, leveraging unique biological features for user identification. Fingerprint recognition, iris scanning, facial recognition, and voice recognition are examples of biometric authentication methods. Biometric data serves as a unique identifier for each user, enhancing security by requiring a physical attribute for authentication. However, it's crucial to handle biometric data securely, ensuring its protection against unauthorized access or compromise. The implementation of biometric authentication in UI design provides a balance between security and user convenience, offering a more seamless and user-friendly experience compared to traditional username-password methods.

In the realm of UI design, the use of single sign-on (SSO) mechanisms has gained popularity, streamlining the authentication process across multiple applications or services. With SSO, users authenticate once and gain access to various interconnected systems without the need to re-enter credentials for each. Federated identity protocols, such as OAuth and OpenID Connect, enable secure SSO implementations. These protocols facilitate the exchange of authentication and authorization data between systems, allowing users to access resources seamlessly while maintaining a centralized and secure authentication mechanism. SSO mechanisms contribute to a more user-friendly experience and reduce the cognitive load associated with managing multiple sets of credentials.

Authorization, the process of granting or denying access rights and permissions to authenticated users, is equally crucial in UI design to control users' actions within a system. Role-based access control (RBAC) is a widely adopted authorization mechanism that assigns users specific roles with corresponding permissions. Administering permissions based on roles streamlines access management, making it more scalable and manageable. UI designs implementing RBAC often present administrators with intuitive interfaces for role assignment and permission configuration, allowing them to define and refine user access rights easily.

Attribute-based access control (ABAC) is another authorization mechanism that considers various attributes about the user, the resource, and the context to make access decisions. ABAC enables fine-grained access control by evaluating dynamic conditions, such as user roles, time of access, and environmental factors. In UI design, ABAC interfaces may include dynamic policy creation tools, allowing administrators to set complex rules based on a combination of attributes. This flexibility makes ABAC particularly suitable for environments with diverse user roles and complex access requirements.

Implementing access control lists (ACLs) is a common practice in UI design to specify which users or system processes are granted access to resources and what operations are allowed on given resources. ACLs are often associated with files, directories, or network services, allowing administrators to define who can read, write, or execute specific actions. UIs for managing ACLs typically provide an interface where administrators can assign or modify access permissions for individual users or groups. Effective ACL management is essential for ensuring that users have the necessary access to perform their tasks while preventing unauthorized actions.

In UI design, graphical user interfaces (GUIs) for managing user accounts and access rights play a crucial role in the overall usability and effectiveness of authentication and authorization mechanisms.

Intuitive and user-friendly interfaces for user account creation, password management, and access permission assignments contribute to a positive user experience. Additionally, administrators should have access to clear and well-designed interfaces for configuring security policies, managing roles, and defining access controls. These interfaces should provide a visual representation of the access hierarchy, allowing administrators to comprehend and modify access rights efficiently.

Token-based authentication mechanisms are prevalent in UI design, especially in web and mobile applications. JSON Web Tokens (JWT) and OAuth tokens are examples of token-based authentication approaches. JWTs are compact, self-contained tokens that encode information about the user and their permissions, enabling secure transmission and storage of authentication data. OAuth tokens, commonly used in authorization processes, provide a way for applications to obtain limited access to a user's resources without exposing their credentials. UI designs incorporating token-based authentication often include interfaces for token issuance, validation, and management, ensuring a secure and seamless flow of authentication and authorization data between clients and servers.

In the context of web applications, session management is a critical aspect of user authentication and authorization. UI designs for session management involve creating, maintaining, and terminating user sessions securely. Session tokens or cookies are often used to associate users with their sessions. UIs for managing sessions typically include options for administrators to view active sessions, revoke sessions, and set session expiration policies. Ensuring robust session management is vital for preventing session hijacking, maintaining user privacy, and enhancing the overall security of web applications.

In UI design, secure password policies contribute significantly to user authentication. UIs for password management should encourage users to create strong and unique passwords while providing clear feedback on password strength. Additionally, password reset interfaces should follow best practices, incorporating multi-factor authentication to verify users' identities before allowing them to reset their passwords. Educating users on password security through informative interfaces contributes to a more resilient authentication mechanism.

The integration of risk-based authentication mechanisms in UI design adds an adaptive layer to user authentication. These mechanisms assess contextual factors such as device characteristics, geolocation, and user behavior to dynamically adjust the authentication requirements. UIs for risk-based authentication often present administrators with dashboards or configuration panels to set risk thresholds and customize authentication policies based on contextual factors. This adaptive approach enhances security by challenging users with additional authentication steps when unusual or high-risk activities are detected.

In the realm of emerging technologies, UI designs for biometric authentication mechanisms involve creating intuitive interfaces for capturing and processing biometric data. Whether it's fingerprint scans, facial recognition, or voice authentication, the user interface should guide users through the biometric enrollment process, ensuring accurate and secure capture of biometric information. Additionally, UI designs for biometric authentication should consider privacy concerns, providing users with transparency and control over their biometric data.

In conclusion, the mechanisms for user authentication and authorization in UI design are foundational elements for ensuring the security, privacy, and integrity of digital systems. From traditional methods like username-password combinations to advanced approaches such as multi-factor authentication, biometrics, and token-based systems, UI designs play a crucial role in providing secure and user-friendly experiences. The interfaces for managing user accounts, access controls, and security policies contribute to the overall usability and effectiveness of these mechanisms. As technology continues to evolve, UI designers must remain attuned to emerging authentication and authorization trends to create interfaces that balance security and user experience in an ever-changing digital landscape.

Discuss the role of secure login procedures and permission management.

The role of secure login procedures and permission management is foundational in ensuring the overall security and integrity of digital systems, applications, and services. Secure login procedures form the initial barrier against unauthorized access, demanding robust authentication mechanisms to verify the identity of users attempting to access a system. Password-based authentication, a traditional method, necessitates strong password policies and secure storage practices. Encouraging users to create complex passwords and employing secure hashing algorithms to store them mitigates the risk of password-related vulnerabilities. Multi-factor authentication (MFA) enhances security by requiring users to provide additional proof of identity, such as a one-time code or biometric data, adding layers of verification beyond passwords. Secure login procedures contribute to the establishment of a trusted user identity, preventing unauthorized access and safeguarding sensitive information.

Permission management, a complementary aspect, is crucial for governing the actions and access rights of authenticated users within a system. Role-based access control (RBAC) is a widely adopted approach that assigns users specific roles, each associated with predefined permissions. Administrators can efficiently manage user access by assigning roles, streamlining the process and ensuring that users only possess the necessary permissions for their tasks. RBAC interfaces in permission management often provide a visual representation of the role hierarchy, allowing administrators to grasp and modify access rights easily. This role-centric approach enhances scalability, simplifies access control administration, and aligns with organizational structures, contributing to a more effective and manageable permission management system.

In addition to RBAC, attribute-based access control (ABAC) is gaining prominence in permission management, offering a more dynamic and flexible approach. ABAC evaluates access decisions based on a combination of attributes, including user characteristics, resource properties, and contextual factors. This fine-grained access control allows for more nuanced and context-aware permission assignments. In permission management interfaces, ABAC systems may include dynamic policy creation tools, enabling administrators to set complex rules based on various attributes. The flexibility of ABAC makes it particularly suitable for environments with diverse user roles and complex access requirements, enhancing the precision and adaptability of permission management.

Access control lists (ACLs) represent another mechanism within permission management, specifying which users or system processes are granted access to resources and what operations are allowed on those resources. ACLs are often associated with files, directories, or network services, providing a granular approach to access control. Permission management interfaces for ACLs typically allow administrators to assign or modify access permissions for individual users or groups, offering flexibility in defining access rights. Effective ACL management is vital for ensuring that users have the necessary access to perform their tasks while preventing unauthorized actions, and UIs for ACL management contribute to achieving this balance.

Graphical user interfaces (GUIs) for managing user accounts and access rights play a crucial role in the overall usability and efficiency of secure login procedures and permission management. Intuitive interfaces for user account creation, modification, and deletion contribute to a positive user experience, guiding users through the process seamlessly. GUIs for secure login procedures often incorporate features such as password strength meters and multi-factor authentication setup wizards to enhance user understanding and compliance with security measures. For permission management, GUIs should provide administrators with clear and well-designed interfaces for configuring security policies, managing roles, and defining access controls. These interfaces should enable administrators to visualize the access hierarchy, making it easier to comprehend and modify access rights.

Token-based authentication mechanisms are prevalent in secure login procedures, especially in web and mobile applications. JSON Web Tokens (JWT) and OAuth tokens are examples of token-based authentication approaches. JWTs are compact, self-contained tokens that encode information about the user and their permissions, enabling secure transmission and storage of authentication data. OAuth tokens, commonly used in authorization processes, provide a way for applications to obtain limited access to a user's resources without exposing their credentials. UI designs for token-based authentication often include interfaces for token issuance, validation, and management, ensuring a secure and seamless flow of authentication data between clients and servers. Token-based authentication enhances security by reducing the exposure of sensitive information and facilitating secure communication between different components of a system.

Session management, an integral part of secure login procedures, involves creating, maintaining, and terminating user sessions securely. UI designs for session management should include options for administrators to view active sessions, revoke sessions, and set session expiration policies. Session tokens or cookies are often used to associate users with their sessions. Proper session management is essential for preventing session hijacking, maintaining user privacy, and enhancing the overall security of web applications. UIs for session management should present information in a clear and organized manner, allowing administrators to monitor and control user sessions effectively.

In the context of secure login procedures, password policies play a critical role in ensuring the strength and resilience of user authentication. UIs for password management should encourage users to create strong and unique passwords, providing clear feedback on password strength. Additionally, password reset interfaces should follow best practices, incorporating multi-factor authentication to verify users' identities before allowing them to reset their passwords. Educating users on password security through informative interfaces contributes to a more resilient authentication mechanism. UI designs that incorporate effective password policies contribute to the overall security posture of a system, preventing unauthorized access due to weak or compromised passwords.

Risk-based authentication mechanisms add an adaptive layer to secure login procedures, dynamically adjusting authentication requirements based on contextual factors. UIs for risk-based authentication often present administrators with dashboards or configuration panels to set risk thresholds and customize authentication policies based on contextual factors. This adaptive approach enhances security by challenging users with additional authentication steps when unusual or high-risk activities are detected. UI designs for risk-based authentication should provide administrators with intuitive tools for configuring risk factors and responses, ensuring that security measures align with the dynamic nature of user interactions.

In the realm of emerging technologies, UI designs for biometric authentication mechanisms involve creating intuitive interfaces for capturing and processing biometric data. Whether it's fingerprint scans, facial recognition, or voice authentication, the user interface should guide users through the biometric enrollment process, ensuring accurate and secure capture of biometric information. Additionally, UI designs for biometric authentication should consider privacy concerns, providing users with transparency and control over their biometric data. Biometric authentication adds an additional layer of security to secure login procedures, relying on unique physiological or behavioral characteristics for user identification.

In conclusion, the role of secure login procedures and permission management is instrumental in establishing and maintaining the security of digital systems. From traditional authentication methods like passwords to advanced approaches such as multi-factor authentication, biometrics, and token-based systems, UI designs play a crucial role in providing secure and user-friendly experiences. The interfaces for managing user accounts, access controls, and security policies contribute to the overall usability and effectiveness of these mechanisms. As technology continues to evolve, UI designers must remain attuned to emerging trends and best practices to create interfaces that balance security and user experience in an ever-changing digital landscape.

Discuss strategies for securing data transmission within the UI.

Securing data transmission within the user interface (UI) is a critical aspect of ensuring the confidentiality, integrity, and privacy of sensitive information as it travels between different components of a digital system. One fundamental strategy for securing data transmission is the use of encryption protocols. Transport Layer Security (TLS) and its predecessor, Secure Sockets Layer (SSL), are commonly employed to encrypt data in transit. These protocols establish a secure communication channel between a user's device and a server, ensuring that data exchanged between them remains confidential and protected from eavesdropping. UI designs that integrate encryption protocols often include visual indicators, such as padlock icons, to reassure users that their data is being transmitted securely. Employing strong encryption algorithms and regularly updating to the latest protocol versions are crucial aspects of maintaining the effectiveness of these strategies.

Additionally, the implementation of secure communication protocols, such as HTTPS for web applications, is paramount in securing data transmission. HTTPS combines the standard HTTP protocol with TLS or SSL to encrypt data during transit, preventing unauthorized interception and tampering. UI designs should ensure that all communications, especially those involving sensitive information like login credentials or payment details, are conducted over HTTPS. Clear and prominent indicators, such as the padlock symbol in the address bar, contribute to user awareness and trust in the security of data transmission. This strategy is foundational for protecting data as it traverses the network, particularly in scenarios where users interact with web-based interfaces.

Securing data transmission also involves the proper validation of server certificates. UI designs should incorporate mechanisms to verify the authenticity of server certificates, ensuring that users are connecting to legitimate servers and not falling victim to man-in-the-middle attacks. Certificate authorities (CAs) play a crucial role in this process by issuing digital certificates that validate the identity of the server. UI interfaces often include visual cues, such as the green address bar, to indicate a valid and authenticated connection. Strategies for certificate validation contribute to the overall trustworthiness of data transmission, assuring users that they are communicating with genuine and secure servers.

Another strategy for securing data transmission within the UI is the implementation of Content Security Policy (CSP). CSP is a security standard that helps mitigate the risk of cross-site scripting (XSS) attacks by defining and enforcing the sources from which content, such as scripts or stylesheets, can be loaded. UI designs incorporating CSP policies reduce the likelihood of malicious code injection and unauthorized data access through scripts. By specifying trusted sources for content loading, CSP enhances the integrity and security of data transmitted between the client and the server.

In the context of web applications, implementing HTTP Strict Transport Security (HSTS) is a crucial strategy for securing data transmission. HSTS is a web security policy mechanism that helps protect against man-in-the-middle attacks and cookie hijacking by enforcing the use of HTTPS. UI designs should include the appropriate headers to instruct browsers to only communicate with the server over secure connections. This proactive approach ensures that even if users attempt to connect via an unsecured HTTP link, the browser automatically redirects them to the secure HTTPS version. HSTS contributes to a more robust and secure data transmission environment within web applications.

Secure data transmission strategies also involve the proper handling of user authentication tokens and session management. UI designs should prioritize the use of secure and widely adopted authentication mechanisms, such as OAuth or OpenID Connect, which facilitate the secure exchange of authentication tokens between the client and the server. Ensuring that these tokens are transmitted securely and are resistant to interception or tampering is crucial for maintaining the confidentiality of user sessions. Session management interfaces in the UI should include options for administrators to monitor and terminate active sessions, preventing unauthorized access and enhancing the overall security of data transmission.

To further secure data transmission, UI designs should consider implementing additional layers of protection, such as Web Application Firewalls (WAFs). WAFs act as a barrier between the web application and the internet, filtering and monitoring HTTP traffic to block malicious activity. UI interfaces for managing WAF settings enable administrators to configure rules, monitor traffic, and respond to potential threats. This strategy provides an additional line of defense against various attacks, including SQL injection, cross-site scripting, and other web application vulnerabilities that could compromise data during transmission.

User education is a pivotal aspect of securing data transmission within the UI. UI designs should include informative interfaces that educate users about secure practices, such as recognizing phishing attempts and verifying the security indicators in their browsers. Providing clear guidance on the importance of secure data transmission and the risks associated with unsecured connections enhances user awareness and encourages responsible online behavior. UI interfaces can incorporate tooltips, pop-up messages, or dedicated sections with security information to guide users in making informed decisions about their online interactions.

In the realm of mobile applications, securing data transmission involves implementing secure communication channels and validating the authenticity of backend servers. Mobile UI designs should prioritize the use of secure communication protocols, such as HTTPS, and ensure that data transmitted between the mobile app and the server is encrypted. Additionally, mobile UIs should include features that verify the integrity of the server's SSL/TLS certificates to prevent man-in-the-middle attacks. Strategies for securing data transmission in mobile UIs align with the principles applied in web-based interfaces, emphasizing the importance of encryption, secure protocols, and certificate validation.

Continuous monitoring and logging are essential components of a comprehensive strategy for securing data transmission. UI designs should incorporate interfaces for administrators to monitor network traffic, review logs, and detect any anomalies or suspicious activities. Proactive monitoring enables the timely identification of security incidents, facilitating a swift response to potential threats. UI interfaces for monitoring and logging should present information in a comprehensible and actionable format, allowing administrators to assess the security status of data transmission effectively.

The adoption of emerging technologies, such as the Internet of Things (IoT) and edge computing, introduces new challenges in securing data transmission within the UI. UI designs for IoT devices should prioritize secure communication protocols and encryption mechanisms, considering the unique constraints and characteristics of IoT networks. Edge computing environments demand UI interfaces that allow administrators to manage and secure data transmission between edge devices and central servers. Strategies for securing data transmission in these contexts involve a combination of encryption, authentication, and access control mechanisms tailored to the specific requirements of IoT and edge computing ecosystems.

In conclusion, securing data transmission within the UI is a multifaceted challenge that requires a comprehensive and proactive approach. Strategies involving encryption protocols, secure communication channels, certificate validation, content security policies, and user education contribute to building a robust defense against various threats. Implementing secure practices in session management, authentication token handling, and continuous monitoring enhances the overall security posture. As technology evolves, UI designers must remain vigilant, adapting and incorporating emerging security standards to ensure the confidentiality, integrity, and privacy of data during transmission within digital systems.

Explore the use of encryption and secure protocols to protect user data.

The use of encryption and secure protocols represents a cornerstone in safeguarding user data, ensuring confidentiality, integrity, and privacy across various digital platforms. Encryption, a process of encoding information in such a way that only authorized parties can access it, plays a pivotal role in protecting sensitive user data from unauthorized access and interception during transmission. Transport Layer Security (TLS) and its predecessor, Secure Sockets Layer (SSL), are widely adopted cryptographic protocols that establish secure communication channels between users and servers. These protocols employ encryption algorithms to scramble data, making it indecipherable to anyone without the proper decryption key. By encrypting data in transit, TLS and SSL mitigate the risks associated with eavesdropping and man-in-the-middle attacks, ensuring that sensitive user information, such as login credentials and financial transactions, remains confidential.

In the context of web applications, the adoption of HTTPS (Hypertext Transfer Protocol Secure) is a prevalent practice to secure the transmission of data between users and servers. HTTPS combines the standard HTTP protocol with TLS or SSL, encrypting the data exchanged between the user's browser and the web server. The use of HTTPS is signaled by the padlock icon in the browser's address bar, providing users with a visual cue that their communication with the website is secure. UI designs for websites and web applications must prioritize the implementation of HTTPS to protect user data from potential threats, fostering trust and confidence among users.

Public key cryptography, a fundamental component of encryption, involves the use of asymmetric key pairs—a public key for encryption and a private key for decryption. This cryptographic method adds an extra layer of security, enabling secure communication without the need to share secret keys. SSL/TLS protocols often leverage public key cryptography during the initial handshake between the user's device and the server to establish a secure connection. UI designs should include interfaces that facilitate the generation, storage, and management of public and private keys, ensuring the seamless implementation of encryption mechanisms and enhancing the security of user data.

End-to-end encryption is a robust strategy that ensures data remains encrypted throughout its entire journey, from the sender to the recipient. This approach is particularly relevant in messaging applications and email services where privacy is paramount. UI designs for end-to-end encryption should provide users with intuitive interfaces for managing encryption keys and verifying the identity of communication endpoints. The implementation of end-to-end encryption prevents intermediaries, including service providers, from accessing the content of messages, thus safeguarding user communications against unauthorized access.

In the realm of mobile applications, securing user data requires the implementation of encryption mechanisms tailored to the characteristics of mobile platforms. Mobile UI designs should prioritize the use of secure communication protocols, such as HTTPS, to protect data transmitted between the mobile app and the server. Additionally, mobile applications often handle sensitive information, including personal identifiers and geolocation data. Implementing encryption for data stored on the device, such as in local databases or caches, is crucial to prevent unauthorized access in the event of device loss or theft. UI interfaces for mobile applications should incorporate options for users to enable or manage encryption settings, contributing to a more secure mobile data environment.

Secure email communication relies on encryption to protect the confidentiality of messages and attachments. Pretty Good Privacy (PGP) and its open-source implementation, GNU Privacy Guard (GPG), are widely used for email encryption. These tools employ a combination of symmetric and asymmetric encryption, allowing users to encrypt email content and attachments for specific recipients. UI designs for email clients should include user-friendly interfaces for key management, encryption settings, and secure email composition. The integration of encryption into email communication interfaces ensures that sensitive information remains confidential and protected from unauthorized access.

Cloud storage services represent a common platform for users to store and share data. Ensuring the security of user data in the cloud involves the use of encryption mechanisms both during transmission and while at rest. UI designs for cloud storage platforms should prioritize the implementation of TLS or SSL for securing data in transit between the user's device and the cloud servers. Additionally, employing client-side encryption, where data is encrypted on the user's device before being uploaded to the cloud, enhances the security posture. UI interfaces should provide users with intuitive options to enable and manage encryption settings, fostering a secure environment for storing and accessing sensitive data in the cloud.

Data at rest encryption is a strategy employed to secure information stored on devices or servers when not in active use. UI designs for applications and platforms that handle sensitive user data should include interfaces for managing data at rest encryption settings. Full disk encryption, file-level encryption, and database encryption are common approaches to protect stored data from unauthorized access. Implementing data at rest encryption ensures that even if physical access to storage devices is compromised, the stored data remains unreadable without the proper decryption keys.

Virtual Private Networks (VPNs) contribute to securing user data by encrypting internet traffic and providing a secure communication channel between the user's device and a VPN server. UI designs for VPN applications should offer users intuitive interfaces for selecting server locations, enabling or disabling the VPN connection, and managing encryption settings. The use of VPNs is particularly relevant when users connect to public Wi-Fi networks, where the risk of unauthorized access and data interception is higher. By encrypting data from the user's device to the VPN server, these applications add a layer of security to data transmission, ensuring the privacy and integrity of user information.

Secure File Transfer Protocols, such as Secure File Transfer Protocol (SFTP) and Secure Copy Protocol (SCP), are essential for protecting user data during file uploads and downloads. UI designs for file transfer applications and platforms should prioritize the use of these secure protocols to ensure that data transmitted between the user's device and the server is encrypted. Providing users with interfaces that facilitate the selection of secure transfer options, key authentication, and secure file management contributes to a more secure file transfer environment.

The adoption of Zero-Knowledge Encryption (ZKE) is a privacy-centric strategy that ensures service providers have zero knowledge of user data stored on their platforms. In a zero-knowledge system, only the end-users hold the encryption keys, and the service provider cannot access the contents of user data. UI designs for platforms implementing zero-knowledge encryption should incorporate interfaces for users to manage their encryption keys securely. While ensuring the privacy of user data, UI interfaces should strike a balance between security and user convenience, providing a seamless experience while maintaining a robust level of encryption.

Continuous advancements in encryption technologies, including post-quantum cryptography, contribute to the ongoing evolution of secure data protection strategies. UI designs must remain adaptive to incorporate emerging encryption standards and protocols to address evolving security challenges. As quantum computing capabilities progress, UI interfaces for encryption should consider the potential vulnerabilities posed by quantum algorithms, prompting the adoption of quantum-resistant encryption algorithms. By staying abreast of encryption innovations, UI designers contribute to the resilience and effectiveness of secure data protection mechanisms, ensuring that user data remains shielded from emerging threats.

In conclusion, the use of encryption and secure protocols is integral to protecting user data across diverse digital environments. Whether securing data in transit through SSL/TLS, implementing end-to-end encryption for messaging, or employing data at rest encryption in storage, UI designs play a central role in ensuring the seamless integration of these security measures. By providing users with intuitive interfaces for managing encryption settings, key authentication, and secure communication, UI designers contribute to creating a secure and trustworthy digital experience, upholding the principles of confidentiality, integrity, and privacy for user data.

Explore the integration of biometric authentication in operating system interfaces.

The integration of biometric authentication into operating system interfaces marks a significant advancement in the quest for secure, convenient, and user-friendly methods of user verification. Biometric authentication leverages unique physiological or behavioral characteristics of individuals, such as fingerprints, facial features, iris patterns, voice, or even behavioral traits like typing patterns, to verify and authenticate their identity. Operating system interfaces have increasingly embraced biometric authentication as a more robust and user-centric alternative to traditional password-based methods. Fingerprint recognition, a widely adopted biometric authentication method, involves capturing and analyzing the unique patterns of ridges and valleys on a person's fingertip. The integration of fingerprint authentication in operating system interfaces often entails dedicated fingerprint sensors or scanners embedded in devices, allowing users to unlock their devices, access applications, and authenticate transactions with a simple touch.

Facial recognition represents another prominent biometric authentication method integrated into operating system interfaces. This technology analyzes and maps facial features, creating a unique facial signature for each individual. Operating systems employing facial recognition typically utilize front-facing cameras or specialized sensors to capture and process facial data. The integration of facial recognition in operating system interfaces enables users to unlock their devices, authorize payments, and access sensitive information by merely looking at the device. The seamless and natural interaction with the device, coupled with the accuracy of facial recognition algorithms, enhances user experience while maintaining a high level of security.

Iris recognition, a more advanced biometric authentication technique, focuses on the unique patterns within the iris of the eye. Operating systems incorporating iris recognition utilize specialized cameras to capture intricate details of the iris, creating a highly secure biometric template for user authentication. The integration of iris recognition in operating system interfaces enhances security by relying on an internal and protected feature, making it more resistant to spoofing attempts. Users can unlock their devices or authenticate transactions by simply looking into the iris recognition camera, offering a convenient and robust authentication method.

Voice recognition, another facet of biometric authentication, analyzes the unique characteristics of an individual's voice, including pitch, tone, and speech patterns. Operating system interfaces that integrate voice recognition enable users to access their devices or authorize actions through spoken commands. Voice authentication can be particularly beneficial in scenarios where hands-free operation is essential, such as in-car systems or smart home devices. The integration of voice recognition in operating systems broadens the scope of biometric authentication, providing users with a diverse set of options based on their preferences and the context of use.

The behavioral aspect of biometric authentication extends to methods such as keystroke dynamics, which analyzes the unique typing patterns and rhythm of individuals. Operating systems can leverage this biometric method to continuously verify the identity of users based on how they interact with keyboards or touchscreens. Keystroke dynamics offer a non-intrusive and continuous authentication method, contributing to a more seamless user experience within the operating system interface. As users type, the system continuously validates their identity, allowing for secure access to applications and services without requiring explicit actions.

The integration of biometric authentication into operating system interfaces also extends to novel methods, such as palm vein recognition. This technique analyzes the unique vein patterns within an individual's palm, adding an additional layer of security to user authentication. Operating systems equipped with palm vein recognition interfaces allow users to authenticate themselves by placing their palm over a sensor, capturing and verifying the intricate vein patterns. This biometric method offers a balance between security and user convenience, contributing to the multifaceted landscape of biometric authentication within operating systems.

Operating systems with biometric authentication capabilities often include dedicated user interfaces for enrolling, managing, and customizing biometric data. During the enrollment process, users register their biometric information, allowing the operating system to create a secure template for future authentication. The user interfaces for biometric enrollment typically guide users through the process, ensuring accurate capture and storage of their unique biometric data. These interfaces may include visual feedback, step-by-step instructions, and quality checks to enhance the reliability of the enrolled biometric information.

The security of biometric data is a paramount concern in the integration of biometric authentication within operating systems. To address this, operating systems implement robust security measures, such as encryption and secure storage, to protect the stored biometric templates. Biometric data is often stored in a highly secure enclave or on a dedicated hardware module within the device, adding an extra layer of protection against unauthorized access. User interfaces for managing biometric data within operating systems should prioritize transparency and educate users about the security measures in place to safeguard their sensitive biometric information.

Multi-factor authentication (MFA) is a complementary strategy often integrated into operating system interfaces alongside biometric authentication. MFA combines multiple verification methods, such as biometrics and passwords, to enhance security. Users may be required to provide a combination of something they know (password) and something they are (biometric data) for more robust authentication. Operating systems incorporate MFA interfaces that guide users through the setup and management of multiple authentication factors, contributing to a layered security approach within the interface.

Operating systems with biometric authentication capabilities extend their integration to various applications and services, creating a unified and seamless user experience. Biometric authentication interfaces are designed to work seamlessly with third-party applications, allowing users to leverage the same biometric data for authentication across a spectrum of services. The integration of biometric authentication in app ecosystems, financial transactions, and secure document access contributes to a more cohesive and user-friendly digital environment.

Accessibility considerations play a crucial role in the integration of biometric authentication within operating system interfaces. User interfaces for biometric authentication should accommodate individuals with diverse abilities and preferences. Operating systems often include options for alternative authentication methods or provide configurable settings to adapt the biometric interface to individual user needs. The design of biometric authentication interfaces should adhere to accessibility standards, ensuring that users with disabilities can effectively and comfortably utilize biometric authentication features within the operating system.

The continuous evolution of biometric technology introduces advancements such as 3D facial recognition, which captures and analyzes a three-dimensional map of the user's face for enhanced accuracy and security. Operating systems adapt to these technological innovations by incorporating interfaces that guide users through the setup and utilization of new biometric features. The integration of cutting-edge biometric technologies within operating system interfaces contributes to staying ahead of security challenges while providing users with the latest advancements in user authentication.

In conclusion, the integration of biometric authentication into operating system interfaces represents a transformative shift in user authentication methods, emphasizing security, convenience, and accessibility. Fingerprint, facial, iris, voice, and behavioral biometrics offer a diverse array of options, allowing users to choose authentication methods based on their preferences and the context of use. The design of user interfaces for biometric authentication involves creating intuitive and secure enrollment, management, and customization interfaces. Security measures, including encryption and secure storage of biometric data, are paramount to instill user confidence in the reliability and privacy of biometric authentication. As operating systems continue to evolve, the integration of emerging biometric technologies and the adherence to accessibility standards will play a central role in shaping the future landscape of user authentication within digital interfaces.

Discuss the advantages and challenges of biometric security measures.

The adoption of biometric security measures presents a paradigm shift in the realm of authentication, offering a multifaceted landscape of advantages and challenges. One of the key advantages of biometric security lies in its inherent uniqueness and individuality. Biometric identifiers, such as fingerprints, facial features, and iris patterns, are highly distinctive to each person, providing a robust and personalized method of user authentication. This uniqueness enhances the security of biometric systems, as it significantly reduces the likelihood of false positives—instances where the system incorrectly identifies an individual as someone else. The inherent individuality of biometric traits contributes to a more reliable and accurate means of verifying identity compared to traditional methods like passwords, which are susceptible to breaches through theft or hacking.

Another significant advantage of biometric security measures is the convenience they offer to users. Biometric authentication methods, such as fingerprint or facial recognition, streamline the authentication process by eliminating the need for users to remember and input complex passwords. This convenience is particularly valuable in the era of pervasive digital interactions, where individuals engage with various devices and services on a daily basis. Biometric security measures contribute to a more seamless user experience, reducing friction and enhancing user adoption of secure authentication practices.

Biometric security measures also excel in providing an additional layer of security through multi-factor authentication (MFA). By combining biometric authentication with other factors such as passwords or security tokens, MFA creates a layered defense against unauthorized access. This layered approach enhances security by requiring attackers to compromise multiple authentication factors, significantly raising the complexity and effort involved in breaching the system. Biometric MFA contributes to a robust security posture, offering both the uniqueness of biometric traits and the diversity of multiple authentication factors.

The integration of biometric security measures aligns with the trend towards enhanced user experience and personalization. As users increasingly expect seamless and user-friendly interactions with digital systems, biometrics offer a natural and intuitive means of authentication. The user-friendly nature of biometric security measures simplifies the authentication process, making it accessible to individuals with varying levels of technical expertise. This accessibility contributes to the democratization of secure practices, as biometric authentication methods cater to a broad user demographic.

In the context of physical access control, biometric security measures provide advantages in terms of non-repudiation. Biometric traits, being inherent to individuals, offer a level of certainty regarding the identity of a person accessing a physical space or facility. This non-repudiation aspect is particularly crucial in scenarios where accountability and traceability are paramount, such as in secure government facilities, financial institutions, or research laboratories. Biometric access control contributes to a more accountable and traceable security infrastructure, reducing the potential for disputes or fraudulent activities.

However, the widespread adoption of biometric security measures also brings forth a set of challenges that require careful consideration. One significant challenge is the issue of privacy and data protection. Biometric data, being inherently personal and sensitive, raises concerns about its collection, storage, and potential misuse. The compromise of biometric data poses unique risks, as unlike passwords or tokens, biometric traits are irreplaceable. Striking a balance between the security benefits of biometrics and the protection of individuals' privacy is a critical challenge that necessitates robust legal frameworks, ethical considerations, and secure storage practices.

The vulnerability to spoofing or presentation attacks is another challenge associated with biometric security measures. Techniques such as fingerprint or facial recognition spoofing, where attackers attempt to mimic or present falsified biometric data to deceive the system, pose a risk to the integrity of biometric authentication. Biometric systems need to incorporate advanced anti-spoofing mechanisms, including liveness detection and multi-modal biometrics, to mitigate the risk of presentation attacks. The ongoing arms race between biometric technology advancements and spoofing techniques underscores the need for continuous innovation in the field.

Interoperability and standardization represent challenges in the deployment of biometric security measures across diverse systems and applications. Different devices and platforms may employ varying biometric recognition methods, making it challenging to establish a universal standard. Interoperability issues can hinder the seamless integration of biometric authentication across devices and services, potentially leading to fragmentation and inconsistencies. Efforts to establish industry standards and promote interoperability are crucial for realizing the full potential of biometric security measures in diverse digital ecosystems.

Biometric template storage and management introduce complexities related to scalability, security, and compliance. Storing biometric templates securely, especially in large-scale deployments, demands robust cryptographic measures and secure storage architectures. Ensuring compliance with data protection regulations and standards becomes crucial, requiring organizations to implement transparent and accountable practices in handling biometric data. The challenges associated with template storage and management highlight the need for secure and scalable infrastructures to support the increasing adoption of biometric security measures.

The susceptibility to biometric template database breaches raises concerns about the long-term security of biometric data. In cases where biometric templates are compromised, individuals face a unique challenge, as unlike passwords, biometric traits cannot be easily reset or changed. The potential for irreversible privacy implications necessitates stringent security measures, encryption techniques, and continuous monitoring to safeguard biometric databases from unauthorized access. Organizations deploying biometric security measures must prioritize the implementation of robust security protocols to mitigate the impact of potential breaches.

Ethical considerations surrounding consent and user awareness present challenges in the deployment of biometric security measures.

Users may be unaware of the extent to which their biometric data is collected, stored, and used, raising questions about informed consent. Transparent communication, user education, and clear policies regarding biometric data usage are essential to address ethical concerns. Balancing the advantages of biometric security with the ethical imperative to respect individuals' autonomy and rights remains an ongoing challenge that requires collaboration between technology developers, regulators, and users.

Biometric diversity and inclusivity are critical considerations in the design and deployment of biometric security measures. Some biometric technologies may exhibit demographic biases, leading to differential performance across various ethnicities, genders, or age groups. Ensuring fairness and accuracy in biometric authentication across diverse user populations requires comprehensive testing, continuous improvement, and the development of inclusive algorithms. Addressing biases and promoting diversity in biometric recognition systems contribute to equitable access and user acceptance.

The potential for mission creep, where originally collected biometric data is repurposed for unintended uses, poses a challenge to the ethical and responsible deployment of biometric security measures. Organizations must establish clear policies regarding the scope and purpose of biometric data collection to prevent its misuse or unauthorized sharing. Legal frameworks and governance structures play a crucial role in defining the boundaries of biometric data usage and ensuring adherence to ethical principles.

In conclusion, while biometric security measures offer a multitude of advantages, they also present a set of challenges that require careful consideration, innovation, and collaboration across various domains. The unique combination of security, convenience, and user-friendly interaction positions biometrics at the forefront of modern authentication methods. Addressing privacy concerns, mitigating the risk of presentation attacks, establishing interoperability standards, and navigating ethical considerations are pivotal in realizing the full potential of biometric security measures. The ongoing evolution of biometric technology calls for a holistic approach, encompassing technological advancements, legal frameworks, ethical guidelines, and user education to create a secure and inclusive digital landscape.

Highlight the importance of user education in maintaining secure UI interactions.

User education plays a pivotal role in maintaining secure UI interactions, serving as a cornerstone in the defense against various cyber threats and promoting responsible online behavior. In an era characterized by pervasive digital interactions and an evolving threat landscape, the importance of educating users about secure UI practices cannot be overstated. One of the primary aspects of user education involves raising awareness about the significance of strong, unique passwords. Users need to understand the vulnerability associated with using easily guessable passwords or reusing the same password across multiple platforms. Educating users on the importance of creating complex passwords, incorporating a mix of uppercase and lowercase letters, numbers, and symbols, contributes to the development of a robust first line of defense against unauthorized access.

Furthermore, user education extends to the concept of password hygiene, emphasizing the need for regular password updates and avoiding the use of easily discoverable personal information. Users should be aware of the potential risks associated with storing passwords in plaintext or using the same credentials for an extended period. Comprehensive user education programs provide guidance on secure password management tools, encouraging the adoption of password managers to generate, store, and manage complex passwords securely. By promoting these practices, user education empowers individuals to take an active role in safeguarding their digital identities and the sensitive information associated with their accounts.

Phishing attacks represent a prevalent and sophisticated threat vector, and user education becomes a crucial defense mechanism against falling victim to such deceptive tactics. Users need to be adept at recognizing phishing attempts, understanding the hallmarks of suspicious emails, links, or messages that may attempt to trick them into divulging sensitive information. User education initiatives should familiarize individuals with common phishing techniques, such as email spoofing, social engineering, and deceptive URLs, enabling them to exercise vigilance in evaluating the authenticity of digital communications. By fostering a culture of skepticism and teaching users to verify the legitimacy of requests for sensitive information, user education contributes significantly to mitigating the impact of phishing attacks.

In the context of secure UI interactions, user education also plays a pivotal role in promoting awareness about the risks associated with public Wi-Fi networks. Users need to understand that public Wi-Fi hotspots, while convenient, can pose significant security risks if not used cautiously. Educational programs should emphasize the importance of avoiding sensitive transactions, such as online banking or accessing confidential work-related information, while connected to unsecured Wi-Fi networks. Users should be educated on the potential threat of network eavesdropping and the importance of using virtual private networks (VPNs) for encrypting data transmission over public networks, thereby enhancing the security of their UI interactions.

Educating users about the implications of software updates and patches is essential for maintaining a secure UI environment. Users may be inclined to postpone or ignore software updates due to inconvenience or lack of awareness about the critical role these updates play in addressing security vulnerabilities. User education initiatives should underscore the importance of timely software updates in patching known vulnerabilities and enhancing the overall security posture of applications and operating systems. By instilling an understanding of the risks associated with outdated software, user education empowers individuals to prioritize and promptly apply necessary updates, contributing to a resilient and secure UI ecosystem.

Social engineering attacks, which exploit human psychology to manipulate individuals into divulging confidential information, pose a significant threat to secure UI interactions. User education programs play a crucial role in equipping individuals with the knowledge to recognize and resist social engineering tactics. Users should be educated about the risks associated with disclosing personal or sensitive information over the phone, through emails, or on social media platforms. Training programs can simulate real-world scenarios to enhance users' ability to identify social engineering attempts and reinforce the importance of verifying the legitimacy of unexpected requests for information. By cultivating a heightened awareness of social engineering tactics, user education becomes a frontline defense against these manipulative strategies.

Secure browsing habits are integral to maintaining a secure UI environment, and user education is instrumental in instilling best practices. Users need to understand the potential risks associated with visiting malicious websites, downloading suspicious files, or clicking on unverified links. Educational initiatives should emphasize the importance of verifying website security through indicators such as HTTPS and recognizing the signs of potentially compromised websites. Users should be educated on the dangers of downloading files from unknown sources and the potential for malware infections. By imparting knowledge about secure browsing habits, user education contributes to the prevention of malware infections and the protection of sensitive data during UI interactions.

User education extends to the realm of physical security, emphasizing the importance of safeguarding devices and maintaining awareness of their surroundings. Individuals should be educated on the risks of leaving devices unattended in public spaces and the potential for unauthorized access. Educational programs can guide users on implementing screen locks, biometric authentication, and device encryption to enhance the security of their personal information. By fostering a sense of responsibility for the physical security of devices, user education contributes to a comprehensive approach to UI security that encompasses both digital and physical dimensions.

In the era of bring-your-own-device (BYOD) policies and remote work, user education becomes even more critical in ensuring a secure UI environment. Individuals need to be aware of the risks associated with connecting personal devices to corporate networks and the potential for unauthorized access to sensitive organizational data. User education programs should guide individuals on implementing security measures, such as device encryption, strong authentication, and adherence to organizational security policies. By educating users about the unique challenges and security considerations associated with remote work and BYOD scenarios, organizations empower individuals to be active contributors to a secure UI landscape.

In the context of financial transactions and online shopping, user education plays a crucial role in fostering secure behaviors. Users should be educated on the risks of sharing financial information over unsecured connections and the importance of verifying the legitimacy of online merchants. Training programs can provide guidance on recognizing secure payment indicators, such as the padlock symbol and HTTPS, to ensure the confidentiality of financial transactions. By instilling a sense of caution and awareness in users engaging in online financial activities, user education contributes to the prevention of fraud and the protection of sensitive financial information.

The ubiquity of Internet of Things (IoT) devices introduces new challenges in UI security, and user education becomes essential in navigating this evolving landscape. Users should be educated on the potential security risks associated with IoT devices, including the importance of changing default passwords, updating firmware, and configuring privacy settings. Training programs can guide users on recognizing signs of potential IoT device compromise and adopting secure practices in their interactions with smart home devices, wearable technologies, and other IoT gadgets. By promoting an understanding of IoT security considerations, user education enhances the overall security posture of interconnected digital ecosystems.

The collaborative nature of user education initiatives involves a partnership between individuals, organizations, and technology developers. UI designers play a crucial role in creating interfaces that facilitate user understanding and adherence to secure practices. User interfaces should incorporate clear and accessible security indicators, provide informative prompts about potential risks, and offer guidance on secure behaviors. Designing interfaces with simplicity and user-friendliness in mind ensures that security features are not perceived as obstacles but as integral components of a positive user experience.

In conclusion, user education stands as an indispensable pillar in maintaining secure UI interactions, offering a proactive and preventive approach to cybersecurity. By instilling awareness, fostering responsible online behavior, and empowering individuals with the knowledge to recognize and mitigate security risks, user education contributes to the development of a resilient and informed user base. In the ever-evolving landscape of digital interactions, user education becomes a dynamic and adaptive strategy, ensuring that individuals are equipped to navigate the complexities of UI security and actively contribute to the protection of their digital identities and sensitive information.

Discuss security best practices and how users can actively contribute to system security.

Security best practices are fundamental principles and guidelines designed to safeguard systems, data, and digital interactions from unauthorized access, cyber threats, and potential breaches. Users play a crucial role in actively contributing to system security by adhering to these best practices and adopting a proactive mindset towards cybersecurity. One of the foundational aspects of security best practices involves the creation and maintenance of strong, unique passwords. Users should adopt the practice of using complex passwords, combining uppercase and lowercase letters, numbers, and symbols to enhance the strength of their credentials. Regularly updating passwords and avoiding the reuse of passwords across multiple accounts are essential practices to mitigate the risk of unauthorized access, as compromised passwords can have cascading effects on various online platforms and services.

Multi-factor authentication (MFA) stands as a pivotal security best practice that adds an additional layer of protection to user accounts. By requiring users to provide multiple forms of verification, such as a password combined with a temporary code sent to their mobile device, MFA significantly enhances the security of accounts. Users are encouraged to enable MFA wherever possible, as this practice mitigates the impact of compromised passwords and provides a robust defense against unauthorized access. Embracing MFA as a security best practice exemplifies a proactive approach towards safeguarding digital identities and sensitive information.

Regular software updates and patch management constitute critical security best practices that users can actively contribute to system security. Keeping operating systems, applications, and software up-to-date ensures that known vulnerabilities are patched, reducing the risk of exploitation by malicious actors. Users should prioritize installing updates promptly, as delayed or neglected updates can leave systems exposed to potential security threats. By actively engaging in the process of software maintenance, users contribute to the overall resilience of systems, creating a fortified defense against evolving cyber threats.

Vigilant awareness of phishing threats is an integral aspect of security best practices. Phishing attacks, which involve deceptive tactics to trick individuals into divulging sensitive information, are pervasive and continually evolving. Users can actively contribute to system security by recognizing the signs of phishing attempts, such as suspicious emails, links, or messages. Verifying the legitimacy of requests for personal or financial information, avoiding clicking on unverified links, and scrutinizing the authenticity of digital communications are essential practices to thwart phishing attacks. User education on phishing awareness plays a crucial role in empowering individuals to exercise caution and contribute to the collective defense against social engineering threats.

Secure browsing habits represent a proactive security best practice that users can adopt to protect themselves from various online threats. Users should be cautious when visiting websites, ensuring that they are secure and encrypted by checking for HTTPS in the website address. Avoiding the download of files from untrusted sources, using reputable browsers with built-in security features, and exercising caution when clicking on advertisements or pop-ups contribute to a secure online browsing experience. By cultivating a mindset of discernment and prudence in their online activities, users actively contribute to maintaining a secure digital environment.

Data backup and recovery planning are essential security best practices that empower users to mitigate the impact of data loss or system failures. Regularly backing up important files and data to external drives or secure cloud services ensures that users can recover their information in the event of unforeseen incidents such as hardware failures, ransomware attacks, or accidental deletions. Establishing a robust backup strategy, including the testing of backup restoration processes, enhances the resilience of data against potential loss or compromise. Users who prioritize data backup contribute to the overall preparedness and recovery capability of systems, minimizing the potential disruptions caused by unforeseen events.

Endpoint security, which involves securing individual devices connected to a network, is a critical aspect of security best practices. Users can actively contribute to endpoint security by implementing measures such as device encryption, biometric authentication, and secure access controls. Encrypting data on devices protects sensitive information in the event of physical loss or theft. Leveraging biometric authentication methods, such as fingerprint recognition or facial recognition, enhances the security of device access. Users should also establish strong access controls, including password protection and device locking mechanisms, to prevent unauthorized access to their devices. By fortifying the security of individual endpoints, users contribute to the overall resilience of networked systems.

Privacy awareness and responsible data sharing represent security best practices that users can adopt to protect their personal information. Understanding the implications of sharing sensitive data online, such as financial details, contact information, or personally identifiable information, is crucial for safeguarding privacy. Users should be discerning about the information they share on social media platforms, online forums, and other digital spaces. Additionally, adopting privacy settings and controls provided by online platforms contributes to a more secure online presence. By exercising caution and promoting responsible data sharing practices, users actively contribute to the protection of their personal privacy and reduce the risk of identity theft or unauthorized access.

Collaboration and communication about security incidents and concerns within online communities or workplace environments are security best practices that enhance collective defense. Users should actively participate in reporting potential security threats, vulner-abilities, or suspicious activities to relevant authorities, IT departments, or community forums. Sharing knowledge about emerging threats, discussing security best practices, and fostering a culture of cybersecurity awareness contribute to a more resilient digital ecosystem. Users can actively contribute to a community-based defense against cyber threats by remaining vigilant, reporting incidents promptly, and participating in collaborative efforts to address security challenges.

Security awareness training and education programs are instrumental in cultivating a culture of cybersecurity within organizations and communities. Users should actively engage in security awareness training sessions, workshops, or online courses to stay informed about the latest security threats, best practices, and emerging trends. Building a foundation of cybersecurity knowledge empowers users to make informed decisions, recognize potential risks, and contribute to a secure digital environment. Organizations should prioritize ongoing security education to ensure that users remain well-equipped to navigate the evolving landscape of cyber threats.

Adopting a zero-trust security model represents an advanced security best practice that users can contribute to by adopting a mindset of continuous verification and authentication. The zero-trust model challenges the traditional approach of trusting entities within a network implicitly and emphasizes the need for continuous verification of user identities and devices. Users can actively contribute to a zero-trust security approach by embracing principles such as least privilege access, where access permissions are granted only to the minimum level required for tasks. Verifying and authenticating users and devices regularly, even within trusted networks, adds an additional layer of security against potential insider threats or compromised entities.

In conclusion, security best practices are essential guidelines that users can actively adopt to contribute to the overall security of systems, data, and digital interactions. By prioritizing practices such as strong password management, multi-factor authentication, regular software updates, and vigilant awareness of potential threats, users play a crucial role in fortifying the collective defense against cyber threats. Embracing a proactive mindset, staying informed about cybersecurity principles, and actively participating in security awareness initiatives contribute to the development of a resilient and secure digital ecosystem. As technology continues to advance, the commitment of users to security best practices becomes increasingly vital in navigating the evolving landscape of cyber threats and maintaining a robust defense against potential risks.

Chapter 8: UI Customization: Tailoring Your OS Experience

Define UI customization and its role in personalizing the user experience.

User Interface (UI) customization is a pivotal aspect of modern digital design, empowering users to tailor the visual and interactive elements of software applications or websites according to their preferences and needs. At its core, UI customization involves providing users with the flexibility to modify various elements of the interface, ranging from color schemes and layout structures to font styles and widget placements. The primary goal of UI customization is to enhance user experience by allowing individuals to create a personalized and intuitive environment that aligns with their aesthetic preferences, workflow habits, and accessibility requirements.

The role of UI customization in personalizing the user experience is multifaceted, addressing diverse aspects of design and usability. One of the key contributions of UI customization lies in accommodating individual preferences regarding visual aesthetics. Users have varied tastes and preferences when it comes to color schemes, contrast ratios, and overall design aesthetics. UI customization empowers users to choose themes or color palettes that resonate with their personal preferences, creating a visually appealing and comfortable interface. This level of customization goes beyond mere aesthetics; it contributes to a sense of ownership and comfort, fostering a positive emotional connection between users and the digital environment.

Accessibility is a critical dimension where UI customization plays a transformative role. Individuals with diverse abilities may have specific requirements related to font size, contrast, or navigation structures. UI customization allows users to adapt the interface to better suit their accessibility needs. For instance, users with visual impairments can adjust font sizes or choose high-contrast color schemes to enhance readability. This customization empowers individuals to create an inclusive and accessible digital experience that accommodates diverse needs, contributing to a more equitable and user-friendly interface.

Moreover, UI customization significantly impacts the efficiency and productivity of users by enabling them to tailor the layout and organization of the interface. Personalizing the arrangement of widgets, menus, or toolbars allows users to optimize their workflow based on individual preferences and tasks. This level of customization enhances user efficiency by reducing the cognitive load associated with navigating through a standardized interface. Users can prioritize and arrange elements according to their usage patterns, resulting in a more streamlined and intuitive interaction model that aligns with their unique workflow.

UI customization extends its influence to the realm of user engagement and satisfaction. Personalization fosters a sense of agency and control, as users can actively shape their digital environment according to their liking. This sense of control contributes to increased user satisfaction and a positive overall experience. Customization options, such as the ability to rearrange dashboard components or choose preferred display modes, empower users to create a digital space that resonates with their individual needs and preferences. This, in turn, enhances user engagement and encourages prolonged interactions with the digital platform.

In the context of software applications, UI customization is particularly relevant for power users or individuals who require specialized tools for specific tasks. Customizable interfaces allow these users to tailor the application to meet their specific requirements, incorporating features or functionalities that align with their professional or personal needs. This adaptability is particularly advantageous in domains such as graphic design, software development, or content creation, where users often have unique workflows and tool preferences. UI customization, in this context, transforms the digital environment into a tailored workspace, enhancing the efficiency and effectiveness of users in their specialized tasks.

Furthermore, UI customization is integral to supporting cross-platform consistency and user familiarity. In today's digital landscape, users engage with various devices and platforms, from desktop computers to mobile devices and tablets. UI customization allows users to maintain a consistent experience across different platforms by adapting the interface to fit the characteristics of each device. This not only ensures a seamless transition for users but also contributes to a sense of continuity and familiarity, irrespective of the device they are using. Consistent and customizable interfaces enhance user confidence and reduce the learning curve associated with switching between platforms.

The role of UI customization extends to social and collaborative platforms, where individuals engage in shared digital spaces. Customizable interfaces enable users to express their individuality within collaborative environments, fostering a sense of identity and community. Users can personalize profiles, choose display preferences, or customize collaboration spaces, contributing to a more inclusive and user-centric collaborative experience. This level of personalization supports the diverse needs and preferences of individuals within a collaborative setting, promoting a positive and engaging digital community.

Despite the myriad benefits of UI customization, designers and developers must strike a balance between flexibility and consistency to maintain a cohesive user experience. Offering too many customization options without thoughtful design considerations can lead to confusion or degraded usability. Designers should carefully curate customization features, ensuring that they align with the overall design principles and usability goals of the application. Striking this balance requires a user-centered design approach, where customization options are intuitive, accessible, and aligned with the core objectives of the digital platform.

In conclusion, UI customization is a dynamic and influential aspect of digital design, playing a crucial role in personalizing the user experience. From enhancing visual aesthetics and accommodating accessibility needs to optimizing workflow efficiency and fostering user engagement, UI customization empowers individuals to shape their digital environment according to their unique preferences and requirements. This level of personalization contributes not only to a positive user experience but also to a sense of ownership, control, and satisfaction. As technology continues to advance, UI customization will remain a central pillar in the pursuit of creating inclusive, user-centric, and adaptive digital interfaces that cater to the diverse needs of individuals across various domains and contexts.

Discuss how customizable interfaces contribute to user satisfaction.

Customizable interfaces play a pivotal role in shaping user satisfaction by empowering individuals to tailor their digital experiences to align with their preferences, needs, and workflow habits. At the core of this contribution lies the ability of users to exercise control over various aspects of the interface, fostering a sense of agency and personalization. This heightened level of control, from visual elements to functional features, contributes significantly to user satisfaction by providing a tailored and user-centric interaction model.

Visual aesthetics stand as a prominent factor in user satisfaction, and customizable interfaces offer users the flexibility to personalize the look and feel of their digital environment. The ability to choose color schemes, themes, and visual styles allows individuals to create a visually appealing interface that resonates with their preferences. This personalization not only enhances the aesthetics but also contributes to a positive emotional connection between users and the digital platform. By aligning the visual elements with individual tastes, customizable interfaces create a more enjoyable and engaging user experience, promoting a sense of ownership over the digital space.

Furthermore, customizable interfaces significantly impact accessibility, contributing to a more inclusive and user-friendly experience. Users with diverse abilities may have specific requirements related to font sizes, color contrasts, or interface layouts. Customization features, such as adjustable text sizes, high-contrast themes, or adaptable layouts, empower individuals to tailor the interface to meet their accessibility needs. This inclusivity enhances user satisfaction by ensuring that the digital experience is accessible to a broad range of users, regardless of their abilities or preferences. The ability to adapt the interface to individual accessibility requirements fosters a more considerate and user-centric design approach, contributing to heightened satisfaction.

Efficiency and productivity are integral dimensions of user satisfaction, and customizable interfaces play a pivotal role in optimizing workflow efficiency. Users can personalize the arrangement and organization of interface elements, such as menus, toolbars, or widgets, based on their unique usage patterns. This adaptability allows individuals to streamline their interactions with the digital platform, reducing the cognitive load associated with navigating through a standardized interface. Customization features that cater to the optimization of workflows contribute to a more efficient and user-friendly experience, enhancing user satisfaction by aligning the digital environment with individual preferences and tasks.

In addition to visual and functional customization, the ability to personalize user interactions with data and content adds another layer to user satisfaction. Customizable interfaces often allow users to create personalized dashboards, choose preferred display modes, or set content preferences. This personalization of content delivery contributes to a more engaging and relevant user experience. Users can prioritize information based on their interests, making the digital interaction more meaningful and tailored to their individual needs. By providing avenues for content personalization, customizable interfaces contribute to heightened user satisfaction through a more relevant and personalized content consumption experience.

User engagement is closely intertwined with satisfaction, and customizable interfaces foster increased engagement by providing users with the tools to shape their digital environment according to their liking. The ability to customize profiles, choose display preferences, or personalize collaborative spaces within a digital platform contributes to a more engaging and interactive user experience. Users are more likely to invest time and effort into a platform that accommodates their preferences, reflects their identity, and offers a personalized interaction model. The social and collaborative aspects of digital platforms are enhanced through customization, fostering a sense of community and shared ownership, ultimately contributing to heightened user satisfaction.

Cross-platform consistency is a crucial aspect of user satisfaction, particularly in a digital landscape where individuals engage with various devices and platforms. Customizable interfaces empower users to maintain a consistent experience across different platforms by adapting the interface to fit the characteristics of each device. This level of flexibility ensures a seamless transition for users, reducing the learning curve associated with switching between devices. Consistent and customizable interfaces enhance user confidence and satisfaction by providing a sense of continuity and familiarity, irrespective of the device they are using. This cross-platform cohesion contributes to a positive user experience and reinforces satisfaction with the digital platform.

In the context of software applications, customizable interfaces cater to power users or individuals who require specialized tools for specific tasks. Customization options allow these users to tailor the application to meet their specific professional or personal needs. Whether it's customizing keyboard shortcuts, arranging interface elements, or incorporating features relevant to a specific workflow, customizable interfaces empower users to create a digital workspace that aligns with their specialized requirements. This adaptability is particularly advantageous in domains such as graphic design, software development, or content creation, where users often have unique workflows and tool preferences. Customizable interfaces, in this context, enhance the efficiency, effectiveness, and overall satisfaction of users engaged in specialized tasks.

Despite the myriad benefits of customizable interfaces, designers and developers must carefully balance flexibility and consistency to maintain a cohesive user experience. Offering too many customization options without thoughtful design considerations can lead to confusion or degraded usability. Striking this balance requires a user-centered design approach, where customization features are intuitive, accessible, and aligned with the overall design principles and usability goals of the application. The challenge lies in providing users with enough customization options to tailor their experience without overwhelming them or compromising the integrity of the user interface.

In conclusion, customizable interfaces significantly contribute to user satisfaction by offering individuals the ability to shape their digital experiences according to their preferences, needs, and workflow habits. From enhancing visual aesthetics and accommodating accessibility requirements to optimizing workflow efficiency and fostering user engagement, customization empowers users to create a personalized and user-centric interaction model. The sense of control, ownership, and agency fostered by customizable interfaces contributes to positive emotional connections, increased engagement, and overall satisfaction with the digital platform. As technology continues to advance, the role of customizable interfaces in shaping user satisfaction remains a dynamic and integral aspect of user-centered design principles, ensuring that digital experiences are inclusive, adaptable, and resonant with individual preferences.

Explore options for customizing the visual aspects of the interface.

Customizing the visual aspects of the interface is a cornerstone of user-centered design, allowing individuals to tailor the look and feel of digital environments to align with their preferences and needs. Various options empower users to personalize the visual elements of an interface, contributing to a more engaging and user-friendly experience. One of the fundamental aspects of visual customization is the ability to choose and apply different color schemes or themes. Users can select from a range of predefined themes or even create their own, adapting the interface's color palette to suit their aesthetic preferences. This level of customization not only enhances the visual appeal of the interface but also fosters a sense of individuality and ownership, as users can create a personalized visual identity within the digital space.

Font customization is another significant option for tailoring the visual aspects of the interface. Users may have specific preferences regarding font styles, sizes, and spacing. Customization features allow individuals to adjust these parameters, ensuring that the text within the interface aligns with their readability and aesthetic preferences. This level of flexibility is particularly beneficial for users with visual impairments or those who simply prefer a specific font style for improved legibility. Font customization contributes to a more inclusive and user-centric design, accommodating diverse preferences related to text presentation within the digital environment.

Beyond color schemes and fonts, users often have the option to customize the layout and arrangement of interface elements. This includes the ability to modify the position of menus, toolbars, or widgets based on individual workflow habits. The flexibility to rearrange these elements enhances user efficiency by allowing individuals to create a layout that aligns with their unique usage patterns. This personalization of the interface layout reduces cognitive load and contributes to a more intuitive and streamlined user experience. It empowers users to optimize the spatial organization of the interface based on their tasks and preferences, fostering a sense of control and adaptability.

In addition to layout customization, users may have the option to personalize the size and positioning of interface elements. This is particularly relevant for users who may benefit from larger buttons, icons, or interactive elements for improved accessibility. Customization features that allow users to resize elements cater to diverse needs related to visual comfort and ease of interaction. Users can adjust the scale of interface components, ensuring that the digital environment is tailored to their individual requirements. This adaptability in size and positioning contributes to a more inclusive and user-friendly interface, accommodating users with varying visual abilities.

The ability to customize the background and foreground elements of the interface adds another layer of visual personalization. Users can choose from a selection of backgrounds or upload their own images to serve as the backdrop for the interface. This option allows individuals to create a visually pleasing and personalized atmosphere within the digital environment. Moreover, customization of foreground elements, such as icons or buttons, contributes to the overall visual coherence of the interface. Users can select or design their own icon sets, fostering a sense of visual unity and consistency within the personalized interface.

Some interfaces provide users with the option to enable or disable animations and transitions. This customization feature caters to users with preferences or sensitivities related to motion effects. For individuals who find animations distracting or uncomfortable, the ability to turn off or customize the speed of transitions contributes to a more comfortable and visually accommodating experience. On the other hand, users who appreciate dynamic visual effects may choose to enhance the interface with fluid animations, contributing to a more engaging and visually dynamic digital environment.

Customization of visual styles extends to the selection of graphic elements and icons used within the interface. Users can choose from different icon sets or even upload their own icons to replace default graphics. This level of customization allows for a more personalized and visually coherent interface, aligning with the user's design preferences and creating a distinct visual identity. Additionally, users may have the option to customize the cursor style, allowing them to choose a cursor design that complements their visual preferences or enhances visibility. These graphic customizations contribute to a visually enriched and personalized user experience.

In the realm of web browsing, customizing the appearance of websites through browser extensions or settings is a common practice. Users can install browser extensions that enable them to modify the color schemes, fonts, or overall visual styling of websites. This level of customization is particularly beneficial for users who prefer high-contrast themes, reduced brightness, or custom styling to enhance readability. Browser-based visual customization features contribute to a more comfortable and tailored web-browsing experience, aligning websites with users' individual visual preferences.

Dark mode or light mode toggles represent a popular visual customization option, allowing users to choose between a dark color scheme with light text or a light color scheme with dark text. This feature caters to individual preferences related to readability and comfort, especially in varying lighting conditions. Users can switch between dark and light modes based on their visual preferences, contributing to a more adaptable and visually pleasing interface. The availability of such toggles adds versatility to the visual customization options, accommodating users with diverse preferences and usage scenarios.

Moreover, the use of custom widgets or gadgets is a prevalent form of visual customization, particularly on desktop or mobile interfaces. Users can add, remove, or rearrange widgets on their home screens, choosing from a variety of functionalities such as weather updates, calendar events, or news feeds. This customization of widget placements allows individuals to create a personalized dashboard that aligns with their information needs and usage patterns. The ability to integrate custom widgets enhances the utility and visual appeal of the interface, contributing to a more personalized and efficient user experience.

Customization of visual aspects may also extend to three-dimensional environments, particularly in virtual or augmented reality settings. Users may have the option to customize the appearance of avatars, virtual spaces, or augmented reality overlays. This level of personalization contributes to a more immersive and enjoyable experience within virtual environments. Users can express their individuality by customizing the visual representation of their digital persona or by tailoring the appearance of augmented reality elements to suit their preferences. Visual customization options in three-dimensional spaces enhance user agency and contribute to a more engaging and user-centric virtual experience.

In conclusion, options for customizing the visual aspects of the interface are diverse and contribute significantly to user satisfaction. From choosing color schemes and fonts to rearranging layout elements and customizing graphic styles, these features empower users to create a personalized and visually appealing digital environment. Visual customization not only enhances the aesthetics of the interface but also fosters a sense of ownership, control, and comfort. As technology continues to advance, the continued exploration and refinement of visual customization options contribute to the development of more inclusive, adaptable, and user-centric digital interfaces across a variety of platforms and contexts.

Discuss themes, color schemes, and icon customization.

Themes, color schemes, and icon customization represent integral aspects of visual customization within digital interfaces, playing a pivotal role in shaping the aesthetic and user experience. Themes serve as overarching design templates that determine the visual style of an interface, influencing color schemes, font choices, and overall layout. Users often have the option to select from a variety of predefined themes or create their own, allowing for a personalized and visually distinct environment. Themes contribute significantly to the overall look and feel of an interface, setting the tone for the user's digital experience. Whether it's a minimalist, vibrant, or dark-themed design, the choice of a theme establishes the visual identity of the interface, fostering a sense of individuality and personalization.

Color schemes play a fundamental role in defining the visual character of an interface, and customization options empower users to tailor these color palettes to align with their preferences and aesthetic sensibilities. The availability of predefined color schemes or the ability to create custom ones enables users to choose combinations that resonate with their visual preferences or even align with specific branding or design principles. The significance of color goes beyond mere aesthetics; it influences user emotions, readability, and accessibility. Customizable color schemes contribute to a more inclusive and user-centric design, allowing individuals to adapt the inter-

face to meet their unique visual comfort, accessibility, and style preferences.

Icon customization represents a granular yet impactful level of visual personalization, allowing users to modify the graphic elements that represent actions, functions, or content within the interface. Icons are visual cues that enhance the navigability and understanding of the interface, and customization options provide users with the flexibility to choose from different icon sets or even upload their own. This level of customization contributes to a more visually coherent and personalized interface, aligning with the user's design preferences and creating a distinct visual language. Icon customization is particularly relevant for users who value a consistent and recognizable visual representation of functions or features within the digital environment, fostering a sense of familiarity and ease of use.

Themes, color schemes, and icon customization collectively contribute to the overall visual identity and user satisfaction within a digital interface. The selection of a theme sets the foundational aesthetic tone, providing users with a starting point for further customization. Themes often encompass color schemes, defining the palette used for various elements such as backgrounds, text, buttons, and accents. Users can choose from predefined themes that cater to different design preferences or create custom themes to express their unique style. This ability to personalize the overarching visual theme is particularly relevant in creating a digital space that resonates with the individual user, fostering a positive emotional connection and a sense of ownership.

Color schemes, as part of the broader theme customization, offer users the opportunity to fine-tune the visual appeal of the interface. Different color combinations evoke varied emotions and aesthetic experiences. For example, a light and pastel color scheme may create a calming and relaxed atmosphere, while a bold and vibrant scheme can convey energy and dynamism. Beyond aesthetics, color customization holds practical significance, especially in terms of accessibility. Users with visual impairments or specific preferences benefit from the ability to adjust contrast ratios, choose high-visibility color combinations, or even enable dark mode for reduced eye strain in low-light conditions. Customizable color schemes thus contribute not only to the overall visual appeal but also to the inclusivity and adaptability of the interface.

Icon customization drills down to the minutiae of visual elements within the interface, offering users the ability to modify the graphical representations of specific actions or content. Icons serve as visual cues that aid in navigation and comprehension, and customization options enhance their relevance and recognition. Users can select from different icon sets that align with their design preferences, ensuring a consistent and coherent visual language throughout the interface. Furthermore, the ability to upload custom icons allows for a highly personalized touch, enabling users to associate specific functions with images that resonate with their understanding or preferences. Icon customization, in conjunction with theme and color customization, contributes to a holistic and user-centric visual experience.

The interplay between themes, color schemes, and icon customization is exemplified in their collective impact on user engagement and satisfaction. A well-designed theme sets the stage for an aesthetically pleasing and cohesive visual environment. When users can further customize color schemes, they infuse their personal preferences into the interface, creating a space that aligns with their taste and style. Icon customization, as the granular layer, enhances the usability and recognizability of the interface, ensuring that users can easily navigate and comprehend the visual cues presented. This collective customization fosters a sense of agency and control, contributing to heightened user satisfaction and a positive overall experience within the digital space.

Moreover, the significance of these customization options extends beyond personal preference to accommodate diverse contexts and use cases. For instance, in professional settings, users may prefer a more subdued and formal color scheme, while in personal or creative contexts, vibrant and expressive themes might be favored. The ability to switch between different themes, color schemes, or icon sets allows users to adapt the interface to the specific demands of their tasks, contributing to a versatile and adaptable user experience.

In the context of mobile applications, where limited screen real estate necessitates efficient design, themes, color schemes, and icon customization become even more critical. Mobile users often interact with their devices in varied environments and lighting conditions, making customizable themes and color schemes essential for optimizing visibility and readability. Icon customization, in this context, aids in creating easily recognizable and intuitive interfaces, enhancing the overall usability of mobile applications. The personalization options cater to the diverse preferences of mobile users, contributing to a more enjoyable and user-centric mobile experience.

Furthermore, the role of themes, color schemes, and icon customization is accentuated in the context of web design. Websites cater to a broad audience with diverse preferences and expectations. Customizable themes and color schemes provide website visitors with the flexibility to adapt the visual presentation to their liking. This level of personalization enhances the user experience by creating a visually appealing and comfortable environment, encouraging prolonged engagement with the website. Icon customization, particularly in the case of interactive web applications, aids in creating an intuitive and recognizable visual language, ensuring that users can effortlessly navigate and interact with the web interface.

Despite the evident benefits of themes, color schemes, and icon customization, designers must strike a delicate balance to avoid overwhelming users with choices or compromising the integrity of the overall design. A thoughtful approach involves offering a curated selection of themes and color schemes that align with different design preferences and use cases. The customization process should be intuitive, with clear options and previews to help users make informed choices. Icon customization, while providing flexibility, should also adhere to design principles that ensure consistency and clarity in visual communication. By maintaining this balance, designers can empower users to personalize their digital experiences while preserving the cohesiveness and usability of the interface.

In conclusion, themes, color schemes, and icon customization collectively shape the visual identity of digital interfaces, contributing to user satisfaction and engagement. The ability to personalize the overarching theme sets the aesthetic tone, while customizable color schemes cater to individual preferences and accessibility needs. Icon customization enhances the recognizability and usability of the interface by allowing users to modify the graphical representations of specific functions or content. The interplay between these customization options creates a dynamic and user-centric visual experience, fostering a sense of ownership, control, and comfort within the digital space. As technology continues to evolve, the exploration and refinement of themes, color schemes, and icon customization options remain crucial in creating inclusive, adaptable, and visually appealing interfaces across various platforms and contexts.

Discuss features that allow users to personalize their preferences.

Personalization features within digital interfaces represent a fundamental aspect of user-centric design, empowering individuals to tailor their digital experiences to align with unique preferences, needs, and habits. The ability to personalize preferences encompasses a wide array of features that cater to diverse dimensions, ranging from visual aesthetics and interaction styles to content delivery and functional settings. One of the foundational elements of personalization is the option to customize the visual aspects of the interface. Users can often choose from various themes, color schemes, and fonts, enabling them to create a visually appealing environment that resonates with their aesthetic preferences. This level of customization fosters a sense of individuality and ownership, establishing an emotional connection between users and the digital space.

In addition to visual personalization, users commonly have the option to customize their interaction styles and preferences. This includes the ability to adjust settings related to input devices, such as mouse sensitivity or touchpad responsiveness. Personalization features extend to input methods, allowing users to define gestures, shortcuts, or keyboard layouts based on their comfort and efficiency. By tailoring interaction settings, users can optimize the digital environment to match their unique workflows, enhancing the overall usability and user experience.

Personalization often extends to the arrangement and organization of interface elements, providing users with the flexibility to personalize the layout according to their preferences. This includes the ability to rearrange menus, toolbars, or widgets, as well as resize and reposition interface components. By allowing users to adapt the spatial organization of the interface, personalization features contribute to a more intuitive and streamlined interaction model. Users can prioritize and arrange elements based on their usage patterns, reducing cognitive load and fostering a digital environment that aligns with individual preferences and tasks.

Moreover, personalization features frequently encompass content preferences, allowing users to tailor the delivery of information according to their interests and needs. This may involve the customization of news feeds, recommendation algorithms, or content filters. Users can specify preferences related to the types of content they want to see, creating a personalized and relevant content consumption experience. By providing granular control over content delivery, personalization features contribute to increased user engagement and satisfaction, ensuring that the digital space caters to individual preferences.

The personalization of notification settings is another prominent feature that allows users to tailor their digital experience. Users can customize preferences related to the frequency, format, and content of notifications, ensuring that alerts align with their communication preferences and priorities. This level of personalization empowers users to manage information flow, reducing potential distractions and enhancing the overall user experience. By allowing users to finely tune notification settings, personalization features contribute to a more focused, efficient, and user-centric interaction with digital platforms.

Furthermore, personalization often extends to the customization of privacy and security settings. Users can define preferences related to data sharing, visibility of personal information, and the level of security measures applied to their accounts. This level of customization provides users with control over their digital privacy, aligning the platform's security features with individual preferences and comfort levels. The ability to personalize privacy settings contributes to increased trust in digital platforms and ensures that users have agency over the protection of their personal information.

Personalization features also play a crucial role in adapting the digital interface to users with diverse abilities and accessibility needs. Customizable accessibility settings allow users to tailor aspects such as text size, color contrast, or screen reader preferences. By accommodating individual accessibility requirements, personalization features contribute to a more inclusive and user-friendly interface. This level of adaptability ensures that users with varying abilities can personalize the digital experience to suit their specific needs, contributing to a more equitable and accessible interaction model.

In the realm of e-commerce and online services, personalization features often revolve around user preferences in product recommendations and shopping experiences. Recommendation algorithms analyze user behavior, purchase history, and preferences to provide personalized product suggestions. Users may also have the option to create wish lists, save favorite items, or define style preferences. These personalization features enhance the shopping experience by tailoring product offerings to individual tastes and interests, contributing to increased user satisfaction and engagement.

Additionally, personalization features may include the ability to create and manage user profiles. Users can set preferences related to account settings, profile information, and communication preferences. Personalized profiles contribute to a sense of identity within digital platforms, allowing users to express themselves and shape their online persona. The customization of profile settings ensures that users have control over how they are represented within the digital space, fostering a more personalized and user-centric experience.

In the context of collaborative and social platforms, personalization features extend to customization options for user profiles, collaboration spaces, and communication channels. Users can personalize their profiles by adding profile pictures, bios, and other personal details. Collaboration spaces may offer features for personalizing layouts, themes, or display preferences. Customization options for communication channels may include the ability to set notification preferences, customize chat appearances, or define privacy settings. These personalization features contribute to a more engaging and user-centric collaborative experience, accommodating the diverse preferences and needs of individuals within a shared digital space.

Furthermore, the personalization of search and browsing preferences is a common feature in digital platforms. Users can customize search settings, filter preferences, and browsing options to align with their information-seeking behaviors. Personalization in search engines ensures that users receive more relevant and personalized search results, enhancing the efficiency and satisfaction of information retrieval. By tailoring search and browsing experiences, personalization features contribute to a more user-centric and adaptive digital environment.

In the context of entertainment platforms, personalization features often revolve around content recommendations and preferences. Users can create playlists, mark favorite content, and customize viewing or listening histories. Recommendation algorithms leverage this personalized data to offer tailored content suggestions, contributing to a more enjoyable and engaging entertainment experience. By allowing users to shape their content preferences, personalization features enhance the discovery and consumption of entertainment media, fostering a sense of individualized enjoyment.

Despite the evident benefits of personalization features, designers and developers must navigate the challenge of providing customization options without overwhelming users or compromising the integrity of the interface. Striking a balance between flexibility and simplicity requires a user-centered design approach, where personalization features are intuitive, accessible, and aligned with the overall design principles and usability goals of the application. By offering thoughtful and well-designed personalization options, digital platforms can empower users to tailor their experiences while maintaining a cohesive and user-friendly interface.

In conclusion, personalization features within digital interfaces are multifaceted, encompassing visual aesthetics, interaction styles, content delivery, notification settings, privacy and security preferences, accessibility settings, e-commerce experiences, user profiles, collaboration spaces, search and browsing options, and entertainment platforms. These features collectively contribute to a user-centric design approach, empowering individuals to shape their digital experiences according to their unique preferences, needs, and habits.

As technology continues to advance, the refinement and expansion of personalization features remain integral in creating inclusive, adaptable, and resonant digital interfaces across a variety of platforms and contexts.

Explore options for customizing layouts, menus, and interactive elements.

Customizing layouts, menus, and interactive elements stands as a cornerstone in user interface design, offering users the flexibility to tailor their digital environments to match their unique preferences and workflow habits. Layout customization provides users with the ability to arrange and organize interface elements in a way that suits their individual usage patterns. This includes the freedom to adjust the placement, size, and grouping of menus, toolbars, widgets, and other interactive components. The customizable layout empowers users to create an interface that aligns with their specific needs, reducing cognitive load and enhancing overall usability.

Menus represent crucial components of digital interfaces, and customization options offer users the ability to personalize menu structures to match their preferences and usage contexts. Users can often rearrange menu items, hide or show specific options, or create custom shortcuts for frequently accessed features. This level of menu customization ensures that users can streamline their interactions with the interface, optimizing efficiency and reducing the time required to access essential functions. Customizable menus contribute to a user-centric design by accommodating diverse workflows and allowing individuals to prioritize the features most relevant to their tasks.

Interactive elements, such as buttons, icons, and widgets, are integral components of digital interfaces, and customization options enhance the user experience by providing flexibility in their appearance and behavior. Users may have the option to choose from different icon sets, button styles, or widget designs, allowing them to align the visual language of the interface with their design prefer-ences. Additionally, customization features often extend to interac-tive behaviors, enabling users to define actions, gestures, or shortcuts that correspond to their preferred interaction styles. This adaptabil-ity in interactive elements fosters a sense of control and ownership, contributing to a more user-centric and engaging interface.

Layout customization extends to the adaptability of the interface across different devices and screen sizes. Responsive design features allow users to customize layouts for desktops, tablets, and mobile de-vices, ensuring a seamless and consistent user experience across var-ied platforms. This level of responsiveness caters to the diverse ways users engage with digital interfaces, adapting layouts to fit the char-acteristics of each device. Customizable layouts contribute to cross-platform consistency, reducing the learning curve associated with switching between devices and providing users with a cohesive and familiar experience.

In addition to visual customization, users often have the option to personalize the functionality of interactive elements through cus-tomization features related to input methods and controls. This in-cludes the ability to adjust parameters such as mouse sensitivity, touchpad responsiveness, or keyboard shortcuts. Users can define gestures or customize touch controls based on their preferences, en-abling a more personalized and efficient interaction model. The adaptability of input methods through customization options con-tributes to a user-friendly interface that accommodates diverse pref-erences and usage contexts.

Furthermore, layout customization features often extend to the spatial organization and arrangement of content within the inter-face. Users can customize the placement of content panes, windows, or panels to suit their individual workflow and multitasking needs. This level of adaptability allows users to create a workspace that aligns with their specific tasks, optimizing efficiency and reducing unnecessary navigation. By providing customizable content layouts, digital interfaces empower users to create personalized workspaces that enhance productivity and user satisfaction.

Customization options for layouts also play a significant role in accommodating users with diverse abilities and accessibility needs. Adaptive layouts allow users to adjust the size, spacing, and arrangement of interface elements, ensuring a more inclusive and user-friendly experience. Individuals with visual impairments or motor control challenges may benefit from the ability to customize layouts to improve readability, increase button sizes, or simplify the arrangement of interactive elements. Layout customization, in this context, contributes to a more accessible and accommodating interface, aligning with the principles of universal design.

Menus, as interactive navigation components, are subject to customization options that go beyond mere visual aesthetics. Users often have the ability to personalize menu structures based on their preferences and usage patterns. This may involve rearranging menu items, creating custom shortcuts, or even hiding less frequently used options. Customizable menus contribute to a more streamlined and efficient navigation experience, allowing users to access essential features with minimal effort. The adaptability of menus through customization options aligns with user-centric design principles, acknowledging the diversity in user workflows and preferences.

Interactive elements, including buttons, icons, and widgets, can be tailored to meet individual design preferences and functional requirements. Users may have the option to select from different icon sets or button styles, allowing them to align the visual appearance of the interface with their aesthetic sensibilities. Additionally, customization features often extend to the behavior of interactive elements, enabling users to define actions, gestures, or shortcuts that correspond to their preferred interaction styles. This adaptability in interactive elements fosters a sense of control and ownership, contributing to a more user-centric and engaging interface.

Customization of layouts, menus, and interactive elements is particularly crucial in the context of software applications used for specialized tasks or creative endeavors. Graphic designers, software developers, and content creators often have unique workflows and tool preferences. Customizable layouts allow these users to arrange interface elements in a way that optimizes their specific workflow, enhancing efficiency and productivity. Additionally, the ability to customize interactive elements, such as toolbars or widgets, ensures that these professionals can tailor the software application to meet their specialized requirements. Customizable layouts and interactive elements contribute to a more personalized and user-centric experience in professional and creative software environments.

The adaptability of layouts across different devices and screen sizes is a key consideration in contemporary user interface design. Responsive design features, which allow users to customize layouts for desktops, tablets, and mobile devices, contribute to a seamless and consistent user experience. Users can adjust the arrangement and appearance of interface elements to fit the characteristics of each device, ensuring optimal usability and visual coherence. Responsive layout customization caters to the diverse ways users interact with digital interfaces, fostering cross-platform consistency and enhancing the overall user experience.

In conclusion, customization options for layouts, menus, and interactive elements are integral components of user-centric design, providing users with the flexibility to tailor their digital experiences to match their unique preferences and workflow habits. The adaptability of layouts allows users to arrange and organize interface elements in a way that suits their individual usage patterns, reducing cognitive load and enhancing overall usability. Customizable menus empower users to personalize menu structures and streamline navigation based on their preferences and tasks. Interactive elements, when subject to customization options, contribute to a more engaging and user-centric interface by allowing users to align the visual appearance and behavior of the interface with their design preferences and interaction styles. As technology continues to advance, the refinement and expansion of customization options for layouts, menus, and interactive elements remain crucial in creating inclusive, adaptable, and resonant digital interfaces across a variety of platforms and contexts.

Discuss adaptive UI design principles for varying screen sizes and devices.

Adaptive user interface (UI) design principles play a pivotal role in addressing the diverse landscape of screen sizes and devices, ensuring a seamless and consistent user experience across different platforms. The essence of adaptive design lies in its ability to intelligently respond to the characteristics of various screens and devices, optimizing the presentation of content and functionality for each context. One fundamental principle involves responsive layout design, where the UI dynamically adjusts to accommodate different screen sizes. Fluid grids and flexible layouts enable content to scale proportionally, preventing visual clutter or awkward formatting issues. This adaptability is crucial for catering to the wide array of devices, from large desktop monitors to tablets and smartphones, providing users with a consistent and visually appealing interface regardless of the screen they are using.

Another key principle in adaptive UI design revolves around flexible images and media. The presentation of images and multimedia elements needs to be adaptable to various screen resolutions and sizes. Adaptive images can be dynamically resized or replaced with higher or lower resolution versions based on the user's device, ensuring optimal loading times and visual quality. This approach not only contributes to a more polished visual experience but also enhances the performance of the interface, particularly on devices with varying bandwidth capabilities.

Typography plays a significant role in user interface design, and adaptive principles extend to the flexible handling of text. Responsive typography involves adjusting font sizes, line heights, and spacing to maintain readability across different screens. Ensuring legibility on smaller screens, such as smartphones, may require larger font sizes and appropriate spacing, while larger screens can accommodate more expansive typography. Adaptive typography contributes to a user-friendly experience by prioritizing readability and visual comfort, irrespective of the device being used.

Navigation is a critical aspect of user interfaces, and adaptive design principles are instrumental in crafting navigation systems that work seamlessly across diverse devices. Progressive disclosure is a key concept, where navigation menus may evolve based on available screen space. On larger screens, traditional menus with multiple options can be displayed, while on smaller screens, compact or collapsible menus might be more appropriate. Additionally, touch-friendly navigation elements are emphasized for mobile devices, recognizing the prevalence of touch interfaces in smartphones and tablets. Adaptive navigation design ensures that users can easily access essential features regardless of the device, enhancing overall usability and user satisfaction.

Context-aware content delivery is another adaptive UI design principle that takes into account the capabilities and limitations of different devices. The prioritization and presentation of content may vary based on factors such as screen size, orientation, or input method. For instance, on smaller screens, content might be condensed or rearranged to fit within a single column, while on larger screens, multiple columns or side-by-side layouts may be employed. Adaptive content delivery ensures that users receive an optimized presentation that takes full advantage of the capabilities of their specific device.

Device-agnostic design is a foundational principle in adaptive UI design, emphasizing the creation of interfaces that are not tied to specific devices or platforms. Instead, the focus is on creating experiences that seamlessly adapt to the capabilities of various devices, embracing the diversity in the digital landscape. This approach involves using flexible coding techniques and adopting design patterns that can adapt to different screen sizes, resolutions, and input methods. A device-agnostic mindset ensures that the interface remains robust and effective, even as new devices with varying specifications and form factors emerge.

Media queries are a fundamental tool in implementing adaptive UI design principles. These CSS techniques enable developers to apply specific styles based on characteristics such as screen width, resolution, or device orientation. By using media queries, designers can create breakpoints where the layout and styling of the interface can be adjusted to cater to different devices. This granular control over styling ensures that the UI remains visually appealing and functional across a spectrum of screen sizes, contributing to a seamless and adaptive user experience.

Touch-friendly design is a crucial consideration in adaptive UI design, given the prevalence of touchscreens in devices like smartphones and tablets. Interfaces need to accommodate touch gestures such as tapping, swiping, and pinching. Larger touch targets and ample spacing between interactive elements are essential for preventing unintentional interactions and ensuring a smooth and intuitive touch experience. Adaptive touch-friendly design not only considers the physical aspects of touch but also incorporates gestures that enhance user interactions, contributing to a more tactile and user-friendly interface.

Cross-browser compatibility is a central tenet in adaptive UI design, acknowledging the diversity of web browsers and rendering engines. Ensuring that the interface functions consistently across popular browsers and devices is vital for reaching a broad user base. Adaptive design principles involve testing and optimizing the interface for compatibility with different browsers, addressing potential rendering inconsistencies and ensuring a uniform user experience regardless of the chosen browser or device.

Accessibility is an integral aspect of adaptive UI design, emphasizing the creation of interfaces that can be easily used by individuals with diverse abilities. This includes considerations for users with visual or motor impairments. Adaptive accessibility features may involve resizable text, high-contrast modes, and keyboard navigation options. Ensuring that the interface is perceivable, operable, and understandable for all users, regardless of their abilities or the devices they use, aligns with the principles of universal design and contributes to a more inclusive user experience.

Performance optimization is a critical consideration in adaptive UI design, particularly in the context of varied devices with differing processing capabilities and network conditions. Adaptive design principles involve strategies such as lazy loading of images, optimizing code for faster rendering, and minimizing unnecessary data transfer. By prioritizing performance considerations, adaptive UI design ensures that the interface remains responsive and efficient across a spectrum of devices, contributing to a positive user experience irrespective of the user's device specifications.

User testing across multiple devices is an essential practice in adaptive UI design, allowing designers and developers to assess how the interface performs and adapts across various devices and screen sizes. Testing involves evaluating usability, visual aesthetics, and functional consistency on different devices to identify and address any issues. User feedback from diverse devices provides valuable insights into the effectiveness of adaptive design strategies, enabling continuous refinement and optimization to enhance the overall user experience.

In conclusion, adaptive UI design principles are instrumental in crafting interfaces that seamlessly adapt to the diverse landscape of screen sizes and devices. From responsive layouts and flexible media handling to touch-friendly design and accessibility considerations, these principles prioritize a user-centric approach that accommodates the varying capabilities and contexts of different devices. Device-agnostic design, cross-browser compatibility, and performance optimization further contribute to creating interfaces that are robust, inclusive, and efficient across the ever-evolving digital landscape. As technology continues to advance, the adherence to adaptive UI design principles remains crucial in providing users with consistent, engaging, and accessible experiences across a spectrum of devices.

Explore how interfaces can dynamically adjust to different platforms.

Dynamic adaptation of interfaces to different platforms is a fundamental aspect of modern user experience design, addressing the diverse ecosystem of devices and platforms that users interact with daily. One key approach involves responsive design, where interfaces are crafted to fluidly adjust their layout, content, and functionality based on the characteristics of the platform. Responsive design relies on flexible grids and media queries, enabling the interface to adapt seamlessly to varying screen sizes and resolutions. This adaptability ensures that users, whether on desktops, tablets, or smartphones, receive an optimal and consistent visual experience, fostering a sense of familiarity and usability across platforms.

Cross-platform consistency is a central goal in the dynamic adjustment of interfaces. Regardless of the platform—be it a web browser, a mobile app, or a desktop application—the interface should maintain a cohesive visual language and functionality. Users often transition between different platforms, and a consistent design ensures a smooth and intuitive experience, reducing the learning curve associated with switching devices. Elements such as color schemes, typography, and iconography should align, creating a unified brand identity and reinforcing the user's connection with the interface, irrespective of the platform.

Device-specific considerations play a crucial role in the dynamic adaptation of interfaces. Tailoring the user interface to the unique characteristics of each platform involves more than responsive layouts. It requires optimizing interactions for the specific input methods and capabilities of devices. Touch-friendly designs are essential for mobile platforms, while desktop platforms may leverage mouse and keyboard interactions. The dynamic adjustment extends to the use of platform-specific UI components and navigation patterns, ensuring that the interface feels native to each platform and leverages the strengths of its underlying technology.

The utilization of native features and capabilities is a key strategy in dynamically adapting interfaces to different platforms. Each platform has its own set of capabilities, from specific sensors and gestures to unique system functionalities. Dynamic adaptation involves leveraging these capabilities to enhance the user experience. For example, mobile apps may incorporate device orientation for dynamic content display, or desktop applications may integrate with system notifications. By intelligently utilizing native features, interfaces become more context-aware and seamlessly integrate into the overall user experience of each platform.

The fluidity of data synchronization is an integral aspect of dynamic adaptation, especially in the context of multi-platform experiences. Users expect a seamless transition between devices while maintaining access to their data and preferences. Cloud-based solutions facilitate the synchronization of user data, ensuring that changes made on one platform are reflected across all others. Dynamic adaptation involves not only adjusting the interface but also orchestrating the underlying data synchronization processes to provide users with a continuous and coherent experience as they switch between platforms.

Optimizing performance for each platform is a critical consideration in dynamic adaptation. Different devices and platforms have varying processing power, memory, and network capabilities. Adaptive interfaces prioritize performance optimization techniques such as lazy loading of assets, efficient data fetching, and minimizing unnecessary computations. This ensures that the interface remains responsive and performs well across a spectrum of platforms, contributing to a positive user experience irrespective of the user's device specifications.

Accessibility considerations are paramount in the dynamic adjustment of interfaces to different platforms. Users with diverse abilities engage with interfaces across various devices, and adaptive design principles extend to ensuring that the interface is perceivable, operable, and understandable for all users. Platform-specific accessibility features and guidelines must be adhered to, encompassing considerations for screen readers, voice commands, and alternative input methods. By dynamically adjusting accessibility features based on the platform, interfaces become more inclusive and cater to a broader user base.

The integration of platform-specific design patterns and guidelines is a key element in the dynamic adjustment of interfaces. Each platform has its own set of design conventions, ranging from navigation patterns to interaction styles. Adhering to platform-specific guidelines ensures that the interface feels native, aligning with user expectations and contributing to a more intuitive and user-friendly experience. For instance, mobile apps may incorporate gesture-based navigation, while desktop applications adhere to standard menu structures. By embracing platform-specific design patterns, interfaces dynamically adapt to the visual language and behavior expected on each platform.

Responsive design frameworks and tools facilitate the dynamic adjustment of interfaces by providing a structured and efficient approach to building adaptable layouts. These frameworks often include pre-built components, style libraries, and responsive grids, streamlining the development process and ensuring a consistent and coherent design language across platforms. Utilizing responsive design frameworks allows designers and developers to focus on optimizing the user experience for each platform while leveraging standardized practices for responsive layout design.

A/B testing and user feedback are integral components of the dynamic adaptation process. By conducting A/B tests across different platforms, designers can gather insights into user preferences, behaviors, and performance metrics. User feedback provides valuable qualitative insights into the user experience on specific platforms, uncovering potential pain points and areas for improvement. Dynamic adaptation involves an iterative process, and continuous testing and feedback collection contribute to refining the interface to better meet user expectations on each platform.

The continuous evolution of technology and the emergence of new platforms necessitate a forward-looking approach in dynamic adaptation. Designers must anticipate changes in user behavior, technological advancements, and the introduction of novel platforms. This forward-looking perspective involves adopting scalable design and development practices that can accommodate future platforms seamlessly. The ability to dynamically adjust to new platforms positions interfaces to remain relevant, innovative, and aligned with the evolving landscape of technology.

In conclusion, the dynamic adjustment of interfaces to different platforms is a multifaceted process that involves responsive design, cross-platform consistency, device-specific considerations, native feature utilization, data synchronization, performance optimization, accessibility considerations, platform-specific design patterns, responsive design frameworks, A/B testing, user feedback, and a forward-looking approach. This comprehensive approach ensures that interfaces seamlessly adapt to the diverse ecosystem of devices and platforms, providing users with a consistent, intuitive, and engaging experience across various contexts. As technology continues to evolve, the principles of dynamic adaptation remain crucial in creating interfaces that are resilient, user-centric, and capable of delivering optimal experiences across the ever-expanding array of digital platforms.

Explore the integration of third-party extensions and plugins for UI customization.

The integration of third-party extensions and plugins for UI customization represents a dynamic and transformative aspect of contemporary user interface design, offering users the ability to tailor their digital experiences by extending the functionality and appearance of applications. These third-party extensions, often developed by independent developers or organizations, serve as modular add-ons that enhance or modify the core features of software applications. This symbiotic relationship between the core application and external plugins fosters a rich ecosystem of customization possibilities, empowering users to mold their digital interfaces according to their unique preferences and needs.

One of the primary advantages of integrating third-party extensions is the diversification of functionality. Core applications may have a set of predefined features, but third-party developers can introduce specialized functionalities that cater to niche requirements or emerging trends. For instance, a web browser might offer basic bookmarking features, but a third-party extension could introduce advanced bookmark management, tagging, or synchronization across devices. This diversification allows users to augment the capabilities of their applications, transforming them into versatile tools that align with their specific workflows or interests.

The extensibility provided by third-party plugins significantly contributes to personalization, a cornerstone of user-centric design. Users can selectively install extensions that resonate with their preferences, introducing features and enhancements that align with their unique needs. In the context of web browsers, users might add extensions for ad-blocking, password management, or language translation, tailoring the browsing experience to their preferences. This personalization fosters a sense of ownership and agency, as users actively shape the functionality and appearance of their digital interfaces, creating an environment that suits their individual requirements.

The collaboration between core application developers and third-party extension creators facilitates a continuous cycle of innovation. Core applications often provide extension APIs (Application Programming Interfaces) that allow developers to interact with and extend the functionalities of the application. This open and collaborative ecosystem encourages developers to experiment with new ideas, introduce novel features, and address specific user needs that might not have been prioritized by the core development team. The constant influx of new and innovative extensions enriches the overall user experience, ensuring that the application remains dynamic and responsive to evolving user expectations.

Moreover, the integration of third-party extensions serves as a testament to the adaptability and scalability of software ecosystems. Instead of relying solely on the development team to introduce new features or improvements, users can tap into a vast repository of extensions to enhance their experience. This flexibility is particularly advantageous in rapidly evolving domains such as web development, where emerging technologies and standards can be quickly embraced through third-party tools and plugins. The collaborative nature of extension development ensures that users can stay at the forefront of technological advancements without waiting for official updates from the core application.

While the integration of third-party extensions brings a myriad of benefits, it also raises considerations related to security and stability. Since these extensions often have access to the core functionalities of the application, there is a potential risk of introducing security vulnerabilities or conflicts with other extensions. Core application developers must implement robust security measures and compatibility checks to mitigate these risks. Similarly, users need to exercise caution when installing extensions, ensuring that they come from reputable sources and undergo regular updates to address potential security issues. Striking a balance between openness to third-party innovation and maintaining a secure and stable user experience is an ongoing challenge in the integration of extensions.

The realm of content management systems (CMS) exemplifies how third-party extensions can transform the user interface and extend the capabilities of a core application. Platforms like WordPress, Joomla, and Drupal offer a wide array of functionalities out of the box, but the addition of plugins allows users to tailor their websites with unprecedented flexibility. Third-party developers create plugins for various purposes, ranging from SEO optimization and e-commerce integration to social media sharing and advanced content formatting. This extensibility transforms these CMS platforms into versatile tools that can cater to diverse use cases, from personal blogs to complex e-commerce websites, showcasing the power of third-party contributions in shaping the user experience.

The integration of third-party extensions is particularly prevalent in the domain of graphic design and creative software. Applications like Adobe Photoshop or Sketch provide a robust set of features for digital design, but third-party plugins allow users to extend these capabilities further. Graphic designers can enhance their workflow with plugins for specialized effects, asset management, or collaboration tools. The availability of an extensive plugin ecosystem transforms these design applications into adaptable platforms that can cater to the specific needs and preferences of individual designers, fostering a vibrant community of plugin developers and users.

Web browsers serve as a prominent example of how third-party extensions can redefine the browsing experience. Browsers like Google Chrome, Mozilla Firefox, and Microsoft Edge provide users with a basic set of features, but the integration of extensions allows for an unparalleled level of customization. Users can install ad blockers for a cleaner browsing experience, password managers for enhanced security, or productivity tools for seamless integration with other applications. The diverse range of browser extensions underscores how third-party contributions can transform a standard browser into a personalized and feature-rich tool that aligns with the user's browsing habits and priorities.

E-commerce platforms also leverage the power of third-party extensions to offer users a tailored and feature-rich online shopping experience. Platforms like Shopify, WooCommerce (for WordPress), and Magento provide essential e-commerce functionalities, but third-party plugins expand the capabilities of these platforms exponentially. Users can integrate payment gateways, implement advanced analytics, or enhance the visual design of their online stores through a vast marketplace of extensions. This extensibility ensures that e-commerce platforms can cater to a wide range of businesses, from small startups to large enterprises, by offering a customizable and scalable solution.

In the context of project management and collaboration tools, the integration of third-party extensions enhances the versatility of these platforms. Applications like Trello, Asana, or Slack offer core features for project organization and team communication, but third-party developers contribute extensions that address specific collaboration needs. Users can integrate time tracking tools, enhance communication with custom integrations, or automate repetitive tasks through these extensions. The modular nature of third-party contributions enables project management platforms to accommodate the diverse workflows and requirements of different teams and industries.

The advent of low-code and no-code platforms has further democratized the development and integration of third-party extensions. These platforms empower users with limited programming skills to create and deploy custom functionalities without delving into complex coding. As a result, the barrier to entry for developing and integrating third-party extensions has been significantly lowered. This accessibility fosters a more inclusive ecosystem, allowing a broader range of users to contribute to the customization and enhancement of digital interfaces.

The integration of third-party extensions has become a fundamental aspect of mobile app development, particularly in the context of app marketplaces such as the Apple App Store and Google Play Store. Mobile applications often leverage third-party SDKs (Software Development Kits) and plugins to incorporate functionalities like analytics, advertising, or social media integration. This modular approach allows app developers to focus on core features while tapping into the expertise of third-party developers for specialized functionalities, contributing to a faster development cycle and a more feature-rich user experience.

The collaborative nature of third-party extension ecosystems extends beyond individual applications to encompass entire operating systems. Platforms like iOS and Android provide app developers with frameworks and APIs (Application Programming Interfaces) to create extensions that seamlessly integrate with the overall system. Users can enhance the functionality of their devices by installing third-party keyboards, widgets, or system utilities. This extensibility ensures that users can tailor the behavior and appearance of their devices, contributing to a personalized and adaptive user experience.

Despite the numerous advantages of third-party extensions, there are challenges and considerations that both developers and users must navigate. Compatibility issues and conflicts between extensions can arise, requiring vigilant oversight from core application developers to maintain a stable ecosystem. Security concerns, such as the potential for malicious code within extensions, necessitate robust review processes and continuous monitoring. The responsibility also falls on users to exercise caution when choosing and installing extensions, verifying their legitimacy and keeping them updated to mitigate potential security risks.

In conclusion, the integration of third-party extensions and plugins for UI customization stands as a transformative force in contemporary user interface design. This symbiotic relationship between core applications and external developers fosters an ecosystem of innovation, personalization, and versatility. From content management systems and graphic design software to web browsers, e-commerce platforms, and mobile applications, the impact of third-party contributions is pervasive, shaping the way users interact with digital interfaces. While challenges related to security and compatibility persist, the benefits of extensibility, diversity of functionalities, and user-driven innovation underscore the integral role of third-party extensions in creating dynamic, adaptable, and user-centric digital experiences. As technology continues to evolve, the collaborative synergy between core applications and third-party developers is poised to remain a driving force in the evolution of user interfaces across a multitude of platforms and contexts.

Discuss the benefits and considerations associated with external modifications.

External modifications, often referred to as third-party modifications or mods, have become an integral part of various digital ecosystems, providing users with the ability to customize, extend, and enhance their digital experiences. These modifications span a wide range of applications, platforms, and technologies, offering benefits that range from increased functionality and personalization to fostering vibrant communities of users and developers. However, along with these advantages come considerations related to security, stability, and the potential for unintended consequences. Examining both the benefits and considerations associated with external modifications provides valuable insights into the nuanced landscape of user-driven customization and its impact on digital interfaces.

One of the primary benefits of external modifications lies in the enhanced functionality they bring to existing applications and platforms. Users can augment the features of software applications by integrating third-party plugins, extensions, or modifications. For example, in the context of web browsers, users can install ad blockers, password managers, or productivity tools to tailor the browsing experience to their preferences. This increased functionality not only meets individual user needs but also allows for the creation of specialized tools catering to niche requirements. The diverse ecosystem of external modifications ensures that users can adapt core applications to align with their specific workflows, enhancing overall efficiency and utility.

Personalization stands out as a key advantage associated with external modifications. Users have the flexibility to tailor the appearance and behavior of digital interfaces according to their individual preferences. This personalization extends to various aspects, including color schemes, layouts, and interaction styles. For instance, users can customize the visual elements of their operating systems, web browsers, or content management systems to create a more aesthetically pleasing and user-friendly environment. The ability to personalize interfaces fosters a sense of ownership and agency, empowering users to create a digital space that resonates with their unique tastes and preferences.

The collaborative nature of external modifications contributes to the formation of vibrant and engaged user communities. Developers and users come together to create, share, and iterate on modifications, fostering a sense of camaraderie and shared enthusiasm. These communities often center around specific applications, games, or platforms, creating forums, repositories, and communication channels where users can exchange ideas, seek assistance, and showcase their creations. The synergy between developers and users in the modification community not only enriches the ecosystem but also serves as a testament to the power of user-driven innovation in shaping digital experiences.

External modifications can breathe new life into older or stagnant software, extending the longevity of applications and platforms. In scenarios where official support may have waned, dedicated communities of modders often step in to revitalize and update software. This preservation aspect is particularly evident in the gaming community, where mods can enhance graphics, introduce new content, or fix bugs in older games, allowing them to remain relevant and enjoyable for a much longer period. The ability to rejuvenate software through external modifications underscores the resilience and adaptability of user-driven customization.

Moreover, external modifications can serve as a valuable resource for educational purposes and skill development. Aspiring developers and designers can delve into the world of modification to learn about programming, design principles, and system architecture. Contributing to or creating modifications provides a hands-on learning experience, allowing individuals to apply theoretical knowledge in practical scenarios. This educational aspect extends beyond traditional learning environments, offering a dynamic and engaging pathway for individuals to acquire technical skills and gain practical experience in software development and customization.

However, along with the benefits associated with external modifications, there are considerations that must be carefully navigated to ensure a balanced and secure user experience. One of the primary concerns is related to security risks. External modifications, particularly those developed by independent third parties, may introduce vulnerabilities or malicious code into the software ecosystem. These security risks can compromise the integrity of user data, expose sensitive information, or create entry points for malicious actors. Both developers and users must exercise caution, adopting best practices such as code reviews, secure development methodologies, and regular updates to mitigate potential security threats associated with external modifications.

Stability is another consideration tied to external modifications, as they can impact the overall reliability and performance of applications. Modifications may inadvertently introduce bugs, conflicts with other modifications, or cause compatibility issues with software updates. This potential instability poses challenges for both users and core application developers, requiring proactive measures to ensure a harmonious coexistence between external modifications and the core software. Establishing clear guidelines, conducting thorough testing, and fostering open communication between developers and the modification community contribute to maintaining stability within the digital ecosystem.

Legal considerations and intellectual property rights add a layer of complexity to the landscape of external modifications. Developers creating modifications may need to navigate licensing agreements, terms of service, and intellectual property laws to ensure compliance with legal frameworks. Similarly, users must be mindful of the legal implications of installing and distributing modifications. The legal landscape surrounding modifications can vary significantly across different applications, platforms, and jurisdictions, necessitating a nuanced understanding of the legal considerations associated with external modifications.

Furthermore, external modifications can pose challenges related to user experience fragmentation. As users customize their interfaces through a variety of modifications, the uniformity and consistency of the user experience may be compromised. This fragmentation can be particularly evident in platforms with open ecosystems, where users have the freedom to extensively modify the interface. Striking a balance between customization and preserving a cohesive user experience requires thoughtful design decisions and considerations for how modifications may impact the overall look and feel of the software.

The sustainability of external modifications is also a consideration, especially when they are created by individual developers or small communities. Changes in the development landscape, shifts in user preferences, or evolving technologies may affect the ongoing maintenance and support of modifications. This raises questions about the long-term viability of certain modifications and the potential for users to be left with outdated or incompatible customization options. Developers and users must assess the sustainability of modifications, considering factors such as community support, update frequency, and responsiveness to changing technological landscapes.

In the context of gaming, external modifications often intersect with issues related to fair play and online multiplayer environments. Mods that provide unfair advantages or disrupt the intended balance of a game can lead to negative experiences for other players. Balancing the desire for customization with the need for fair and equitable gameplay requires careful consideration of how modifications may impact the multiplayer experience. Game developers often implement policies or tools to manage the use of modifications in online environments, striking a balance between user creativity and maintaining a level playing field.

In conclusion, external modifications play a transformative role in user interface customization, offering numerous benefits such as enhanced functionality, personalization, community engagement, and educational opportunities. However, navigating the considerations associated with security, stability, legal implications, user experience fragmentation, sustainability, and fair play requires a nuanced approach. Striking the right balance between customization and maintaining a secure, stable, and cohesive user experience is an ongoing challenge that involves collaboration between core application developers, modification communities, and users. As technology continues to advance, the landscape of external modifications will evolve, requiring adaptive strategies and frameworks to ensure that user-driven customization remains a positive and enriching force in the digital ecosystem.